God without the Supernatural

Cornell Studies in the Philosophy of Religion

EDITED BY WILLIAM P. ALSTON

A full list of titles in the series appears
at the end of the book.

Peter Forrest

God without the Supernatural

Supernatural

A Defense of Scientific Theism

Cornell University Press, Ithaca and London

First published 1996 by Cornell University Press.

Printed in the United States of America

⊗ The paper in this book meets the minimum requirements
of the American National Standard for Information Sciences—
Permanence of Paper for Printed Library Materials, ANSI Z39.48–1984.

Library of Congress Cataloging-in-Publication Data

Forrest, Peter, b. 1948
    God without the supernatural : a defense of scientific theism /
Peter Forrest.
        p.   cm. —(Cornell studies in the philosophy of religion)
    Includes bibliographical references and index.
    ISBN 0-8014-3255-3 (alk. paper)
    1. Theism. 2. Religion and science. I. Title. II. Series.
BL200.F65   1996
211'.3—dc20   96-1044

In memory of my daughter Caroline,
and my mother Monica.

Contents

Contents

Preface

This book might have been called *The God-Centered Understanding of Things* or, simply, *Against Atheism*. For my aim is indeed to exhibit the theocentric understanding of this beautiful but flawed world. And that does indeed provide a case against atheism. I especially want to emphasize, however, that this is quite compatible with the rejection of supernatural explanations. Hence the title.

Because I am presenting an argument against atheism, it could seem that I have some special animus toward atheists. This is not so. I do not believe that any religion is better than none, and I think that atheism, when it is a high-minded love of the truth and not just a prolonged adolescent rebellion, is more faithful to the Judaeo-Christian tradition than many a superstitious corruption of that tradition.

I am indebted to the Center for Philosophy of Religion at the University of Notre Dame, where I worked on an early draft as a visiting fellow in the fall semester of 1990. I am also grateful for the continued support, by means of internal research grants, of the Faculty of Arts at the University of New England.

David Armstrong, James Franklin, Barry Miller, an anonymous referee for Cornell University Press, and the series editor, William P. Alston, have painstakingly commented on various drafts. I am most grateful for their encouragement and their comments.

I would like to thank Alison Manion for proofreading.

Last, love and thanks to my wife, Felicity, and my children, Joseph, Stephen, Alice, and Nicholas.

PETER FORREST

Armidale, Australia

God without the Supernatural

Introduction

In recent years there has been a resurgence of scientific theism. By that I mean belief in a god as the explanation of various features revealed by, or implicit in, modern science. Of these features the best known is the *fine-tuning* of our universe for life, namely the fact that various quantities must be almost exactly as they actually are if the universe is to be suited to life.[1] It is natural enough to see the hand of God in this fine-tuning. Now there is a tendency for scientific theists, like many of the deists of earlier centuries, to reject belief in the personal and caring God worshiped by the majority of human beings. Thus Paul Davies writes: "There must, it seems to me, be a deeper level of explanation [of the physical universe]. Whether one wishes to call that deeper level 'God' is a matter of taste and definition" (1992, p. 16). Again, John Leslie writes, "There is no need to think of God as a person who exists reasonlessly. God may not be a person at all" (1989, p. 165). Although this book is itself a work of scientific theism, one of my aims is to defend belief in a personal and caring God—the sort of God to whom devotion is appropriate.[2]

I take as my starting point scientific realism and, more generally, what I consider the scientific attitude. The mark of scientific realists such as myself

---

[1] Although fine-tuning has been relied upon by most scientific theists, it is not something I endorse without qualification. See Chapter 2 for a discussion of the theocentric understanding of the suitability of the universe for life, which does not depend on fine-tuning.

[2] I am not, of course, a pioneer in this regard. Richard Swinburne, who is an orthodox Christian, treats fine-tuning as significant evidence for the existence of God (1990). And the physicist turned theologian John Polkinghorne has offered a lucid defense of theism in the context of scientific realism (1986, 1988, 1989).

is that they believe in the entities posited in scientific theories, such as neutrons, even when these entities are not observable (Forrest 1994a). Thus scientific realism is opposed to instrumentalism, the position that the unobservable entities are convenient fictions useful for making predictions but not to be taken literally. In both the dispute over the unobservable entities posited by scientists and the dispute over whether there is a God, there is, of course, an agnostic position, namely suspending judgment.[3] I acknowledge this as a worthy intellectual alternative to the position I defend. My purpose is to defend theism and to argue against atheism, rather than to argue against agnosticism.

The method by which I defend scientific realism is a common enough one—an appeal to inference to the best explanation, or some variant. That is, we are entitled to believe in unobservable entities such as neutrons because they provide the best way of understanding what is observable. To take an oversimplified example, the tracks left by charged particles in a cloud chamber are sometimes best explained by positing various uncharged particles such as neutrons. Likewise, I defend theism and argue against atheism by exhibiting theism as the best way of understanding various truths we are already confident of. And since I am defending theism within the context of scientific realism, most of these truths are in one way or another to do with science and mathematics.

The use of best-explanation apologetics, as I call it, to defend theism and argue against atheism might suggest that I am positing supernatural explanations. This work is, however, part of a larger antisupernaturalist program in which I aim to avoid both poles of the naturalism-versus-supernaturalism dichotomy: I am an antisupernaturalist without being a naturalist.[4] Let me explain, then, what I mean by naturalism and supernaturalism. I start by assuming that we have an idea of the *familiar*, by which I mean the observable things around us. Here I stipulate that the familiar includes what we know about ourselves, even if we are not purely physical things. Both naturalism and supernaturalism are programs for understanding the familiar. And both programs permit explanations in terms of unfamiliar, even quite peculiar, entities. They differ, however, as regards the kinds of entities that are considered ac-

[3] The agnostic position concerning the unobservable entities posited by scientists has been ably defended by Bas van Fraassen (1980). In Forrest 1994a I present some arguments against van Fraassen's position, but as the phrase "most of us" in the title of that article indicates, these arguments are audience-specific.

[4] In this work I use "naturalist" as a noun to mean "advocate of naturalism" and occasionally as an adjective to mean "naturalistic." Obviously naturalists in the sense of students of nature could endorse any or none of the rival programs I am discussing.

ceptable and in the ways they interact. The ideal for naturalists is to provide explanations that satisfy two constraints: (i) no entities are posited unless well-confirmed scientific theories provide a *precedent* for them; and (ii) no well-confirmed law of nature is violated. Naturalists may have to compromise with that ideal, in the ways discussed in Chapter 3. Nonetheless they aim to stay as close as they can to it. Notice that naturalists are permitted speculative hypotheses provided the well-confirmed theories establish a precedent for them. (In Chapter 6 I explicate the relevant sense of a precedent using the idea of a *theoretical niche*.) Thus naturalists may, and do, help themselves to all sorts of speculations about evolution because well-confirmed examples of evolution set a precedent for these speculations.

Supernaturalists differ from naturalists because they resort, in their explanations, to either or both of (i) entities for which neither the familiar entities around us nor those mentioned in the natural sciences establish a precedent; and (ii) violations of laws of nature.[5] Typically such explanations involve persons without bodies, or, sometimes, persons with bodies made of quite unfamiliar stuff. For instance, God, angels, and demons would be examples of the supernatural in my sense of the word, if and only if either they are unprecedented entities or they violate the laws of nature.

As I have characterized them, naturalism and supernaturalism are contraries but not contradictories. That is because naturalists aim to restrict themselves to explanations for which there is scientific precedent, ignoring—and typically denying the success of—nonscientific explanations for which the precedent lies in the familiar world. By antisupernaturalism I mean the contradictory of supernaturalism, namely the insistence that all explanations be in terms of entities that (i) have a precedent in either the ones we are familiar with or the novel kinds posited by the sciences; and (ii) operate without violating the laws of nature that scientists have discovered.[6] What is wrong, though, with supernaturalism? To be sure, the supernatural is popularly identified with the magical and the occult. Consider for instance *The Dictionary of the Supernatural: An A to Z of Hauntings, Possession, Witchcraft, Demonology and Other Occult Phenomena* (Underwood 1978). Those theists who pride themselves on their

[5] If we consider the combined statement of all the laws of nature to be qualified by a "nihil obstat" or "ceteris paribus" clause, then violating the laws of nature must be interpreted as producing a state of affairs inconsistent with the unqualified statement.

[6] Antisupernaturalism does not, let me stress, imply the rejection of the thesis that our final destiny is "supernatural" in the sense of being more than God could reasonably be expected to provide for beings with our natures. Nor does it imply the rejection of the thesis that human beings are offered "supernatural" assistance ("grace") in moral and intellectual struggles. What antisupernaturalism does require is that neither our "supernatural" destiny nor the "supernatural" graces we receive be given a genuinely supernatural explanation.

common sense are probably relieved when they note that this work has articles on Glastonbury, Glossolalia, and Golem, but none on God. However, all that has about as much to do with the supernatural characterised above, as the "Metaphysics" section of the bookstore, where the occult and the magical are to be found, has to do with *The Review of Metaphysics*. A more serious reason is required to reject supernaturalism.

What is wrong, then, with the supernatural, provided we distinguish it from the magical and the occult? Here I submit that there is an Ockhamist presumption in favor of positing only entities of kinds we are familiar with. Likewise, I consider there is a presumption that the ways in which things interact will be quite compatible with the ways of interacting with which we are familiar and which we extrapolate by induction. A certain sort of empiricist considers these presumptions are never overcome.[7] I disagree, considering that the presumption is overcome in two ways. First, the sciences, especially physics, overcome both presumptions because of the precision and variety of the phenomena explained. This leaves us with a presumption against positing unfamiliar entities not mentioned in well-confirmed scientific theories and a presumption against violations of the laws of nature scientists have discovered. I further submit that even this presumption is rather weak, and so quite easy to overcome, in cases where the posited entities have a precedent in those we already believe in. In cases where there is no precedent, however, I consider the presumption to be a strong one. Hence I aim to avoid positing supernatural beings, and I aim to avoid the assumption that God has actually exercised any divine power to break the laws of nature.[8] I appeal to readers who consider this an excess of caution at least to grant its ad hominem value. For my impression is that the rejection of the supernatural is second only to the argument from evil as an obstacle to theism.

But how can theists avoid supernaturalism? I gave God, angels, and demons as examples of the supernatural, provided they have no precedent. Let us consider this proviso. It is easy enough for Cartesian dualists to find a precedent for God, for they can interpret God as being a mind like ours but vastly greater in power.[9] This suggests a strategy for antisupernaturalist theists, even

---

[7] *The Scientific Image* (van Fraassen 1980) is a presentation of the first of these presumptions as it applies to the sciences. The second presumption may be both compared and contrasted with Hume's discussion of miracles in Section 10 of *An Enquiry Concerning Human Understanding*.

[8] I would maintain these *aims* even when considering the details of Christianity (which are beyond the scope of this work). I am, however, less confident of the tenability of Christianity without the supernatural than of anthropic theism without the supernatural.

[9] Since Descartes argued that our idea of God could have originated only from God, not from introspection, he himself could not take our human minds to be a precedent for God.

if they reject Cartesian dualism. There is something about ourselves, namely being conscious, with which we are all familiar by means of introspection but which, I argue, cannot be understood by means of the natural sciences. Theists may avoid supernaturalism by treating our own consciousness as a precedent for God. I adopt this strategy in Chapters 6 and 7, and I do so in a way that meets two important objections. The first is that, whether or not we are purely physical things, our varied mental states depend on enormously complex brain processes. We may contrast this with the extreme Cartesian position that takes the full range of human mental states as independent of brain processes and considers the brain to be merely the organ by which the mind interacts with the body. The first objection, then, is that this extreme Cartesian position is properly outmoded. If God is likened to some nonphysical aspect of ourselves, then we must abandon anthropomorphic views of God as having a humanlike mind, just as we long ago abandoned anthropomorphic views of God as having a humanlike body. God would have to be some kind of unrestricted consciousness or pure awareness—Brahman maybe. I grant all that but argue that such a God still explains the various phenomena I treat, and may still be considered a personal and caring God.

The second objection to my strategy for antisupernaturalist theism is that God must be supposed to have powers quite unlike those we humans have, which is itself, the objection goes, something supernatural. For if God does not have such supernatural powers, then how can there be creation out of nothing? Furthermore, my defense of my preferred version of theism requires an afterlife. That, too, might seem to imply that God has supernatural powers. I aim to avoid supernaturalism even as regards the divine power by presenting a unified account of divine and human power. Thus the divine power has a precedent in the familiar power we humans possess. It is, therefore, not something supernatural, provided, as I claim, God both creates the universe and ensures an afterlife without any violation of the (divinely ordained) laws of nature.

The most straightforward aim of this book, then, is to defend theism and argue against atheism. A subsidiary aim is to do so without invoking supernatural explanations. A third aim is to illustrate a Kant-inspired, but not Kantian, account of the role of metaphysics as speculation.[10] Rarely, if ever, does metaphysics provide us with information about actual things. Instead it shows us ways things might be. In particular, like Robert Nozick (1981, introduc-

---

[10] Metaphysical speculation has, in my case, little to do with the tradition of "speculative metaphysics" exemplified by Hegel. I am using the word "speculate" in its contemporary sense.

tion), I use metaphysical speculation to answer various "How is it possible?" questions.[11] Thus we may ask how creation is possible, requesting an account that avoids ascribing supernatural powers to God. Another "How is it possible?" question is raised by the problem of evil: How is it possible that a good God has created a universe with so much evil in it? Here again I rely on metaphysical speculation.

---

[11] The possibility here is not logical possibility (i.e., consistency), which is usually unproblematic. Rather it is *genuine epistemic possibility*, about which I say more in Chapter 1.

[I]

The Apologetics
of Understanding

To argue against atheism and to defend theism, I rely on the *apologetics of understanding*. By that I mean the project of defending the belief component of faith by showing what it enables us to understand. A combination of the apologetics of understanding and an appeal to religious experience would establish belief in God beyond all reasonable doubt for those who have had the appropriate experience. The apologetics of understanding is, however, just part of that overall case.[1] Alternatively, or in addition, the apologetics of understanding may be thought of as background to an informed assessment of the claims of various religious traditions. By itself, however, the apologetics of understanding does not exclude agnosticism. It is, nonetheless, sufficient to show atheism to be unwarranted.[2]

Often theocentric understanding begins by being inarticulate, but, as objections are raised and replies given, it becomes articulate and hence philosophical. Are there, we ask, better explanations than that provided by God? Moreover, isn't it extravagant, supernaturalist even, to posit a nonphysical God when all our ordinary experience of personal beings is of them as embodied? And, of course, there is the problem of evil: initially it is astounding that God does not prevent suffering. Objections occur to us once we begin to think

---

[1] For a recent defense of the role of religious experience in establishing the warrantedness of theism, see Alston 1991.

[2] Atheists who accept my case that theocentric understanding is superior to rivals are, I submit, unwarranted but not necessarily failing in their intellectual duties. For if moderate fideism is correct there is no duty to have only warranted beliefs. See Section 2.

about theocentric understanding. So, however distasteful philosophy might be, we have reason to become philosophers.[3]

1. On Our Conception of God

It is appropriate to begin with the conception of God used in this work, so as to distinguish belief in a personal deity from belief in an impersonal one. I restrict the word "God" to mean a personal deity, and "theism" to mean "belief in a personal deity." Hence believers in an impersonal deity will, strictly speaking, be considered atheists.

Among theists, that is, believers in a personal deity, I distinguish two sorts. The first sort holds the thesis that one of the chief reasons for creation is the well-being of us humans, and any other embodied persons there may be. Hence our existence is not an accident or a by-product or merely a means to some further end. The other sort rejects that thesis as anthropocentric. I extend the scope of the word "anthropos" to cover any extraterrestrial embodied persons there may be, not just human beings. Hence I use the word "anthropic" to mean "of or to do with embodied persons." So I call the first sort of theists, among whom I number myself, *anthropic* theists. (Anthropic theism should not be confused with the version of naturalism, discussed in Chapter 3, that relies on anthropic explanations.) The other sort of theists I call *ananthropic*. Among these I include Davies, who seems to consider that our existence is merely the means to some further end, when he provides the almost Hegelian speculation that conscious organisms exist so that "the universe has generated self-awareness" (1992, p. 232). Another form of ananthropic theism worth considering is the belief in a God whose motive is purely aesthetic. My aim is not merely to defend theism and argue against atheism but to defend anthropic theism and argue against ananthropic theism.

Theism, whether anthropic or not, may be contrasted with belief in an impersonal deity, such as Brahman is sometimes taken to be,[4] or the deity of pantheism.[5] The importance of these contrasts is affective as much as intel-

---

[3] Philosophy is here characterized as the public discussion of controversial issues, typically by means of objections and defenses and not merely by rhetorical means. Many find philosophy distasteful not merely because it involves exposing ourselves to often unsympathetic critics but also because the historical record suggests that philosophers tend to get things wrong. My response is that the fault is with philosophers, not philosophy.

[4] When it is described as Nirguna Brahman, that is, ultimate reality devoid of all attributes.

[5] Pantheism would be a form of theism if it resulted from a combination of physicalism with Grace Jantzen's thesis that God is an embodied person whose body is the Universe (1984). But I am contrasting theism with the nontheistic pantheism expounded by Michael Levine (1994).

lectual. For anthropic theism, far more than ananthropic theism or belief in an impersonal deity, generates devotion and gratitude to God as one who has created for our sakes.[6]

Whether based on anthropic or ananthropic theism, the theocentric understanding of things that I expound requires a God who is personal and who also has sufficient power to create the physical universe with the characteristics it has. Again, God must have sufficient knowledge to create. Beyond saying that God is personal, sufficiently powerful, and sufficiently knowing, I have little need to specify the divine characteristics. Thus I am not committed to the classical doctrines of the necessity, eternity, and simplicity of God. As part of my case for theism I speculate about the nature of God, and these speculations indeed support something like these classical doctrines. Let me emphasize, though, that I am not committed to belief in my speculations, which are provided to answer "How is it possible?" questions.

I should, however, say something about divine freedom, to avoid seeming to commit myself to the controversial thesis that God is radically free in the sense that God acts in ways that are neither random nor necessary in the circumstances. Both for God and for human beings, I say that an act is free if it is neither causally determined by external factors nor random. In the case of the act of creation there would presumably be nothing external, so the phrase "by external factors" is redundant. In both the human and the divine case I am neutral on the question whether the free act could also be necessary in the circumstances, or whether it is radically free. I merely note that its being uncaused by external factors is compatible with its being necessary in the circumstances. For a person could act in a way that was necessary but still free, provided the balance of reasons made all but one act unreasonable. Indeed, if we ever act in ways contrary to the balance of reasons, then, I submit, we are not free but compelled by some neurotic urge. To illustrate this I use the example of the postdoctoral fellow who is offered both a position with and a position without tenure. The tenured position is, it so happens, in a more exciting department and better paid. In short the postdoctoral fellow is in the happy position that all reasons incline toward just one of the two choices. I submit that, in circumstances in which the postdoctoral fellow is free, the choice will necessarily be to take the tenured position. Hence the choice is free even though the outcome is necessary in the circumstances. Applying this to God, we have, then, no reason to exclude the speculation

---

[6] It should be noted, however, that belief in a human incarnation of an impersonal deity would also generate religious devotion. The question here, though, is whether we can make sense of an incarnation of an impersonal deity.

that God's free choices are necessary. But neither do we have reason to insist on that speculation, for perhaps there is no balance of reasons requiring the choice.

There is one further point of clarification about which I feel most strongly. I reject any theory that would, in the tradition of Durkheim, treat God as a social construct, or in some other way dependent on us. As far as I am concerned, the claim that God is a social construct should be read with the clear implication "and so there is no God." I insist that God is not even partially dependent on us. In that sense God is totally and without qualification *objective*. Now it is fashionable among postmodernists to deride this insistence upon objectivity, as if it required us humans to take up a "God's eye" point of view, or as if it was the symptom of some nasty disease caught from Plato. Here it suffices to make two remarks. The first is that in saying God is objective I do not imply that there are publicly acceptable tests for deciding whether there is God—philosophical discussion is not like that. My other remark on the objectivity of God is that one of the driving forces behind much contemporary rejection of objective standards for truth and morality is the Nietzschean argument that there is no God and therefore there are no objective standards. I am not myself persuaded about this, but let us suppose that atheism indeed supports subjectivity about truth.[7] Even so, we should not excuse theologians for waking up from their dogmatic slumbers halfway through the argument, and saying, "Ah! Then God is subjective."

My rejection of God-the-social-construct might be thought dogmatic. My purpose, however, is to articulate and defend a theocentric understanding of, among other things, the suitability of the universe for life. Because there has to be life for there to be social constructs, I cannot take God to be a social construct, on pain of circularity. I therefore treat worshipers of God-the-social-construct as atheists—atheists who go around humming Handel's *Messiah*.[8]

Since I am noting commitments and noncommitments, I mention—without any further comment until Chapter 6—the possibility of objective but nonobjectual theism. This may be expressed by saying that there is no such *thing* as God or that God does not *exist*. For that reason I say "There is a God" rather than "God exists." Another advantage of this formulation is that it does not exclude versions of polytheism that allow that there are many Gods, not just many gods. I discuss these in Chapter 5.

---

[7] Philip Devine (1989) has argued that indeed without theism we are prey to relativism and nihilism.

[8] I am indebted to Max Deutscher for pointing out the incongruity of atheists humming the *Messiah*.

2. Why We Still Need Apologetics

Before we reflect critically on our beliefs, we already have (i) various beliefs about what is true, but also (ii) various beliefs about the standards beliefs should satisfy. (If beliefs satisfy these standards, then I say they are *warranted* beliefs.) Epistemology concerns, among other things, the interaction between (i) and (ii) which results when we engage in critical reflection. Three factors complicate this interaction. The first is that it is widely agreed that our beliefs, unlike some of our actions, are beyond our direct control. The second is that disagreement about the standards for warrant can seldom be resolved by appealing to those standards without circularity. (The exception here is when standards are self-refuting.) The third is that critical reflection is not merely the application of standards to beliefs but can instead result in the modification of our standards.

Given these three complications it would be absurd for me, in a single section, to adjudicate between rival epistemologies. Rather I reach two conclusions that will hold, I say, for any reasonable epistemology. The first is that there is a place for apologetics generally and arguments in support of theism in particular. The second is that such arguments for theism need not amount to *proofs* in the sense of arguments that will convince any reasonable person.

I reach the second conclusion by considering the main epistemological theory that might seem to demand proof if we are to believe in God. This is the position Alvin Plantinga calls *classical foundationalism*. It tells us that there are only three ways in which a belief can be warranted: (i) self-evidence, that is, being obvious once we think of it, such as $2 + 2 = 4$; or (ii) being evident to the senses; or (iii) being warrantably inferred from beliefs that are self-evident or evident to the senses. Now few hold theism to be self-evident, and even fewer that it is evident to the senses. That makes theism depend for its warrant on the third way, which leads to apologetics. To avoid this, theists might try to broaden the second way of being warranted to include religious or mystical experience, but there is a well-known difficulty in relying on such experience unless it is supported by some further argument. This is the difficulty that having an experience that confirms belief in a personal rather than an impersonal deity might well be itself the product of a culture of belief in a personal deity.[9] Given classical foundationalism, then, apologetics seems to

---

[9] In calling this a difficulty, I am not endorsing the objection, merely describing a case that might be made for apologetics. For recent discussions of the significance of mystical experiences, see Katz 1978, Almond 1982, and Foreman 1990. For a discussion of religious experience more generally, see Alston 1991.

be required because without it theism would be unwarranted. Let us call this the *classical case for apologetics*.

Some of the antipathy to apologetics derives, I suspect, from the assumption that the only reason for engaging in it is the classical case. If that were so, then to engage in apologetics is to assume classical foundationalism. Let me make it quite clear, then, that in defending the project of apologetics, I am making no such assumption. Rather I am arguing that believers need apologetics even if they reject classical foundationalism. For the moment, however, I am investigating what does follow from classical foundationalism, and I am going to argue that either it is self-refuting, as Plantinga has charged (1983), or that some inferences must be considered warranted which do not amount to proof.

Classical foundationalism might have seemed self-evident to some, but to defend it as such is to water down self-evidence to mean whatever we are inclined to believe without further justification. In that case theism is, after all, warranted as self-evident for those who are inclined to believe in God. And classical foundationalism is obviously not evident to the senses. So if it is not to be self-refuting, then it must be warrantably inferred from premisses that are either self-evident or evident to the senses. The only candidates for such premisses are uncontroversial judgments that such-and-such beliefs are warranted and such-and-such are not warranted.[10] From these self-evident judgments we may then infer an epistemological theory on the grounds that it enables us to understand them in a systematic fashion. (Compare Plantinga 1983, p. 76.)

Classical foundationalism is self-refuting if it insists on higher standards than the ones used in its own defense. And clearly which epistemological theory is supported as the best way of systematizing and understanding uncontroversial judgments of warrant will itself be a matter of controversy, not something which can be proved in the sense of convincing any reasonable person. Moreover, the procedure used to systematize the uncontroversial judgments of warrant is not mere extrapolation. It is precisely the procedure that forms the basis of the apologetics of understanding, namely that we are warranted in believing what (best) enables us to understand. I reach the conclusion, therefore, that any version of classical foundationalism which would insist upon a proof of theism, or which would exclude the propriety of the apologetics of understanding, is indeed self-refuting.

So much for the requirement of proof. But isn't it anachronistic in this postmodern era to bother with any sort of apologetics? I argue that, apart

---

[10] For a discussion of which judgments of warrant might count as self-evident, see Quinn 1985, Plantinga 1986, and Quinn 1993.

from extreme fideists, all should recognize the value of making a case for theism. But first I note that my purpose is not just to defend theism but to criticize atheism, something for which apologetics is clearly required.

The most moderate of antiapologists are the reformed epistemologists, notably Nicholas Wolterstorff (1976) and Plantinga (1983). They articulate the widespread conviction that arguing for theism misses the point of faith. Thus Plantinga defends the thesis that beliefs held on faith may be treated in much the same way as beliefs directly based on perception. That is not to say that faith is treated as a perceptual or quasi-perceptual experience of God, but rather that they have a similar status. More precisely, Plantinga holds that a religious belief (e.g., that God is to be thanked and praised) that directly entails that there is a God may well be *properly basic* (i.e., warranted but in no need of further justification). And here we may indeed compare beliefs directly based on perception. Suppose, for instance, I see a red toadstool with white spots as I walk along. My belief that there is a toadstool is not based on any inference and requires no justification. Likewise, according to Plantinga, my belief that God is to be thanked is not based on any inference and requires no justification. Although these beliefs are basic, they are not, however *groundless*, and if they were they would not be warranted. In the case of the toadstool the grounds are the shape, texture, and color as well as the particular environment. The grounds for the belief that God is to be thanked would include the ordered beauty of the world, the sense of being protected, and so on. Subsequent work by Plantinga suggests that beliefs are grounded in a given set of circumstances precisely if the belief has resulted in those circumstances from the proper functioning of the person who comes to believe.[11]

Furthermore, Plantinga holds that for religious beliefs to be warranted, they should not be *dogmatic*, any more than beliefs in toadstools should be dogmatic. For the person concerned may, and should, take seriously various objections to them. Thus if it were pointed out to me that plastic toadstools had taken over from gnomes as the preferred suburban garden ornament, I would have doubts as to whether the object in a tidy garden was indeed a toadstool. And I might then notice how suspiciously like all the other toadstools it was. Likewise, the absence of a reply to the argument from evil might be so serious an objection that theism would cease to be warranted.[12]

Even if we follow Plantinga and reject the classical case for apologetics, there is still a use for the apologetics of understanding. For a start, attack is

---

[11] See Plantinga 1993b for a theocentric account of proper functioning.

[12] Or at least anthropic theism would be. Presumably one of the prima facie advantages of ananthropic theism is that it is less vulnerable to the argument from evil. In my defense of apologetics I am, however, considering anthropic theism.

often the best defense. Hence a good argument for theism provides an excellent way of replying to the argument from evil. And, more messily, a combination of an argument for theism with a partial undermining of the argument from evil might well be an adequate defense, even if the reasons for rejecting the argument from evil were not enough by themselves.

That use for apologetics would perhaps be redundant if every known version of the argument from evil was shown to be faulty. There is, however, a further reason why reformed epistemologists need apologetics. It concerns a standoff between the grounds for theism and the grounds for atheism. Atheists should be allowed their own properly basic beliefs, which might well be grounded in the experience of the overwhelming horror of evil. Although there are ways of reducing this horror, such as a lively sense of the beauty of the world around us, or, more effectively, faith that God incarnate has shared human suffering, I judge that the experience of evil provides grounds (rather than reasons) for not believing. More precisely, the experience of evil might ground not atheism as such but beliefs that obviously entail atheism. For instance, atheists might have a properly basic belief that the evils around us are such that God would not permit.[13]

Because of this standoff, belief in God is significantly different from our beliefs in the material objects around us. Reformed epistemologists should (i) adopt an explicitly pluralist position according to which theists and atheists are equally warranted, or (ii) suspend judgment, or (iii) as I advocate, rely on apologetics.

Some might complain at this point that the experience of evil does not ground atheism because properly functioning thinkers would not draw atheistic conclusions. This might even seem obvious if proper functioning is a matter of performing as God intended. I deny this. Our circumstances, in particular the sheer amount of evil around us, might not be as God intended, and in circumstances other than the designer intended, something that functions properly may well have unintended results. For example, properly functioning adults have sexual drives, yet, because of their circumstances, these drives often have results unintended by God.

Those are the chief reasons why arguments for theism, such as those of the apologetics of understanding, have a role to play even if we reject classical foundationalism.[14] But there are two additional reasons worth noting. First,

---

[13] This is my interpretation of those otherwise perplexing remarks, noted but not endorsed by George Schlesinger (1988, pp. 70–73), to the effect that the Holocaust has somehow rendered theism untenable even though, it is implied, such all-too-common tragedies as women dying in childbirth did not. As a matter of psychological fact, rather than philosophical argument, certain kinds of evil are more likely than others to ground beliefs that obviously entail atheism.

[14] Compare the discussion between Philip Quinn (1985) and Plantinga (1986, pp. 310–11).

the fact that some of those whom we respect disagree with us, in this case by being atheists, provides grounds for doubt. Such grounds for doubt are best countered by means of an argument for theism. Finally, as Plantinga acknowledges (1983, pp. 82–83), there could be some who come to believe in God as a result of intellectual arguments, even if that is not the only warranted way of coming to believe. Now it is widely held that few ever do come to believe in God as a result of argument.[15] So this is thought of as a special case. But one reason why so few come to believe in God as a result of argument could be that theologians never resort to it. I am reminded of the sensitive New Age cat who never eats meat and never hunts birds and lizards. Does it, I ask, ever get the chance? Likewise, it is no wonder that intellectual conversion to religion is rare—no one ever tries.

A related explanation of why so few come to believe in God as a result of apologetics might be that all sorts of pressures, which believers should join with others in lamenting, have prevented people from thinking rationally about religious issues. For example, fear of damnation for unbelief is not especially conducive to the peace of mind required for rationality. Again, certain aspects of a religious upbringing—those brutal brothers and killjoy sisters of forty years ago—can leave scars that hinder any reasoned assessment of religion. Thus we might well hope that progress could lead to a mature society in which more people than at present are swayed by argument in religious matters. For often the contrast is not between faith and reason but between maturity and adolescence.

I have made a case, then, for the place of apologetics within reformed epistemology. I now turn to fideism. And here I distinguish a moderate from an extreme version of fideism. Moderate fideism, the position I incline toward myself, is based on the denial that our intellectual duty is to have warranted beliefs.[16] It is based instead on the widely accepted thesis that belief is not directly under our control but that what we attend to often is. Therefore instead of, or as well as, discussing the warrantedness of religious beliefs, we should investigate whether the faithful have violated their intellectual duty, which is, I say, precisely to give *informed assent*. That is, we are to attend, as

---

Plantinga argues that grounds for belief may sometimes be sufficient to overcome inconclusive but weighty objections. He gives as an example the religious experience reported in the Old Testament in which God was described as speaking to Moses in a burning bush. Like Quinn (1993, p. 39), I would say that the typical believer has religious experiences that are sufficient to count as grounds but are not enough by themselves to overrule objections. In the Pollock/ Plantinga terminology they are not such as intrinsically defeat the objections that threaten to defeat belief in God.

[15] James Franklin has suggested to me that apologetics might have been less of a failure in retaining believers than in converting unbelievers.

[16] See Plantinga 1993a, chap. 1, for a case against the assimilation of warrant to intellectual duty.

carefully as time and ability permit, to the intellectual considerations that bear upon our beliefs. Here an analogy might be helpful. Being warranted is like getting a pass on an assignment. Students do not, I say, have a duty to pass, but merely to study as well as time and circumstances permit. If they perform this duty, then it is possible, but exceptional, for them to fail. Likewise, if people perform their intellectual duty of giving informed assent, then it is possible, but exceptional, for them to have unwarranted beliefs.[17]

Unlike extreme fideists, I say we have this duty to give informed assent even though we are aware of the general risk to our beliefs in thus exposing them. Moderate fideists are not committed, however, to "following the argument wherever it leads." The case I made for the importance of apologetics within the context of reformed epistemology applies to moderate fideists also. For it would be absurdly one-sided to give arguments against the faith an honest hearing but not bother with the arguments for it. Likewise, atheists who are moderate fideists are at no fault in persevering with their atheism provided they have given both sides of the argument an honest hearing.

Extreme fideism is best thought of as the rejection of any intellectual duty to consider arguments for and against religious faith. Often, like Kierkegaard and Tertullian, fideists glory in the supposed irrationality of religious convictions. Sometimes, as with Barth, they even condemn apologetics as sinful. Or, more eirenically, extreme fideists might allow that the removal of intellectual obstacles by means of apologetics would in fact be helpful for intellectuals, just as appointing as prison chaplain someone who has had a few brushes with the law might be helpful for criminals. This would be an incidental or accidental use for apologetics, not the central role I give it.

I have argued, then, that only extreme fideists are in a position to reject apologetics. I, in my turn, reject extreme fideism. Here I have three arguments: the anti-Pascal objection, the implausibility of brain zaps, and the bath water problem. First, I argue against extreme fideism by diagnosing it as based on an implicit—and illicit—use of Pascal's wager. Faith, the fideist assumes, is so important that we should not risk its loss by taking seriously grounds for doubt. This could in turn be based on the thought that to lose faith is a sin, perhaps even with the threat of damnation. Alternatively, faith in God could have been the result of a major and serious decision when younger, so the loss of faith, even if not thought of as sinful, would be a devastating blow to one's choice of a path in life.

I grant that atheism that resulted from vanity, arrogance, or even, in some

[17] Alas! Things are not as straightforward as the analogy suggests. For I doubt if it is possible, with undivided mind, to believe something and not believe it to be warranted. This is not, however, the place to untie the intellectual knots that make up epistemology.

confused way, hatred of God would be a serious matter, a grievous sin. But that is quite beside the point. The nonbelievers I have in mind are those whose unbelief is based on a careful consideration of the evidence. If this were the place for a sermon I would direct it against those believers so benighted as to think that loyalty to the truth is sinful. Putting the matter in terms familiar to most fideists, faith can itself become an idol, and the worship of the true God could require the honest rejection of faith, even if one comes from a Protestant tradition that sees faith, contrasted with works, as justifying.

My second reason for rejecting fideism is the implausibility of brain zaps. For readers whose education needs completing in this respect, a *brain zapper* is a science-fiction device that when pointed at a person's brain "zaps" it. This results in the severing of old and the formation of new connections between neurons, thus altering a person's character or, in this case, beliefs. My complaint is that extreme fideists seem to suppose that faith is implanted by God in a way that is contrary to the natural processes operating in the brain. Now God has indeed the power to go around giving us brain zaps to make us kind, considerate, better tempered, and so on. One version of the problem of evil can be expressed by asking why God does *not* exercise that power. A good question. But it is quite manifest that God does not in fact intervene in this way. The obvious complaint is that God is too subtle, too respectful of both our autonomy and the natural order. Therefore I find it rather implausible to suppose that when it comes to the gift of faith God would go in for brain zapping.

My third and final reason for rejecting extreme fideism is the bath water problem. Many fideists consider that liberal theologians threw out the baby with the bath water, and there I sympathize with the fideists. But extreme fideists too have trouble distinguishing bath water from baby. Fideism can appear attractive enough when it comes to belief in God, but we should not overlook its dark side. If you just trust in faith, spurning the—God-given, I say—normal human ways of reasoning, then you are in danger of all manner of ugly superstition. For a start Lactantius was a fairly typical fideist of his day when he wrote a book called *On the False Wisdom of the Philosophers*. Today's extreme fideists might like the sound of that title. But, where I live, not many of them would endorse his twenty-fourth chapter, "devoted to heaping ridicule on the doctrine of the spherical figure of the earth and the existence of the antipodes" (Dreyer 1953, p. 209). But there are far worse superstitions to which fideists are prone. I have in mind such teachings as the everlasting suffering of infants who die unbaptized.

Passing from rhetoric to argument, fideists are faced with the obvious problem of other fideists who disagree with them on matters of faith. Of course all of us have this problem whenever we respect others who disagree with us.

Extreme fideists, unlike the rest of us, have denied themselves all use of reason in handling this problem. For example, a Christian fideist who devoutly believes that this life is the last chance we have for salvation and that the next life lasts forever must be perplexed by an equally devout Vaisnavite fideist who believes in any number of reincarnations. Here there is obvious scope for philosophical argument. Is either position tenable? Perhaps both require modification. Would the modified positions be compatible? Moderate fideists may well be moved by such considerations, but extreme fideists have no way of resolving that problem, except by literally denying the *bona fides* of those they would otherwise respect.

A rather different group of extreme fideists are those who recognize the need for something to defeat the grounds for doubt but who seek such defeaters in areas other than argument. There are those who would stress the possibility of knowing God through a mystical or other religious experience. I have no quarrel with those who rely on extraordinary religious experiences to support faith even in the face of serious reasons or grounds for doubt. Ordinary religious experiences, such as most of the faithful can report, are, however, inadequate as defeaters of reasons (or grounds) for doubt.[18] For it would be irrational not to consider, in all seriousness, the possibility that such experiences occur only because of prior faith.

It might not, however, be any special experience that warrants faith even in the face of unanswered grounds for doubt, but that natural capacity to know there is a God (the *sensus divinitatis*) which Calvin proclaims. So let us concentrate on this capacity, and, patronizing though it sounds, let us suppose that those without this capacity are analogous to color-blind people. It would follow then that there is certainly a place for apologetics for the "God-blind." I argue, though, for the stronger conclusion that even those who have this capacity are in need of apologetics if they are to know their beliefs are warranted. But before I do so, I would like to suggest that this natural capacity is in fact an ability to reason implicitly to theism. This suggestion is borne out by the way Calvin, for instance, at the very beginning of the *Institutes*, says: "It is perfectly obvious, that the endowments which we possess cannot possibly be from ourselves; nay, that our very being is nothing else than subsistence in God alone" (Book I, p. 37). This bears the marks of implicit reasoning along the lines of the cosmological argument. Quite generally those who insist that we just know there is a God without further justification will nonetheless often sketch such a justification. (E.g., "There is no need for any philosophical argument. I just know there is a God. There must be some

---

[18] As above, I note that this is effectively Quinn's (1993) response to Plantinga (1986).

explanation for things, mustn't there?") That is evidence that the sensus divinitatis is itself a piece of implicit reasoning.

Let us put these preliminaries to one side and grant Calvin and others that we do have a sensus divinitatis, which, if it is not illusory, is indeed a natural capacity to know there is a God. We may liken this to our natural capacity to know the colors of things. The leaves are shades of green, and clouds at sunset are shades of pink. What could be more obvious? Unfortunately we have excellent reason to believe the pink of the clouds at sunset to be an optical illusion. Moreover, many philosophers follow Locke in denying that the leaves are green except in the sense of causing in us the appropriate sensations. And whether we accept or reject their arguments, we should not dismiss them on the grounds that the leaves are *obviously* green. There is a moral in this for those who rely on the sensus divinitatis to avoid the project of apologetics. I grant that in some fashion it seems obvious to the faithful that there is a God. There is an initial puzzlement as to why anyone should doubt it. I further grant that if there were no grounds for doubt, then that it seems obvious would warrant the belief that there is indeed a God. Moreover, the analogy between the "God-blind" and the color-blind might undermine the grounds for doubt provided by our respect for atheists. Objections such as the argument from evil nonetheless threaten to show God to be an illusion, like the blue sky. And there is no shortage of explanations as to how such an illusion might arise.[19]

Even when it seems obvious that things are a certain way, we should consider the objections to taking them that way. And, as I have already said, the combination of an argument for God with a reply to objections provides the best way of handling the grounds for doubt. I conclude that even those who follow Calvin and rely on the sensus divinitatis need apologetics.

I have argued for the importance of apologetics, then, by noting that believers were subject to various grounds for doubt. At this point it could be urged that, whatever there might be by way of apologetics, few believers avail themselves of it. So, it could be objected, they are condemned as irrational dogmatists. In reply to this I concede that some believers, like some atheists, are indeed irrational dogmatists, but there are two ways in which believers might be warranted in maintaining their religious convictions even without articulate apologetics.

First there is secondhand apologetics, that is, the reliance on others to argue on their behalf. For just as atheists whom we respect provide, I submit, some grounds for doubt, theologians and philosophers whom the faithful re-

---

[19] Marx and Freud are somewhat out of fashion. So I cite Durkheim in this regard.

spect, and who have adequate apologetics, provide grounds for resisting that doubt. Such apologetics at one remove is more convincing if the faithful can at least understand the apologetics in outline, even if they cannot follow the details.

Next there is the way of implicit reasoning. Perhaps the faithful reason implicitly in ways that, when put into words, would provide an apologetic.[20] Here the apologetics of understanding could well be interpreted as the articulation of their previously implicit reasoning, based on implicit understanding and an implicit use of inference to the best explanation. Now the idea of implicit reasoning might seem controversial for it is not subject to critical reflection. What distinction, therefore, can we draw between reasonable and unreasonable implicit reasoning? There is danger that the appeal to implicit reasoning will be used to justify all sorts of irrationality. Because of this danger I consider that, where possible, we should not rely on implicit reasoning but should attempt the task of articulating our reasoning in the form of arguments. Nonetheless, if there is an acceptable apologetic based on the articulation of the ways the faithful reason implicitly, then that apologetic will show that they were reasoning well in their implicit fashion. They were warranted all along but not in a position to know they were warranted.

3. The Goal of Articulation

There is a place, then, for arguments for theism. And I explore one line of argument that defends theism generally, and anthropic theism in particular, as a way of understanding. At this point the faithful could grant all this but quote Pascal's dictum that the heart has reasons of which reason knows nothing, and insist that their understanding of things should not be subjected to the (often unsympathetic) scrutiny of philosophers. In response I offer a defense of the philosophical articulation of theocentric understanding, where by articulation I mean the putting into words as clearly as we can something that was previously obscure. Taken with my case for apologetics this amounts to a defense of that traditional but unfashionable project, philosophical apologetics.

Scientific understanding is inevitably articulate because of its public character and its mathematical form. At the other extreme, aesthetic appreciation is notoriously difficult to articulate and for that reason is seldom recognized as a mode of understanding (Forrest 1991b). Somewhere in between, we tend to think, is the understanding of oneself, the understanding of others, and,

---

[20] That religious convictions are rational in part because of implicit reasoning was a favorite theme of Newman's. See his "Implicit and Explicit Reason," pp. 258–59.

assuming there is such a thing, religious understanding. These can and often do persist in inarticulate form, generating explanations when questions are asked but without any effort at systematic or detailed examination. For example, almost everyone is able to offer some answer to such questions as "Why did you change careers?" or "Why do you like to go swimming?" but few live examined lives. The process of articulation requires a serious and sustained inquiry, not just the readiness to answer questions when asked. But why should we be articulate?

In this section I present four arguments for resisting the privatization of religion, whereby a person's religious beliefs and attitudes are not open to general scrutiny and criticism. And such scrutiny requires that the understanding provided by faith be articulated. One of the differences between science and religion is that scientific articulation requires mathematics whereas religious articulation requires philosophy. But at a very general level I am arguing for an attitude toward faith which is "scientific" in the sense of publicly assessable. And that requires articulation, which in the case of religion amounts to philosophical articulation.

My first argument for articulating the understanding provided by faith is directed against those who, in the spirit of Thomas à Kempis (Book One), resist out of fear of arrogance. I ask, What sort of learning is in fact likely to make us arrogant? Perhaps the ability to expound the teachings of various more or less obscure thinkers. But that is not philosophical articulation, which turns out to be a humbling project. There are always loose ends, always points that seemed clear enough initially but are subsequently found to be both obscure and controversial. The humbling character of philosophy applies with special force to its application to religion. And, since à Kempis (Book One, chap. 1) used the Christian doctrine of the Trinity as an example, I ask, What Christian on being asked to expound that doctrine could possibly be satisfied with the result? Not the Christian philosopher bent on articulation but rather the "learned" person who would quote you Augustine, Aquinas, and others without understanding, or the childish Christian with Sunday School answers off pat. And the same goes both for other religions and for nonreligious world views. Those who honestly attempt an articulate understanding know best what truly defies articulation. I conclude that one excellent reason for attempting the philosophical articulation of religious understanding is that the effort to do so is the best remedy for intellectual arrogance, not pious protestations of humility.

My first argument in defense of the philosophical articulation of theocentric understanding was directed only at those who, usually for religious reasons, consider it arrogant to philosophize. Here is a more general argument. Articulation, I say, is the enemy of self-deception. Now self-deception is a difficult

topic, which I shall spare both myself and my readers. I merely remark that
something often called self-deception involves a belief expressed in words
which conflicts with an inarticulate belief. Consider the ambitious bank manager in a small country town, with the offer of a position in the big city. It
could happen that the obvious advantages of the move, such as the income,
the prestige, and the opportunities for further promotion, are all that is put
in words. Yet, we may suppose, there is also, at a "deeper" level, the belief
that it was not worthwhile uprooting oneself and one's family for the sake of
those advantages. That "deeper" belief is based on an inarticulate understanding of life and what is valuable in life. Because it is inarticulate there is danger
that it will not affect action as it should. And if it does not, then we may say
that the ambitious bank manager is the victim of one kind of self-deception.
To call this phenomenon self-deception might suggest, however, that it is
always the inarticulate beliefs that ought to prevail. Sometimes it is the other
way round. Let us say, then, that the bank manager suffers from *divided beliefs*,
rather than talking of self-deception. A while back it was fashionable to contrast the verbally proficient left brain with the more intuitive but inarticulate
right brain. No doubt that is too crude as a piece of neuroscience. But it is
a useful metaphor, and we can think of much that is called self-deception as
the refusal of the dominant left brain to pay due heed to the right brain, with
the result that the person has divided beliefs, the left believing one thing and
the right another.

Among both theists and atheists there are some who are not entirely at ease
with their convictions. In this circumstance it is rather easy for theists and
atheists to accuse each other of self-deception. If we abandon the phrase "self-
deception" and use instead the less loaded phrase "divided beliefs," there may
be something to these mutual accusations. Although it is hard to discover the
truth on such matters, it may well be that many theists and many atheists have
divided beliefs. If this is granted, and if it is further granted that divided belief
is an unsatisfactory state,[21] then there is a strong case for the articulation of
beliefs. For once I have put in words what I think I believe, then I can ask
the question, And do I really believe it? Moreover, the contradiction involved
in believing and disbelieving the same thing is much harder to sustain if belief
and disbelief are brought together by articulation, rather than existing in isolation.

My third argument for articulating theocentric understanding is that if we

---

[21] This is not obvious, for it would seem that undivided true beliefs are preferable to divided
beliefs, which in turn are preferable to undivided false beliefs. I am assuming, however, that
articulation, although somewhat hazardous, is more likely to heal the division of beliefs by
achieving truth than by achieving falsity.

do not articulate our beliefs and submit them to critical scrutiny, then there is considerable danger of uncritical inference. For example, it is held by some believers that whatever happens, including what is manifestly evil and apparently preventable by us, happens because it is the will of God. Now I suppose there are those who hold that pernicious doctrine after having carefully examined the issue. My present quarrel is not with them. But I fear many have reasoned in ways that if made articulate would be expressed thus:

> Either God did or did not want the events in question to happen. If God had not wanted them to happen, then, being all-knowing, God would have known what was needed to stop them happening, and being all-powerful, God could have done what was needed. So God did want them to happen.

Surely that is not the humble rejection of the intellect, but merely poor reasoning. Once it is made articulate, then it is open to objections. One of these is to point out the possibility that God wants *us* to prevent the evils in question. That in turn raises further philosophical problems—I am not saying the issue is clear cut. But what I am saying is that one excellent reason for attempting the philosophical articulation of religious understanding is that human nature inclines us toward making inferences. Therefore it is of advantage to make them in as articulate and self-critical a fashion as possible to avoid poor reasoning masquerading as the humble rejection of the intellect.

My fourth argument in defense of articulation is based on the *problem of myth*. (See Watts and Williams 1988, pp. 137–40.) Many religious people are drawn to the sophisticated position of interpreting traditional religious doctrines as myths, by which they mean, I think, continued metaphors. For example, the idea of the incarnation of God as a human being is central to Christianity and, in a different way, much of Hinduism. It would be crass to deny the appeal of the idea that God, out of love for us, became one of us. But it is equally crass to make light of the intellectual difficulty of holding this. How is it possible for someone to be truly divine and truly human? We are tempted to treat this doctrine as a beautiful myth illustrating something about God's love and something about human worth.

The problem is that myths seem to lose their emotional impact once they are judged fictitious. For that reason, perhaps, some, in the tradition of Kierkegaard, cling to the doctrine while insisting it is contrary to reason. But that results in strain, even a kind of self-deception in which believers become make-believers. The best possible solution of the problem of myth is to provide a way of understanding how the doctrine can be held as more than metaphorical without any retreat from reason. But to do this requires philosophical articulation. For such questions as "How is it possible for someone to be truly divine and truly human?" are recognizably philosophical ones.[22]

In this way philosophical articulation can protect the emotional impact of religious doctrine. The application of this general point to the topic of this work is straightforward enough. For some are attracted to accounts of God and creation that interpret them as mythical. Thus one eminent contemporary theologian, Don Cupitt, writes in criticism of literal theism, "The stronghold of dogmatic realism is no doubt the doctrine of Creation and the postulation of an objective metaphysical God as world-ground" (1984, p. 159). Cupitt proposes that religious belief be understood in a nonliteral fashion as an ethical project and a spirituality. Now there is indeed a spirituality without belief in an objective personal God. It is to be found in some, but not other, strands of both Buddhism and Hinduism. Like Cupitt, I respect this nontheistic spirituality, but what it lacks is *bhakti*, as Hindus call it—the love of devotees for their God. In this case the problem of myth is that if God is really just a myth, the love of God is illusory. The problem is solved by means of the philosophical articulation of theocentric understanding, which enables a fairly conservative religion to be reconciled with all that is valuable in our intellectual heritage. Spirituality is indeed far more central to religious life than philosophical articulation, but without philosophical articulation spirituality is in mortal danger.

I have argued in four ways that the apologetics of understanding should be made both articulate and public. Some might respond with the *objection from ineffability*. As a result of mystical or other religious experience, because it is part of a tradition, or because it just seems plausible, many would insist that God cannot be known or understood in human terms. For instance, Aquinas, after a certain experience, is said to have called his theology chaff.[23] If he could have read this book, he would surely not have said, "My work is indeed chaff, but this is spot on." No doubt his comment would have been, "Chaffier chaff." The objection from ineffability, then, is that my project requires us to understand the nature of God, which is impossible. Now I am prepared to grant that the nature of God is beyond an articulate understanding, such as I propose in this book when I equate God with unrestricted consciousness. Nonetheless I have two ways of defending myself from this objection. The first is to grant that my project is ultimately a failure but to insist that it serves an ad hominem purpose. Taking that line, I would say that I cannot really provide an articulate understanding of things in terms of God because the

---

[22] For a recent discussion, see Morris 1986.
[23] Or "straw." For an account of Aquinas's breakdown and subsequent refusal to write any more theology, see Weisheipl 1974, pp. 320–21.

divine nature is indeed mysterious. I would go on, however, to say that I can provide an attempt at understanding that meets secular standards. Compare the anecdote told of Picasso, who, it is said, had to pass an art examination in which he was given a month to produce a fully representational classical painting. Cynics might have thought that he, a practitioner of only partly representative nonclassical art, would have been unable to meet the challenge. In fact, the anecdote goes, his result, painted in but a single day, excelled by the representational standards he himself rejected. And that is impressive. Likewise, theists can defend their position much better if they provide explanatory accounts meeting secular standards than if they merely plead that God is beyond our understanding.

My second, and preferred, reply to the objection from ineffability is to insist that a purely speculative understanding can serve the purpose of supporting a nonspeculative explanatory account. In particular, my discussion of the divine nature is frankly speculative. But, as I explain, that is all I need to support the theocentric understanding of certain features of the universe, such as its suitability for life. Hence I am committed not to claiming to have actually understood God, merely to having a tenable speculation. It might, however, be further objected that not all of what I say is proposed as mere speculation. And that might renew the objection from ineffability. For instance, I liken God to someone who wants to share something good just because it is good. Is not this a presumptuous claim to know what is in fact beyond our grasp?

In reply to this further objection I distinguish knowing the nature of something from knowing some truths about it. Thus for thousands of years we have known many truths about gold, such as that it is ductile, but only in this century have we come to know its nature, namely that gold atoms are those with nuclei containing seventy-nine protons. To assert, rather than merely speculate, that God is unrestricted consciousness is to make a claim about the divine nature and so would be open to the objection from ineffability. But likening God to someone who wants to share something good, just because it is good, is not open to that objection. For it is comparable to knowing that gold is ductile, not to knowing that gold nuclei have seventy-nine protons. To be sure, there are philosophical problems about how we can talk about God at all, but they are not the substance of the objection being considered.[24] I conclude, then, that the explanatory account provided by an articulate theocentric understanding does not require us to know the divine nature, and any discussion I provide of that nature is speculative.

I have made a case for the philosophical articulation of the apologetics of

[24] I have attempted to address these in Forrest 1991a. For an account I now prefer, see Alston 1985.

understanding. As a first step in this process of articulation I divide understanding, and hence the apologetics of understanding, into three parts. First,
there is explanation in a narrow sense, in which we explain one thing in terms
of others. In the present case various features of ourselves and of the universe
as a whole are explained by its being created by God. Understanding is not,
however, just the explanation of one thing in terms of another. There is also
the attempt to understand the *terminus* of explanation, by which I mean that
which we use to explain but which is not itself explained by means of something else. Ideally the terminus of explanation, in this case the fact that there
is a God, would be something self-evident. Now I cannot show that it is self-
evident that there is a God, and obviously if I could I would have no further
need for apologetics. But what we can hope to show is that the terminus of
explanation is what I call a *genuine epistemic possibility*. By that I mean a hypothesis that is not too improbable on background evidence. This is contextual in two ways. The first is that just how improbable the terminus of
explanation could be without being too improbable will depend on just how
good an explanation it is in other respects. The second is that the background
evidence can shift: what we are considering is the probability prior to the
consideration of what we are explaining.

The second part of my apologetic project, then, is to present a case for the
genuine epistemic possibility of theism. Finally, there is the further defensive
task of replying to objections to this explanatory account, such as the argument
from evil.

4. Versions of the Apologetics of Understanding

There are several ways of articulating the principle that understanding is
the guide to truth. One version of the apologetics of understanding is based
on inference to the best explanation, as Gilbert Harman calls it. So I call it
best-explanation apologetics. In some respects, however, the title "inference to
the best explanation" is misleading. For we are concerned not with explanation in the day-to-day sense but rather, I submit, with ways of understanding. As I use the terms in this work, the difference between understanding
and explanation is that we always explain one thing in terms of others, whereas
some truths (e.g., that $2 + 2 = 4$) could be intelligible in the sense of not
requiring explanation in order to be understood.[25] The difference between
having explained and having understood would then be analogous to the
difference between a belief being justified by means of other beliefs and a

---

[25] In addition explanation often has a pragmatic character. See van Fraassen 1980.

belief being warranted. For properly basic beliefs are warranted without being justified.[26]

We survey, then, various theories that enable us to understand what we already know, and, making "an inference to the best explanation," we come to believe the theory that best enables us to understand. Best-explanation apologetics is the program of defending theism generally and anthropic theism in particular by showing that (i) belief in a caring God who creates partly for our sakes enables us to understand various things, and (ii) it is a better way of understanding than its rivals, including ananthropic theism. No doubt already included in (i), but worth making explicit, is (iii), the requirement that objections to anthropic theism be met. In addition it is worth making explicit the assumption that, other things being equal, the more that is understood the better. When comparing anthropic theism with its rivals I stress the *breadth* of what it enables us to understand.

One difficulty with reliance on inference to the best explanation is that reasonable people can disagree about what "demands explanation," or, more precisely, what does and what does not need to be explained if it is to be understood. Simple arithmetic truths may perhaps be totally understood without further explanation. More relevant to the present work are hypotheses whose truth, supposing they are true, is less in need of explanation than their falsity, supposing they are false. I call these *intrinsically intelligible* hypotheses. The criterion for deciding what is intrinsically intelligible is the subjective one that we would feel more need to explain their falsity than their truth. An example of an intrinsically intelligible truth would be the conservation of mass, if it were true. For we would have been less inclined, I assume, to ask why no matter comes into or passes out of existence than we are to ask why it in fact does come into existence and pass out of existence.

We should resist the temptation to equate intrinsic intelligibility with high a priori probability. For there might well be truths we know a priori but which lack any intrinsic intelligibility. For instance, there seems nothing incoherent in the claim that we know a priori that inductive extrapolation is on the whole reliable while, having read our Hume, finding this reliability rather hard to understand.

There is a judgment of intrinsic intelligibility which I find attractive and which would save me some of the work of Chapters 6 and 7. It is that we have a store of archetypal ideas or, better, hypotheses which, modified by cultural influences, tend to recur in human thought, and that, although these

[26] A foundationalist theory of understanding could be developed and compared with foundationalist theories of warrant. That would, however, be beyond the scope of this work.

are not known a priori, they are intrinsically intelligible. And among these archetypal hypotheses I would include belief in a deity, although not necessarily a personal God. Unfortunately the assessment of intrinsic intelligibility is subjective in the sense that reasonable people might disagree about the need for explanation. For that reason I refrain from claiming that the termini of my explanations are intrinsically intelligible.[27] I am, for instance, quite prepared to treat consciousness as a mystery. But it is, I say, a mystery we have to accept anyway. Therefore it may be taken for granted when one is giving a theocentric explanation.

I do, however, respond to claims by naturalists that the termini of *their* explanations are intrinsically intelligible. In this regard I note two plausible necessary conditions for intrinsic intelligibility. The first is lack of change: though the existence of unchanging things such as laws of nature might be intrinsically intelligible, changing or transient things like the Big Bang could not be. The second mark is simplicity. More precisely, if a hypothesis is more complicated than some rival, then we will not take it as intrinsically intelligible. Thus Swinburne gives the example of the Vedic pantheon of 333 gods as less simple than monotheism. For that reason we would definitely not take the existence of 333 gods as intrinsically intelligible.

A serious difficulty with reliance on inference to the best explanation is the *threat of the unknown hypothesis.* We cannot survey all the theories that might enable us to understand what we already know (van Fraassen 1980). Even if we grant that the best available explanation is a theocentric one, might that not be due to our having overlooked some better explanation? It is mere caution, not irrationality, to take seriously the possibility of as yet undiscovered explanations. Best explanation apologetics cannot, therefore, exclude agnosticism. If indeed the best available way of understanding is theocentric, however, then we do have a strong case against atheism. (Here I am assuming that the various objections to God have been met, for otherwise theocentric understanding would not be the best available.) For there would be no support for the *belief* that there actually is an as yet undiscovered, better, and nontheistic explanation. But it is just such a belief, as opposed to suspense of judgment, that would be required for atheism.

If the best available way of understanding is theocentric, then the only way of resisting the argument above against atheism would be by an appeal to some kind of mystical experience that implies there is no personal God but only, say, the impersonal Nirguna Brahman. I am skeptical of any such athe-

---

[27] Note, though, that both the characterization of God as a perfect being and the classical theistic doctrine that God is a necessary, simple, and eternal being could be used to support this claim.

istic appeal to mystical experience. For the atheist's experience should be interpreted as an overwhelming sense of the nonpersonal aspects of something that, for all the atheist knows, is a personal God. It is not part of theism to say that the personal aspects of God are the only significant ones.

Having rejected atheism, we should be either theists or agnostics. Although best-explanation apologetics cannot be used to show agnosticism to be unwarranted, it can be used, more defensively, to show that theism is itself warranted. For there are no rules about how cautious we should be intellectually. So we have to rely on good sense. I grant that good sense permits a high enough degree of belief in the existence of undiscovered explanations to warrant suspense of judgment, but I judge that good sense also permits a low enough degree of belief in undiscovered explanations to warrant theism. Hence agnosticism and theism are both warranted positions.[28] The difference between the two applications of best-explanation apologetics is that the case for theism requires a further judgment, namely that it is unlikely there is an undiscovered and superior nontheistic way of understanding. For similar reasons, best-explanation apologetics cannot show unwarranted a suspense of judgment between anthropic and ananthropic theism, but it can be used to show anthropic theism to be warranted and ananthropic theism unwarranted.

I have been expounding the project of best-explanation apologetics. But what warrant is there for reliance on inference to the best explanation itself? We could give examples in which the way we reason is indeed by means of such inferences. Citing these examples does not, to be sure, provide some further justification, for the skeptic could properly treat the examples themselves as instances of natural but unreliable reasoning processes, like the gambler's fallacy ("The more often I have lost in the past, the more likely I am to win next time"). Rather the point of these examples is to persuade us that inference to the best explanation is something we already accept without further justification.

For instance, consider the inference used by a paleo-anthropologist investigating hominid remains in a site a million years old. There are heaps of broken marrow bones, plenty of charcoal, and stones of the right shape for cracking the bones. It is surely reasonable to infer that this was some sort of campsite, that the hominids used fire, and that they were not strict vegetarians.

Yet again, consider van Fraassen's example of the mouse in the wainscoting. He says, "I hear scratching in the wall, the patter of little feet at midnight,

[28] Translated into the rather artificial language of degrees of credence, best-explanation apologetics aims to show that the range of warranted degrees of credence in theism includes high values (i.e., fairly near 100 percent) but excludes low values (i.e., fairly near 0 percent). It does not aim to show that the range excludes intermediate, agnostic values (i.e., near 50 percent).

my cheese disappears—and I infer that a mouse has come to live with me"
(1980, pp. 19–20). Unless we are singularly skeptical, we shall judge all these
inferences to the best explanation to be warranted. On further reflection we
shall, I assume, judge that inference to the best explanation is quite generally
a warranted way of reasoning.

That inference to the best explanation needs no further justification is,
however, open to an objection, derived from Kant via Hans Vaihinger,[29]
namely that our ordinary ways of reasoning should be restricted to what is
observable. A recent exponent of this restriction-to-observables tradition is
van Fraassen, who grants that we reason correctly using inference to the best
explanation when it comes to inferring observable items such as mice behind
the wainscoting. He points out, however, that in these cases there is no difference between believing the conclusion of an inference to the best explanation, on the one hand, and believing that everything observable is *as if* that
conclusion is correct, on the other. For in these cases the conclusion of the
inference is itself observable, though not observed. Or, to be more precise,
the conclusion concerns entities of a kind we can observe, even if we do not
observe those particular instances. Thus to believe that everything observable
is as if there is a mouse behind the wainscoting is to believe there is indeed
a mouse, for mice are observable things. Hence, van Fraassen argues, the most
we need grant in favor of inference to the best explanation is that it supports
conclusions about what is observable, namely that the observable things will
be as if the best explanation was correct. When it comes to unobservable
items such as neutrons, he advocates an agnostic position, namely suspending
judgment between the thesis that there are neutrons and the instrumentalist
thesis that there are no neutrons but it is just as if there are.

I disagree with van Fraassen and do indeed rely on inference to the best
explanation to justify belief in unobservables such as neutrons. But this is not
the place to discuss this. Instead I claim that best-explanation apologetics is
less vulnerable to the restriction-to-observables criticism than is the use of
inference to the best explanation to criticize van Fraassen's scientific agnosticism. That is because I am arguing against atheism and defending theism
rather than arguing against agnosticism. I could, therefore, concede that inference to the best explanation is less secure for unobservable than observable
entities. I could even concede that God is not observable (by us, in this life).
It would follow from these two concessions that we have less strong reasons
for believing there is a God than for believing there is a mouse behind the

---

[29] In Western thought, that is. Arguably the madhyamika dialectic of the great Buddhist
thinkers Nagarjuna and Candrakirti made similar points more than a thousand years before
Kant. See Murti, 1980, chap. 12.

wainscoting. But how much less strong? To make much the same point as I made when considering the threat of the unknown hypothesis, there are no rules governing the diminution of confidence as the hypothetical entities become less observable. We must rely on good sense, and good sense dictates neither that we believe rather than suspend judgment nor that we suspend judgment rather than believe. But, I say, any who grant that theocentric understanding is superior to its rivals would be lacking in good sense if they remain atheists.[30]

There is a further objection to reliance on inference to the best explanation as a defense of theism. It might be taken as a mark of mental instability, paranoia perhaps, to insist that there are explanations when good sense leaves much unexplained. I mention that objection because it is one that might well occur to those who know of traditional cosmological arguments for God and detect a resemblance between best-explanation apologetics and such arguments. My reply is that the objection is based on a natural enough misunderstanding. The phrase "inference to the best explanation" suggests we should believe the best available theory even if it is a rather silly one, just because all the rivals are even sillier. But that is not how I interpret it. Inference to the best explanation is really inference to the best way of understanding if it is good enough. With that gloss I insist I am not demanding a way of understanding, merely seeking one. And to seek to understand where we can is a sign of intellectual health, not mental instability.

Similar to the above is the Kantian objection that there are limits to what can be understood and that reliance on inference to the best explanation threatens to transgress these limits. Now this is not the place to write an "anti-Kant." It suffices to make four remarks and then simply announce that there will be no further discussion of Kantian objections to best explanation apologetics:

(i)   The great philosophers are the original and thought-provoking ones. I see no reason to assume that originality is a guide to truth. In fact we might suspect that, for the most part, original philosophy is false. Hence the undoubted greatness of Kant does not make him an authority.

(ii)   Kant, like every philosopher, was philosophizing in a historical context. The primary object of his critique, therefore, was the tradition of Leibniz and Wolff with its reliance on the Principle of Sufficient Reason and its pretensions to have achieved knowledge about various metaphysical issues.

(iii)   Inference to the best explanation may resemble the Principle of Suffi-

---

[30] For a further discussion of some of these issues in the context of scientific realism, see Forrest 1994a.

cient Reason in some ways, but it is not based on the assumption that everything can be understood. Moreover, it operates not as a method for discovering knowledge but in the context of discussions of which beliefs are warranted.

(iv)   Although acknowledging a debt to Hume, Kant overestimated the role of the a priori. It is not surprising, therefore, that he legislated a priori against various attempts at understanding. We should prefer, I suggest, a more "empirical" approach in which we decide what can be understood by attempting to understand it. Perhaps after we have failed to understand, we might then indulge in Kantian speculations about this failure.

I have replied to various objections to best-explanation apologetics. I now consider some variants, partly to accommodate any who are not convinced by my replies. First, many believers cannot explain just how they came to believe. For them the role of apologetics would be more concerned with the maintenance of belief. Given that believers do have some grounds for doubt, the question now arises as to what sort of justification we need to provide in order to maintain our beliefs. And my suggestion here is that one justification is provided by the following rule of maintaining the best explanation.

> The maintenance of beliefs because they provide a satisfactory way of understanding, is warranted, unless we know of a better way of understanding.[31]

Even if, for some reason, inference to the best explanation be rejected, the rule of maintaining the best explanation should be accepted.

There is another way of weakening inference to the best explanation and so arriving at what might be a more generally acceptable way of reasoning. This is to adopt the Verisimilitude Principle, which tells us that the better the explanation the nearer it is to the truth.[32] One reason for adopting that principle is that if the truth is some hypothesis we have not thought of, then it is no surprise that a similar or approximating hypothesis, which is thus not true but merely near the truth, should explain things fairly well. The idea of one hypothesis being near another may be illustrated by the way classical

---

[31] It is a matter of some subtlety just what sort of connection is permitted between the capacity to understand and the maintenance of belief. For there might be various wayward causal connections. Consider someone who, to preserve the intellectual pleasure of understanding, arranged for some abnormal procedure such as "brain washing" to fix the beliefs that provided the understanding. Such beliefs would not remain warranted.

[32] In recent philosophy of science the concept of verisimilitude became widely discussed as a result of Karl Popper's work. See Oddie 1986 for details.

mechanics is near quantum mechanics in the sense of being a good approximation when Planck's constant is negligible.

Notice that although this intuitive motivation would suggest the best available explanation is near the truth, I have formulated the principle in comparative terms, as indicating that one explanation is nearer the truth than some other. That is largely because what counts as near is contextual, and in the context of theory choice it is hard to assign any meaning to "near" other than "nearer than any other available account." There is an additional advantage in stating the Verisimilitude Principle in this comparative fashion. For if there is no best explanation but merely competing fairly good explanations, we could conclude that they are all about as near the truth. That theism is about as near the truth as its rivals might provide a fall-back position if, as I do not accept, other ways of understanding were about as good as the theocentric.

Given the Verisimilitude Principle, the apologetics of understanding would provide a way of explicating the tradition, often called apophatic, that stresses that God is totally beyond human comprehension. We would arrive at the conclusion that theism is nearer the truth than its rivals, including naturalism, but is nonetheless false. Conversely, to say there is no God would be strictly true but would nonetheless suggest something false, namely the assertion that theism is no nearer the truth than rival ways of understanding. Or putting it another and equally traditional way, we could retain the thesis that there is a God but with the gloss that when, for instance, we say God is personal, that is not strictly true but merely nearer the truth than various rival descriptions of the deity, for instance that it is a principle of order.[33]

The verisimilitude qualification might also help reconcile the sort of theism appropriate for my antisupernaturalist theocentric understanding with the sort of theism generated by reflection on religious tradition and experience.[34] If, as I rather doubt, there is a problem of reconciliation, then we might well take both versions as near the truth and nearer than recognizably nontheistic accounts.

The obvious objection to the verisimilitude qualification is the difficulty in making sense of being near the truth but not true when it comes to God.

---

[33] The difference between these two ways of making a verisimilitude qualification reflects different accounts not of God but of the word "God." First suppose the word "God" is analyzed as a definite description. In that case, if it is merely near the truth that there is a being with the traditional divine attributes, then, strictly speaking, there is no God. Suppose, however, the word "God" is a proper name. Then, presumably, we should not say "There is a God." It could be true, however, that God exists even if we are mistaken about the divine attributes, just as it could be true that Abraham really existed even if the account of his life in Genesis is false. See Kripke 1980; Devitt and Sterelny 1987, pp. 39–66.

[34] The claim that there is need for reconciliation would be an adaptation of Pascal's complaint that the God of the philosophers is not the God of Abraham, Isaac, and Jacob.

(Contrast theories in mathematical physics, where we can rely on numerical approximations.) I note that if it is a genuine difficulty, it should encourage us to accept inference to the best explanation in an unqualified fashion when it comes to theism, even if we adopt the verisimilitude qualification when it comes to science. That is because the problem with inference to the best explanation without the qualification is that a theory near the truth could explain a great deal without being true. Therefore, we think, it is prudent to believe that the best available explanation is either true or near the truth, rather than believing it true. But if, in the case of theism, there could be nothing that was merely near the truth, then there is no problem.

As I indicated, the chief problem with applying verisimilitude to theism is that it is hard to think of how theism could be merely near the truth.[35] Perhaps, though, we should claim that the truth is near theism in ways we cannot even speculate about. Now, as an attempt at understanding, it would be ludicrous to appeal to what we cannot even speculate about. But as a gloss on what we can infer from our best attempt at understanding, it is by no means ludicrous. Quite generally—and not just for the case of theism—we might conclude that the best available theory is nearer the truth than its rivals, but is near the truth in ways we cannot comprehend until and unless we have a better theory. To illustrate this let us suppose, to take our previous example, that quantum mechanics is itself true. Then classical mechanics is near the truth in that it holds as a good approximation when Planck's constant is negligible. There is, however, no mention of Planck's constant in classical mechanics. We required, therefore, quantum mechanics in order to understand the way in which classical mechanics is near the truth and the way in which it fails to be true.

I have now provided several different articulations of the principle that understanding is the guide to truth. It is worth listing the consequences of these for apologetics, assuming that theocentric understanding is indeed the best available way of understanding various features of the universe. Straightforward inference to the best explanation leads to the rejection of atheism as

[35] Following a suggestion of Barry Miller's, we might gain some idea of the way various assertions about God can be nearer or further from the truth by considering the concept of the *limit*. The limit of a polygon as the number of sides increases is no longer a polygon but a circle. Likewise, the limit of a person as various restrictions are removed would no longer be a person, strictly speaking. Now it would be nearer the truth to describe a circle as an infinigon (i.e., a polygon with infinitely many sides) than as a chiliagon (i.e., a polygon with a thousand sides). Likewise, it would be nearer the truth to say that God is a person without any restrictions than to say that God is a person with just a few restrictions. (This is not in fact the thesis Miller propounds, for he uses the concept of a limit to explicate a traditional theory of analogy, according to which the term 'person' is predicated truly of both God and human beings, but in a way that is neither univocal nor casually ambiguous.)

unwarranted but permits agnosticism as well as theism. The maintenance of the best explanation would warrant theism, but only for those who are already theists. Weakening inference to the best explanation by means of the verisimilitude qualification would result in believers being warranted in claiming theism as not strictly true but as nearer the truth than rivals.

5. In Defense of Speculation

In this work I attempt an articulate understanding of various features of the universe. Now much of that attempt, especially in the later chapters, is speculative. Often what I am providing is a way things could be understood, without claiming to have discovered the correct way of understanding. For instance, I provide a double aspect account of human beings according to which mental states are just the consciousness of physical processes. If asked to defend that account, I would begin by pointing to difficulties with what I call reductive physicalism. That indeed motivates my own account; but the considerations I provide in favor of it are not sufficient for me to believe that it, rather than various other possible accounts, is the truth. I have to suspend judgment. Hence my account of human beings is speculative. Later I use my speculation about human nature to speculate, in turn, about the divine nature.

What point, you may ask, is there in mounting speculation upon speculation in this way? The role of speculation in understanding may be illustrated by means of an example. That some species of animal and plant were descended from others, and that not all species were able to survive, is the current, and I submit correct, way of understanding the fossil record. It also provides a way of understanding why species we tend to classify together often have additional characteristics in common beyond those initially used to classify them. This is most remarkable where these common characteristics have no survival value. Thus the vast majority of mammals, I am told, have seven vertebrae in the neck. It is hard to believe that for many species some other number would not have been equally conducive to survival.[36]

That there has been evolution is not, I submit, speculation but rather a well-established truth, arrived at using inference to the best explanation. This explanation is, however, successful only because the evolution of one species from another is a genuine epistemic possibility. By that I mean that even apart from an examination of the fossil record it should be judged as not too improbable. Now Darwin can be interpreted as arguing for the genuine epistemic possibility of evolution on the grounds that we humans have bred new

[36] For many more examples of the explanatory power of evolutionary theory, see Gould 1980, chaps. 1–3.

varieties of animals and plants. He could have conceded that this was sheer speculation, because humans had not bred new species and because it was not known whether the origin of new species was relevantly similar to the breed-ing of new varieties. He could also have conceded that the probability of evolution was fairly low given just the background knowledge, before we look at the detailed evidence. But if he had not provided even a speculative understanding of evolution, then the probability would have been so low that the detailed evidence would not have been sufficient for him to claim that evolution is in fact the correct explanation. Let me stress that it would not have been sufficient for Darwin to insist on the mere logical possibility of the descent of one species from another. (As far as I know, it is logically possible, that is, free from contradiction, for babies to hatch out of coconuts.) Specu-lation is here being used to establish a genuine epistemic possibility.

The example of evolution can also be used to illustrate the role of specu-lation in defending a theory against objections. Certain facts, such as the wide-spread absence from the fossil record of missing links (i.e., intermediate species), which would not otherwise be puzzling, become problematic in the context of evolution. We could handle the implied objection by means of the further speculation that missing links were at a disadvantage compared to competitors and thus could occur only in the rather unusual circumstances where there was lack of competition. It scarcely matters that this is speculative, provided it is a genuine epistemic possibility. For it shows that the difficulty could be handled, whether or not we have hit upon the correct way of handling it. But it would not be enough to provide a mere logical possibility— say, the logical possibility that antievolutionists had secretly dug over all the fossil beds carefully removing all missing links.

Examples such as the above illustrate how speculation can support under-standing by establishing genuine epistemic possibilities and by handling ob-jections. It is important, though, not to treat everything as speculative. My aim is to defend the truth of theism, not merely that it is a genuine epistemic possibility.

Speculation, then, plays an important although subsidiary role in the apol-ogetics of understanding. Now I shall be piling speculation on speculation, and there is a prima facie objection to such iterated speculation. It is a special case of a more general objection to philosophical argument, noted, but mis-diagnosed, by Hume (A Treatise of Human Nature, Book One, Section XIII). The trouble with philosophy is not that philosophers present interesting ar-guments of some weight which are, however, inconclusive. The trouble is that they will insist on moving on to other issues, taking for granted what had not been conclusively established. Or they rely on premises for which their teachers argued in an inconclusive fashion and then present inconclusive arguments from those premisses for theses their students take as premisses. Let us suppose that a well-received philosophical argument typically has a probability of 90 percent—highly persuasive but not conclusive. Then a succession of seven such arguments would have a probability equal to the seventh power of 90 percent, which is less than 50 percent. Fortunately there are ways of handling this difficulty as it applies to philosophical arguments. One is to rely on a consilience of several different lines of argument. But perhaps the best is not to rely on chains of argument but always to go back to the beginning.

The diminution of probability as we pass along a chain of arguments becomes quite catastrophic if we are merely speculating. In response to objections I might add to my initial speculation three further ones. Even if each one had a probability as high as 10 percent, the overall effect would be a speculation a thousand times less probable. How, then, do I justify my reliance on iterated speculations? Let me first formulate a general principle and then defend it. The principle is that improbability that results from the accumulation of detail should not be held against the genuine epistemic possibility of a speculation. My defense is based on the fact that there are, no doubt, very many detailed articulations of a given speculation, but we are in no position to survey them. In that circumstance the presumption is that the ones we are able to articulate are *representative* ways of developing the speculation. Unless that presumption is overcome, the relevant probability is not that of the actual result of piling speculation on speculation but rather the sum of all the possible ways of satisfactorily articulating that speculation. For instance, when it comes to theodicy the relevant probability is not that of the favorite speculations of the quirky author of this work but the probability of there being *some* adequate theodicy.

We have, of course, no accurate estimate of just how many other detailed speculations there are as good as those we have thought of. Nonetheless, in the absence of a survey of all possible speculations, it is entirely reasonable to provide one line of speculation in defense of, or otherwise supporting, theocentric understanding. For the speculations we can think of are representatives or samples of a larger range of speculations most of which we have not thought of. Therefore to insist that any one detailed account is extremely improbable is to miss the point.

6. A Survey of Theocentric Understanding

Let us survey some of the things that can be understood by means of theism generally or, in some cases, anthropic theism in particular. First, there is the ambitious project of understanding why there is something rather than nothing. I mention it to stress that it is not my present concern, for I am neither demanding nor offering an understanding of everything.

Only a little less ambitious is the project of understanding why the physical universe exists. I offer a partial explanation of why there is a physical universe, namely that God intended there to be embodied persons. But this is only partial. For I quite explicitly assume that the situation in which God creates is one in which a whole range of physical universes is possible, and to gain a fuller understanding of why there is a physical universe we would have to understand how the physical is even possible. One explanation would be provided by a Berkeleian theistic subjective idealism, according to which physical things, including those we humans cannot observe, exist because God perceives them. (The slogan is, Quarks are qualia.) But all such explanations strike me as just too speculative to add much weight to best-explanation apologetics. They would serve to establish the physical as a genuine epistemic possibility if that should be doubted, but I am assuming that the physical is not in doubt.

Next in my survey I come to the main topic of the next chapter, namely the theocentric understanding of the suitability of this universe for life. Before I expand on it I need to say what I mean by the phrases "a universe" and "this universe." Here I am following the usage of recent speculation about cosmology (Leslie 1989). The *large "u"* Universe is the sum total of everything physical. It may or may not be composed of more than one *small "u"* universe. When I talk of *this universe,* or where it is not confusing, *the universe,* I mean the small "u" universe to which we belong, including the most distant galaxies that astronomers have or ever will observe. When I talk of *a universe,* I mean one of the small "u" universes. A universe in this sense is an extremely large region that can, without artificiality, be considered in isolation from everything else in the Universe.

With this terminology in place, then, we can note the remarkable fact that this universe, the one we are in, is suited to life. There are several possible explanations for this. One of them is the theocentric account that it is suited to life because God intended it as the home of embodied persons, including ourselves. A rival explanation is the many-universes hypothesis, namely that there are many universes that vary a great deal. As a consequence it is to be expected that some of them will be suited to life. And, of course, we must be in one of the ones thus suited. So if there is some universe suited to life, *this* universe, in the sense of the universe we are in, must be suited to life.

In Chapter 4 I give some attention to the ordered beauty of the universe. From the pre-Socratics it has been assumed that the universe around us must conform to some plan we can comprehend. But on reflection this is not something we should simply take for granted. And it can be given a theocentric understanding. Indeed there are two quite different things that can be understood. The first is that this universe is orderly enough for us to lead meaningful lives, able to form projects knowing that various means will lead to various ends. The second is the occurrence of laws of nature, whose discovery by scientists is one of the genuine glories of Western culture. The former can be explained in terms of God's intention to create embodied persons. For a fairly orderly universe is required if there is to be life as we know it and hence embodied persons like us.

We have reason to believe that the order revealed by the laws of nature extends throughout our universe and so is more than that required for the existence of life or for us to lead meaningful lives. It is best understood, I claim, aesthetically. This leads to the more general topic of the understanding of beauty. If I had to choose one feature of the universe that most clearly supports theism, it would be the beauty of things rather than the suitability of the universe for life. Beauty, I believe, needs to be emphasized as part of the theocentric understanding of things for four reasons. The first is that it is harder to understand in naturalistic terms than is the suitability of the universe for life. The second is that, as I argue, beauty is best understood as the result of divine generosity, and, like all the best gifts, its enjoyment is an end, not a means. This supports belief in anthropic rather than ananthropic theism. The third is that a sense of the beauty of creation acts as a counterweight to the emotional impact of suffering and malice, which, as I concede, provide prima facie grounds for atheism even after the undermining of all articulate formulations of the argument from evil. Finally, the theocentric understanding of beauty results in the emotional responses of both awe and gratitude, which is important because religious faith is widely granted to involve the emotions as well as the intellect.

In addition to the theocentric understanding of the beauty of created things, we can understand the beauty of that which does not depend on creation. I have in mind the serendipity of mathematics, which, being necessary, would seem not to be created. Theists should hold that necessary truths, when they are not mere products of our human ways of thinking and speaking, reflect something of the nature of God. In that case mathematics reveals the beauty of God.

There is such value in art, including drama, and in humor that it is reasonable to suppose that God has deliberately enriched our lives by endowing us with artistic capacities and a sense of humor. I could have considered these abilities, but I concentrate on the theocentric understanding of another, namely the capacity to discover scientific theories. God wants us to achieve various worthwhile goals by our own efforts, "mixing our labour with them," as Locke puts it. To that end, God so arranges the course of genetic and social

evolution as to equip us with faculties that, if we exercise due care, will lead
to worthwhile knowledge. Like the beauty of the universe, this capacity to
discover the truth is best understood in terms of anthropic theism, as a gift
from a generous personal God.

There are several features of morality that could be given a theocentric
understanding. In Chapter 4 I concentrate on just one of them. This is *moral
supremacy*, namely the way moral considerations override others. I explain it
as a result of an implicit divine command. Understanding morality in this
fashion serves to underpin the important, though often overemphasized, aspect
of God as demanding moral uprightness. In addition I argue that the theocentric understanding of moral supremacy requires that we be rational in
trusting God, come what may. Such trust seems more appropriate in the
context of anthropic theism. Hence the consideration of moral supremacy
provides a further reason for preferring anthropic over ananthropic theism.

I now turn to some features that I have decided not to discuss. First, there
is the meaning of life. Many hold—rightly, I say—that life has abundant
meaning and that this abundance of meaning is not just the result of good
fortune for a few but available to all. I could argue for the theocentric understanding of that belief in the abundant and available meaning of life. Wish-
ful thinking is, however, too obvious an explanation for this to be of much
worth as a piece of apologetics.

Again, many people have what they interpret as experiences of God. And
one way of explaining this is by treating these as genuine experiences. This
has been given an important role by Basil Mitchell (1973, p. 44) and has been
argued to be a form of perception by William P. Alston (1991). I do not,
however, rely on religious experience as a phenomenon to be understood.
That is because, however persuasive it might be to someone having the experience, others may interpret it as due to a combination of an underlying
experience of a deity in the broad sense with the prior belief that if there is
a deity then it is a personal God. Hence that others have a certain kind of
religious experience does not provide much support for theism as I have
characterized it. The chief role, I submit, for religious experience in apologetics is as a private confirmation of a faith that is publicly supported by best-
explanation apologetics.

Yet again, anyone who has actually witnessed an apparent miracle is likely
to be impressed and should take seriously some theocentric understanding of
miracles as genuine. There is considerable work to be done here in discussing
whether miracles involve violations of laws of nature and what reasons God
might have for working miracles, whether or not they are strict violations of
laws. But I do not investigate these questions, for the simple reason that there
would seem to be naturalistic explanations of why honest people sincerely

believe they have witnessed miracles even if they are mistaken. The obvious naturalistic explanation is that they are in fact just extremely unlikely coincidences, in which, for example, a spontaneous recovery from bone cancer— itself a rare but possible event—coincides with the going to Lourdes on pilgrimage. Another explanation that comes to mind is the parapsychological one that some people have powers of healing not explained by current medicine. This would be of great interest but of little theological consequence. More difficult to explain naturalistically is the collective religious experience of those who witness the miraculous, but that experience, although shared, is as hard to articulate as more private religious experiences. I do not therefore discuss the miraculous.

The things for which I offer a theocentric understanding, then, are the suitability of the universe for life; the order and beauty of the universe, especially as revealed by the sciences; the serendipity of mathematics; our ability to discover scientific truths; and moral supremacy. In addition, in Chapter 7, I offer a rather speculative explanation of the objectivity of values.

7. A Comparison with Other Apologetic Projects

I conclude this chapter by noting the differences between the apologetics of understanding and some similar projects. Two traditional arguments that resemble the apologetics of understanding are the teleological argument and the argument from design. A more recent approach is Bayesian apologetics.

The proper context of the teleological argument is the Aristotelian idea of something having a *telos*. To make that idea accessible, I interpret the claim that something has a telos in non-Aristotelian terms as the claim that it is *as if intended for some purpose*. The teleological argument starts, then, from the premiss that many, perhaps all, things are as if intended for some purpose. From that it is inferred that they are indeed intended for some purpose, which implies that there is a personal being so intending them. This could be construed as an inference to the best explanation, namely that the best explanation of a thing's being as if intended for some purpose is that it is indeed intended for some purpose. (Quite generally one excellent explanation for things being as if X is that they really are X.)

Although I have no great quarrel with the teleological argument, thus interpreted, it strikes me as unnecessary to go the trouble of first pointing to various features of the universe in order to argue that things are as if intended and then seeking to understand why they are as if intended. The apologetics of understanding is more direct in its approach.

The argument from design I take to be the argument propounded by Cleanthes in Hume's *Dialogues*. It is an argument by analogy in which we are invited to grant the many respects in which the things that are not designed by human beings are nonetheless *like* the things that are. Once again, this could be reconstructed as an inference to the best explanation: the best explanation of the respects in which things are like the results of human design is that they are the products of divine design. (Treating the argument by analogy in this way has the advantage that we do not have to rely on the *like effects like cause principle* of Cleanthes.)

As is well known, many of the remarkable examples of apparent design in nature concerned the way species of animal and plant were adapted to their environment. For that reason the argument from design fell out of favor when Darwinian evolutionary theory became accepted, with its claim that such adaptation would arise as a result of the "survival of the fittest." Now if I considered planets suitable for life to be few and far between, I could take issue with any attempt to explain the marvelous adaptations of plants and animals in Darwinian or neo-Darwinian fashion, on the grounds that on any one inhabitable planet these marvelous adaptations would be an incredible fluke. I do not pursue this line of argument, however. For inhabitable planets, although far between, are not, as far as I know, few. Given enough inhabitable planets, it is not surprising that evolution has resulted in complex and subtle adaptations in some of them, and only where such adaptations have occurred could there be animals, such as ourselves, capable of marveling at these adaptations. The version of the apologetics of understanding I provide has the advantage of making no mention of the adaptation of species.

I now turn to more recent apologetic projects. I have already discussed how my project can be fitted into reformed epistemology if desired, so I do not treat that as a rival apologetic project. A genuine rival is *Bayesian apologetics*, by which I mean the project of establishing that theism has a fairly high numerical probability by appealing to the standard calculus of probabilities. Thus Swinburne (1979) claims that various features of the universe, such as its regular, law-governed character can be shown to be probable given that there is a God, but that these features would otherwise be improbable. By Bayes's theorem this has the effect of amplifying the probability of theism. Schlesinger has presented a similar discussion (1971; 1988, chap. 5). More is required, however, to establish a high probability of theism. In the first place, other considerations might have the opposite effect. Thus the sheer amount of evil might reduce the probability of theism.[37] This is a minor point, for even if they granted it, Bayesian apologists could argue that this reduction is less significant than the previous amplification.

---

[37] Swinburne (1979, p. 219) expresses "considerable initial sympathy" for this claim, but his final position is that the evil leaves the probability unchanged (1979, p. 277).

The second reason why more is required to show theism to be probable is that, as both Swinburne and Schlesinger concede, we must start off with a non-negligible probability if the amplification is to result in a final probability that is high. This is not an easy point to express with precision, for the greater the amplification the less the initial probability has to be in order to arrive at a high final probability. Schlesinger does not have a great deal to say about the initial probability of theism, other than pointing out the difficulties in assigning initial probabilities. Swinburne, however, argues for that non-negligible initial probability by first arguing that human beings are not purely physical or material things. He then infers that an immaterial person-like being or god is quite plausible. Further considerations of theoretical simplicity favor there being one all-powerful God rather than, say, the 333 gods of the Vedic pantheon.

My version of the apologetics of understanding resembles Swinburne's and Schlesinger's Bayesian apologetics in several respects. So let me begin by acknowledging their influence and noting the similarities.

(1)   Both Bayesian apologetics and the apologetics of understanding are conceded to be inconclusive. In that sense they are both versions of probabilistic apologetics.

(2)   My concern to establish theism as a genuine epistemic possibility is parallel to Swinburne's need to establish a non-negligible initial probability for theism. The explanatory power of theism then raises its status to a theory that it is warranted to accept as true and not warranted to reject as false. This parallels the amplification of probabilities in Bayesian apologetics.

(3)   I follow Swinburne in seeing a discussion of human nature as crucial to establishing the genuine epistemic possibility, or initial non-negligible probability, of theism.

There are differences, however. First, I am not an enthusiast for the calculus of probabilities. In part this is because of the artificiality of precise numerical probabilities.[38] If, for example, the probability of theism on the available evidence turned out to be 80 percent, then that would imply that, for ideal rationality, a person must believe in God but without a great deal of confidence. It seems to be far more plausible that the case for theism would permit a whole range of positions varying from belief with almost complete confi-

---

[38] In addition I have scruples about the Multiplication Principle, namely that the probability of P-and-Q is the probability of P given Q times the probability of Q. This principle can be justified using the Dutch book argument. But that, I think, merely shows that it is irrational not to give odds in accordance with the Multiplication Principle. Giving odds is one thing, having degrees of credence another. See Forrest 1989b, p. 281.

dence to the agnostic position. To remedy this artificial precision resulting from the calculus of probabilities, we might adopt a more subtle account, such as Isaac Levi's (1980), but the gain in fidelity to the actual situation of human reasoners is at the expense of technical complexity. Instead I take the calculus of probabilities as a heuristic device that, on the whole, gives us results in accordance with our intuitions about inconclusive reasoning.

A more important difference between the apologetics of understanding and Swinburne's Bayesian apologetics is that Swinburne typically contrasts the probability of something on the supposition of theism with its probability on the supposition of atheism. He argues that the former is high and the latter low. This seems to be oversimplified, for there are many different nontheistic speculations, and on some of them the probability of the feature in question might be quite high. So we are in no position to insist on the low probability of some feature on the supposition of atheism until we have examined these rivals to theism. In Chapters 3 and 5 I aim to give a fair hearing to a variety of alternatives to theism. Moreover, the hypothesis that there is no God is not just the disjunction of the known rivals. We need also consider the "catch-all," as John Earman calls it (1992, p. 168)—in this context the hypothesis that some as yet unknown atheist theory is correct. And the probability of some feature of the universe on this catchall hypothesis is, as Earman puts it, "anybody's guess."

The third notable difference between my approach and that of Swinburne is that he is nearer to being a Cartesian dualist. He argues that humans have a nonmaterial part, which could survive death disembodied (Swinburne 1986) and to which God can be likened. By contrast, I allow that we humans might be essentially embodied. Indeed I do not reject physicalism, the thesis that we humans are purely physical things. This results in two problems for me. The first is that if the only persons we know of are essentially embodied, then, assuming God not to be essentially embodied, it is prima facie implausible that there is a God. I argue that, in spite of this, theism is a genuine epistemic possibility. The second is that an afterlife, which I believe to be required both to speculate about the motive for creation and to reply to the argument from evil, is likewise prima facie implausible if humans are essentially embodied. Here again I argue (in Chapter 2) that an afterlife could be purely physical.

A further difference between Bayesian apologetics and the apologetics of understanding is that the latter can exploit situations in which there is a theocentric understanding of some feature but in which we cannot assign any probability (high or low) to that feature in the absence of an explanation. Bayesian apologetics does not apply to such cases. This is important, because the explanation of the suitability of the universe for life may well be just such a situation. To show that life is improbable in the absence of any explanation would require me to show that a large proportion of the infinity of possible universes are lifeless. And it is hard to make sense of proportions in an infinite population, so the probability of a universe being suited to life might well be undefined.

These differences between the apologetics of understanding and Bayesian apologetics show that I am following Mitchell, who says of his cumulative argument that "it does not take the form of [either] a strict proof or argument from probability" (1973, p. 39). Here by an argument from probability he means, presumably, an argument concerning numerical probabilities as provided by Swinburne or Schlesinger.

[2]
The Theocentric
Understanding of Life

In Chapters 6 and 7 I argue that (anthropic) theism is a genuine epistemic possibility even before we consider what can be explained in terms of God. But my aim in this and the next three chapters is to compare theism—and anthropic theism in particular—with rival explanations, on the assumption that it is indeed a genuine epistemic possibility.

1. The Suitability of Our Universe for Life

The topic of this chapter is the universe's suitability for life and, more specifically, for embodied persons. I am using the phrase "embodied persons" to emphasize that I attach little significance to the fact that these persons are human beings. For we might well suppose that it was mere chance that led, on Earth, to the evolution of mammal persons rather than dinosaur persons. Furthermore, it might be mere chance that animals who are persons evolved anywhere within a billion light-years of here.[1] The fact I am concerned with, then, is that embodied persons came to exist somewhere or other in this universe.

We can divide possible universes into those suited to life, that is, the ones in which life can continue to exist once it has arisen, and those unsuited to life. That there is at least one physical universe, and that it is suited to life, can be explained by saying God created it in order that there be embodied persons. Anthropic theism goes on to say that creation was primarily for the sake of the embodied persons, not for some further divine purpose.

[1] See van Inwagen 1988 for a discussion of chance in the context of theism.

This piece of theocentric understanding is often supported by the noting of various physical constants that have to be fine-tuned if our universe is to be suited to life. (See Leslie 1989, chap. 2.) By a *constant* I mean some numerical quantity which is assumed as part of the statement of current scientific theories. A constant is said to be *fine-tuned* just in case had that constant been different by a small proportion, then the universe would not have been suited to life. For example: "If the weak fine structure constant . . . were slightly smaller, . . . no stars would have evolved; if it were slightly stronger, supernovae would have been unable to eject the heavy elements necessary for life" (Smith 1994, p. 373). That was just a specimen. Indeed it seems that just about every fundamental constant must be fine-tuned if there is to be life. (See Leslie 1989, p. 32, and Smith 1994, p. 373, for further examples.)

I am reluctant to offer a direct theocentric understanding of the fine-tuning of the constants for life, although this has considerable rhetorical appeal. My reluctance is based on the *optimistic induction*: so often there have been purely scientific explanations of what seemed inexplicable that it is reasonable to suppose there will be scientific explanations in this case too.[2] This is supported by the way the inflationary Big Bang theory provides explanations for the "smoothness" and "flatness" of the universe, which were previously taken as evidence for theism. (See Leslie 1989, pp. 29–32.)

Clearly the optimistic induction requires some restriction. There are limits to what can be explained scientifically. But, impressed by the past success of science, I prefer to offer a theocentric understanding of the things science could not explain rather than the things science does not now explain. Another reason for not relying on fine-tuning is that I expect God to order the universe in ways that are not merely providential but elegant. And the need for fine-tuning is, I think, a rather inelegant way of creating. For what it is worth, my opinion is that God would choose a system of laws that did not need fine-tuning because they did not involve any numerical constants at all.

I mentioned the optimistic induction. Let me be an optimist, then, and speculate about what physicists might hope to establish. They might well derive all the "laws of nature"[3] from an elegant system of fundamental laws, without any fine-tuned constants, and, moreover, show that it is probable that any universe that obeys these laws they have posited would indeed contain

---

[2] W. H. Newton-Smith (1981, p. 14) has used the title *pessimistic induction* for the argument that scientific theories have been overthrown so often in the past that we should expect current theories to be likewise overthrown.

[3] For the first and last time in this chapter I put the phrase "laws of nature" in scare quotes. It is, I claim, a piece of controversial metaphysics to call the fundamental order and structure discovered by scientists *laws of nature*. See Forrest 1985b and van Fraassen 1989. So when I speak of laws, I mean the fundamental order and structure scientists seek to discover.

regions suited to life. We may further hope that they would have exhibited the marvelous way in which the richness and complexity of the universe arises out of these elegant fundamental laws.

So what would there be left to explain? This much: although a scientific theory might explain the suitability of the universe for life by assuming the occurrence of an appropriate set of laws, it cannot explain why there are life-friendly rather than life-hostile laws. Here by life-friendly laws I mean ones that make it probable that a universe in which they hold will be suited to life. That there are life-friendly laws can, however, be explained in terms of the divine purpose in creating. (It can also be explained using various rival metaphysical theories discussed in later chapters.)

To make the discussion more concrete we could consider the fantasy of the Book of Laws. On each of its pages is the statement of a system of laws. The index to the Book of Laws tells us which pages are statements of life-friendly laws and which are not. On page 84, say, we find the elegant system of laws that hold for this universe. It is life-friendly. Now we are tempted to ask what proportion of pages are indexed as life-friendly. If the correct answer was that the proportion is high, then indeed we could say that just about any system of laws will result in life, so there is no point in the attempt at a further explanation of the laws. That would make redundant the theistic explanation of the suitability of the universe for life. If, however, we should not assert that the proportion is high, then it is reasonable to seek an explanation of why there are life-friendly laws.

Let us examine, then, what if any proportion of systems of laws are life-friendly. There is, I submit, a strong case against the claim that there is a proportion that is high. To start off with an intuitive point of limited value, we might say life is just so intricate and delicate that we should rather be tempted to the position that life is physically impossible and its occurrence a continuing miracle than that it occurs with a high proportion of systems of laws.[4]

The intricacy and delicacy of living systems might well have suggested that the proportion of possible universes suited to life is low. But that is merely a preliminary. I now turn to the serious obstacles in the way of showing that a high proportion of systems of laws are life-friendly. The first obstacle is that there are, presumably, infinitely many possible systems of laws. So unless you boldly claim that all but a finite number of those systems were life-friendly (or equally boldly that only a finite number of those systems were life-friendly), you could not argue that the proportion of life-friendly laws was

---

[4] But note how lifelike complexity can arise in a quite simple system, namely the *Game of Life* (Gardner 1970, pp. 120–23).

obtained by straightforward division: infinity divided by infinity is not defined.[5]

This obstacle might be surmounted by arranging the systems of laws in a
natural order, so that the proportion could be defined as a limit. The natural
order would be that of increasing complexity. We could, therefore, think of
the Book of Laws as divided into infinitely many chapters corresponding to
the positive integers (Chapter 1, Chapter 2, etc.) such that later chapters contain more complicated systems than earlier ones. Each chapter has, we shall
assume, a finite number of pages, each of which is a statement of laws. (If this
assumption is incorrect, that is a further obstacle.) We can make sense of the
claim that a high proportion of systems of laws are life-friendly by considering
the sequence p_1, p_2, etc., where p_n is the proportion of life-friendly laws in
the first n chapters, and by using standard mathematical limit procedures. If
for all large enough n, p_n is high, then we may say that the proportion of all
life-friendly universes is high, even if there are infinitely many of them. On
the other hand, if for all large enough n, p_n is not high, we may say that the
proportion of life-friendly universes is not high.[6]

The next obstacle in the way of considering the proportion of laws is that
these mathematical limit procedures do not always succeed. We might have
a run of p_n less than 10 percent, followed by a few p_n that are over 90 percent,
followed again by a run of p_n less than 10 percent, and so on indefinitely. In
that case it is neither true that there is a high proportion of life-friendly
universes nor true that there is not.

Let us suppose, however, that these obstacles can be surmounted and it is
either true that the proportion of life-friendly universes is high or true that
the proportion is not high. Clearly we could never survey all the systems of
laws to show in some direct fashion that the proportion is high rather than
not high. We would have to rely on an inductive extrapolation from the
proportion of laws that are life-friendly among those in, say, the first hundred
chapters of the Book of Laws.

There is little prospect of anyone actually being in a position to perform
this extrapolation and so conclude that a high proportion of systems of laws
are life-friendly. In any case the induction would be hazardous. But should
not we still be worried by the thought that perhaps there is a high proportion
even though we cannot show there is? Yes, we should be worried by this in

[5] Or, in nonstandard arithmetic, infinity divided by infinity is not defined until we know
which infinities we are considering.

[6] More precisely, the proportion is greater than r if and only if there is some integer N and
some $s > r$, such that for all $n > $ N, $p_n \geq s$. The proportion is less than r if and only if there
is some integer N and some $s < r$, such that for all $n > $ N, $p_n \leq s$. Note that in neither case
need the sequence $\{p_n\}$ converge.

much the same way as we should be worried by the threat of the unknown hypothesis. There is no argument to show that there is such a high proportion, but the thought that there might be one is yet another reason why the apologetics of understanding is better directed against atheism than against agnosticism.

We have, then, no reason for saying that there is a high proportion of systems of laws that are life-friendly. But we have no reason for saying that there is a low proportion either. Rather we have no way of deciding whether there is a proportion at all, or if it is high or low. In this situation of radical ignorance we should not, I submit, rely on Bayesian procedures, which would require there to be a probability that an arbitrarily chosen system of laws should be life-friendly. For the only guide to such probabilities are the proportions. Nor will it do to interpret the probability as a subjective degree of confidence. For in a situation of radical ignorance we should not rely on whatever confidence we happen to feel.[7]

Because there are neither proportions nor degrees of confidence to guide us, it is important that I am relying not on Bayesian apologetics but on the apologetics of understanding. I am contrasting understanding with lack of understanding, not a high probability with a low probability. The fact that this universe is suited to life can be given a theistic explanation but cannot be explained by saying that a high proportion of possible universes are thus suited.

Some readers might protest, at this point, that I ought to have considered the proportion of life-friendly systems of laws that are no more complicated than the actual ones, rather than considering the proportion of all laws. My reply is to counsel patience. The appeal to simplicity is discussed in the next chapter.

I have carried out the discussion using the concept of a law of nature. But should laws play as important a role in scientific understanding as they are commonly said to?[8] It is worth, therefore, presenting an alternative. Instead of seeking to understand the life-friendly character of laws, we could seek to understand the power of matter to generate life. We traditionally think of matter as like the clay the potter works into a shape—passive inert *stuff*. But we may maintain this way of thinking only if we think of matter as being ordered from without, in accordance with the laws of nature that scientists

---

[7] But, you say, I must have *some* constant degree of confidence, or else a Dutch book can be made against me, that is, a set of bets such that I am bound to lose overall. I disagree: in a situation of radical ignorance I might well select betting odds and keep to them (to avoid a Dutch book), but these odds would not express degrees of confidence, because there are no degrees of confidence to express.

[8] For a critique of the fundamental character of scientific laws, see van Fraassen, 1989.

seek to discover. In the alternative way of thinking, which does not require laws, the various particles must have causal powers attributed to them. (See Harré and Madden 1975, chap. 2.) That is, their natures are such that they affect one another in various ways. So instead of wondering as to the life-friendly character of the laws, we should wonder at the power of these particles to form a series of systems (atoms, molecules, organelles, cells, organs) that result in life as we know it. Thus the shift from thinking of external laws to thinking of particles with causal powers does not affect the discussion of the suitability of the universe for life. For convenience I use the language of laws, allowing readers to make the necessary adjustments.

2. On the Motive for Creation

I have been assuming that God has a motive for creating embodied persons. But what sort of motive might that be? Many of our motives are ones we have just because we are human. As Hume put it in the *Dialogues*, "All the sentiments of the human mind . . . have a plain reference to [our] . . . state and situation. . . ." (Part III, p. 30). Hume includes in his list such sentiments as pity, blame, emulation, and envy. And I am inclined to agree that these are such as we would not expect God to feel. Hume also includes love and friendship in the list, and if he has in mind love based on sexual or parental bonding, or friendships based on the need for company, then indeed he is correct. For it would be an ad hoc complication to the proposed theocentric understanding to insist that God had some need or lack. There is, however, a motive that does not require that there be any lack, namely the judgment of certain states of affairs as valuable. Not only altruism but also artistic and intellectual dedication attest to this. And we may rely on that human motive to speculate about the divine motive for creation.

Here it is worth pausing to consider the common enough cynicism about human motives which treats them as nothing more than the selfish desire to satisfy real or imagined needs. This cynicism does not, I submit, arise because we find anything absurd about the idea of altruism or dedication: judging a state of affairs to be valuable must provide *some* reason for bringing it about, we think. Rather we tend to be cynical about human motives either because of bitter experience or because we are well aware of just how pressing real or imagined needs are. I submit, then, that what has a "plain reference to [our] . . . state and situation" is the prevalence—if indeed it is prevalent—of needs-based motives. Hence we should anticipate that God, or any other beings who know that their needs are satisfied, will act out of the recognition of what is valuable in a fashion comparable to the altruism and the artistic and intellectual dedication that are, perhaps, exceptional for us needs-bound creatures.

We may speculate, then, that the motive for creation is the recognition of values. I am not suggesting, though, that God has no sentiments or passions and that the divine action is governed by a pure unfeeling recognition of values. Rather I am saying that we need not speculate about what it feels like to be God.

We can now sketch an account of why God has brought about at least one universe with life-friendly laws. On this account creation is a "good deed" performed not necessarily out of a sense of duty or obligation but just because of the recognition of the goodness of the outcome. And, since I am defending belief in a personal deity, it is worth noting that to ascribe such a motive is to reject any idea of the deity as an impersonal force or merely the universe as a whole. One obvious candidate for the value of there being embodied persons is the well-being of such persons, and not some further end. In that case this explanatory account requires anthropic theism.

Anthropic theism itself has two versions. One asserts that God is motivated in utilitarian fashion, concerned with the total value of the well-being of all embodied persons. The other asserts that God is concerned with the well-being of them as individuals. The difference concerns the way in which the value of a whole universe depends on the value of its parts. At one extreme is the straightforward utilitarian proposal that the value of the whole is the sum of the values of the parts. At the other would be a refusal to accept any formula for the value of the whole. Now, without making any proposal of my own concerning the way the value of the whole depends on the parts, I reject the utilitarian proposal in favor of an account of overall value in which God is not straightforwardly motivated to sacrifice some for the sake of others. I say "not straightforwardly" because when I come to consider the argument from evil, I shall be concerned with the constraints under which some such sacrifice is not of disvalue. This involves *virtual consent*, but I postpone the details until then. For the moment it suffices to say that I take the divine recognition of value to result in creation for the sake of individuals and not just the overall good.

There are two reasons why we should prefer the nonutilitarian version of anthropic theism. One is that the utilitarian account may well be incoherent. For God has, presumably, the power to create universes of infinite sum total value not because anything especially valuable occurs in them but just because they contain an infinity of parts of some specified but small value, say some slight aesthetic value. In that case the overall value of what is created would not provide a motive to create a universe suited to life. For, as a result of aesthetic considerations, types of universe much like ours except not suited for life might have the same, infinite, value as ours does. The other reason is that my proposed theocentric understanding of moral supremacy is based not merely on anthropic theism but on the hypothesis that God cares for individuals.

One objection to the account I have sketched is that it does not really explain why God creates *animals* who are persons—which is what we are. Why should God not create immaterial beings, such as angels or lesser gods? Or even if the decision is made to create embodied persons, why should not they be embodied in complex configurations of intergalactic plasma? The short reply is that there may well be very many different ways of being a person, but one of these—our way—is being an animal. In the absence of any reason to suppose God would prefer to create angels or persons who were complex configurations of intergalactic plasma, we have explained why this universe is suited to life by noting that one way in which God can create persons is to create a universe suited to animals.

That short reply is, I think, an adequate one, but it can be strengthened. For if God has a motive to create persons at all, then it is plausible that there is a motive to create persons of many different kinds. In that case God would have indeed created persons who are configurations of intergalactic plasma but would still have a motive for creating animals who are persons as well. The plasma persons would be valuable in their way and we animal persons valuable in our way. This reply does not require any detailed account of what embodied persons are, but merely the rejection of some extreme form of dualism, according to which the kind of body we have does not affect the kind of person we are.

A more serious objection to my account of the divine motive for creation is that it seems to require the objectivity of values, namely that what is valuable is a matter of fact, independent of how we humans think of it. For if it just depends on how we think of it, then, it could be urged, we have no reason to believe that God would make similar value judgments to us. This is an important objection, to which I have three replies. One is to provide a rather different account of the motive for creation which does not involve the recognition of values. That I do in the next section. Another reply is to defend the objectivity of values. That I do in Chapter 7, by relying on my somewhat speculative account of the nature of God as unrestricted consciousness. The third reply, which I now give, is to deny that theocentric understanding requires the objectivity of values. For theocentric understanding could be based on the claim that God values the existence of other persons, who will be suitably fulfilled, rather than on the claim that the existence of other persons is objectively good and that God recognizes what is objectively good. Putting it another way, that creating persons is good does not have to be independent of the divine evaluation of it as good. God could, on this account, have valued complete isolation instead and so created nothing whatever. God's valuing isolation would not, however, explain why the universe is suited to life, which is, however, explained on the hypothesis that God values persons. Furthermore, theists may speculate that God has seen to it that, when our minds/ brains are functioning properly, we shall, for the most part, judge those things to be valuable which God judges to be valuable. So although values would be in some sense quite subjective, human values would tend to coincide with divine values. Hence we may assume that God does in fact judge it very good that there are other persons who are suitably fulfilled.

Another serious objection to this theocentric explanation of the life-friendly character of the laws that govern this universe is that the persons we know of, namely us, are not obviously fulfilled and that many lead quite miserable lives. And the mere existence of persons living lives with varying mixtures of joy and suffering does not seem the sort of thing we would expect God to value. My reply to this objection illustrates my general strategy of relying on speculation in order to defend what is not itself put forward as speculative. The speculation in this case concerns the afterlife. Now if at this stage I were to adjoin belief in an afterlife to my theism, then I would be accused[9] of complicating the theistic hypothesis and so rendering it much less probable. I submit, however, that it is merely the genuine epistemic possibility of an afterlife which is required as part of the apologetics of understanding, in order to exhibit a motive God might have.

I discuss how an afterlife can be part of an antisupernaturalist account of religion later in this chapter. For the moment I take it for granted. I shall also assume that part of the afterlife is the awareness of God, which I judge to be a very great good. Now it has been objected[10] that I have no right to assume that the awareness of God would be a joyful experience—bliss—rather than, say, an experience of terror. My answer is that I take religious experience to be authoritative as to what the awareness of God is like if it occurs. In almost all traditions those who have had a mystical or religious experience express great enthusiasm for it. Indeed the trouble with being a mystic seems to be that all else becomes insipid. An analogy might support my reliance on the experience of mystics in this way. Suppose a patient complains to the local doctor about an alarming chest pain. The doctor might dismiss these complaints as hypochondria. But if the aim was to discover what the patient might be suffering from, *if anything*, then the complaints are worth listening to.

We may speculate, then, that the divine motive in creating embodied per-

<hr/>

[9] By William Rowe, among others. See my discussion of Rowe's dilemma in Chapter 8.
[10] By Robert Elliot, in conversation.

sons is for them to lead lives that will find fulfillment after death. If, contrary to what I here assume, this is treated as more than mere speculation, then theists are already committed to anthropic rather than ananthropic theism. Further reasons for preferring anthropic theism are provided in Chapter 4.

3. Creation as the Overflow of Joy

There is an Indian speculation according to which God (Isvara) creates the universe out of play (lila).[11] Or if play sounds too childish, we could think of God's creation as like an exuberant dance.[12] I am not here thinking of dance as aerobic exercise, as an excuse to put your arms round your partner, or even as artistic performance. I am thinking of a dance that is the sheer expression of joy. Initially this speculation might seem to be frivolous. It is, however, worth further consideration. We can think of creation as a spontaneous manifestation of what God is, rather than as the result of being aware that it would be a good thing to create embodied persons.

Such spontaneous, playful creation could be understood as like the way in which human beings on those occasions when they are genuinely enjoying themselves want to share their joy. Joy and happiness overflow, as it were.[13] On such occasions there is no need to reason out that it would be good if others were happy too. The lack of reasoning does not, however, imply any lack of providence or rationality. For God, we may suppose, is already aware of all the possible universes and is already aware of what they are like. The spontaneity of creation occurs in the context of that awareness.

Now God could be joyless and yet still be the source of great joy. So the fulfillment provided by an afterlife does not require that there be any divine joy to share. But here I am indeed committed to the thesis that God experiences joy, or at least something similar to joy. Even if I could give no reason for believing that the divine consciousness is joyful, I would not significantly weaken my case by assuming that it is. For there is nothing implausible about that as a hypothesis. We could say that it might or might not be, and so if the hypothesis that it is enables us to explain various features of the universe, including its suitability for life, then we should assume that the divine consciousness is joyful. Nonetheless best-explanation apologetics is strengthened if we can argue that we should expect the divine consciousness to be joyful.

---

[11] This speculation was held by some in the Nyaya-Vaisesika school. See Dasgupta 1975, p. 324.

[12] Another Indian image—typically associated, however, with Siva, who destroys as well as creates.

[13] Barry Miller has drawn to my attention the scholastic saying, "Bonum est diffusivum sui." God as Goodness itself would spontaneously diffuse goodness.

One consideration here is the phenomenon of joie de vivre. Most of us, at times, feel joy without having any particular reason for feeling it, but simply because we experience no suffering. My explanation for this is that it does not require anything positive for people to enjoy being conscious; it is enough that the all-too-common obstacles be removed. Consciousness is intrinsically joyful.

In this and in the previous section I have expanded on the theocentric explanation of the suitability of the universe for life, by means of two rather different accounts. According to both of them, God creates this universe to share the divine joy with embodied persons. The accounts differ in that according to the first the motive for creation is awareness of what is valuable. According to the second, creation is more spontaneous: it is the divine "game" or an overflowing of joy. In both cases we can explain why the universe is suited to life.

4. The Afterlife without the Supernatural

If God creates for the sake of embodied persons such as us, then it must be that there is something supremely valuable about the lives we lead. Now I hold the traditional Christian doctrine that it is not for this life alone that God has created us, but so that we might find individual and collective fulfillment in a life to come. In this work, however, I am merely defending this doctrine as a genuine epistemic possibility, in order to present one speculation about the motive for creation.

Readers might well wonder why I have chosen to develop theocentric understanding in this fashion. The reason is that I have submitted that God is motivated either by something like altruism or by a more spontaneous tendency to share the divine joy. (The alternative to that account is to suggest that God is motivated in a way that is not such as we would call morally good, perhaps in a purely aesthetic way. I discuss such ananthropic theistic explanations in Chapter 5, along with some other non-naturalistic metaphysical speculations.) Assuming, then, that God's reason is such as we would consider morally good, what alternative is there to an appeal to life after death? We might refuse to speculate, but that would be contrary to my strategy of developing, as best I can, one version of theocentric understanding as a representative of all those I have not considered. So the only alternative to speculating about an afterlife is to claim that it is for the sake of this life that God creates us. Now it is fairly plausible that many people do have the opportunity for a life worth living even if there is no life after death. But I find it quite implausible that everyone does. Indeed the suggestion is insulting to those crushed by misfortune, for it amounts to saying, "Cheer up, my friend, no matter how desperate your situation, no matter how painful, life is good." The question then arises as to whether the opportunity of a life worth living for some, perhaps even the majority, justifies others suffering lives not worth living (through no fault of their own). I judge that the unmerited and uncompensated suffering of some would provide a strong motive for not creating a universe like this, even if life was very good for others. But if readers disagree, then indeed I have no need to defend the possibility of an afterlife.

I am speculating, therefore, that God created us partly for the sake of a life to come. But does not that make this life worthless by comparison? If the answer is that it does, then a firm conviction that this life is worthwhile might provide an objection to the occurrence of an afterlife and hence to theocentric understanding as I develop it. But I insist that creating us partly for an afterlife does not rob this life of value. To say it does is to commit the fallacy of invidious comparison. It is fallacious to argue that Singapore is not hot because Madras is much hotter. Likewise, that God can provide vastly more than we can ever hope to achieve does not rob our efforts of their significance. Moreover, the details of the afterlife and indeed the quality of the mental state enjoyed in it could depend rather critically on what we, both individually and collectively, have made of this life. If so, then the prospect of an afterlife actually increases the importance of this life.

A speculative account of the divine motive for creating may be provided, therefore, by establishing the possibility of an afterlife in which we, individually and collectively, find fulfillment. And if the ordinary human ways of being fulfilled are judged insufficient, we may suppose there is in addition something similar to the union with the divine that mystics seem to achieve momentarily. It is important, though, that this speculation is accepted as a genuine epistemic possibility, not a mere logical possibility. In this section and the next, therefore, I argue for the genuine epistemic possibility of an afterlife. I do so by arguing that God can ensure an afterlife without any divine intervention of a sort that breaks the laws of nature and so counts as supernatural.[14]

It is worth digressing to explain why we should avoid positing a supernatural breaking of the laws of nature, when arguing for the genuine epistemic possibility of an afterlife. In addition to the general reasons for antisupernaturalism, discussed in the Introduction, there is a further reason, which applies to the afterlife and to purported miraculous interventions in history but does not apply to creation itself. One of the things modern science has shown us is that the world around us is beautiful not only in a sensuous fashion— important though that is—but in the mathematical elegance of its previously

---

[14] My position in this regard may be contrasted with that of Stephen Davis (1986), who stresses the role of such divine intervention in his account of the afterlife.

hidden structure. This may be given a theocentric understanding, and in being thus understood it confirms the antecedently plausible claim that God will bring about the divine purpose in as elegant a manner as possible. I grant that if there was no other way of ensuring an afterlife, divine providence might result in a violation of the divinely instituted natural order. It seems rather unlikely, however, that God is forced to act in this inelegant fashion.

We have reason, then, to suppose that God will provide us with an afterlife without breaking the laws of nature. There are, I submit, several ways in which this could be achieved. First, God might rely on the fact that many so-called impossibilities are just highly improbable. For example, thermodynamics assures us that, in a closed system, energy is conserved and entropy never decreases. Now the increase of energy in a closed system might well be physically impossible, but, it is widely claimed, the decrease of entropy is not impossible, just of incredibly low probability. God could, therefore, have ensured that the motion of individual molecules resulted in a decrease in entropy, in which a vacuum was created in half the room while the air pressure doubled in the other half. There would be no reason, of course, to do such a thing. God might, however, rely on such improbable but possible occurrences to bring about events that we would treat as miracles.

Perhaps, then, in a distant part of the universe in the distant future, there would be, apparently by chance but really because God so intended it, a paradise replica of Earth. There are animals in this paradise that look very human, although their offspring grow up without challenges or education, and indeed with very little worth remembering. When these beings are children, their neuronal connections are influenced by the surroundings only to the extent of recording vague memories of their uneventful lives. Instead their brains develop so that, apparently by chance, the events that occurred to us, in our lives, are stored as apparent memories. And perhaps they could relive such "remembered" events in a rather vivid way. Likewise, their character, habits, and capacities would effortlessly develop so as to be just like those we had. When they mature they have, therefore, apparent memory of having been us, and they have the appropriate character and so on. For consistency we may suppose that what is recorded is a positive trait, not a mere lack. A further detail might be that whatever neuronal mechanism underlies consciousness operates only at the end of the whole process, by which time the life of a human being on Earth is totally recorded in one of these replicas. That would ensure an apparent psychological continuity between a life on Earth and the life in this paradise. Finally, and again apparently by chance, there is just one replica of each of us.

Some may find puzzling the idea of beings whose neuronal connections do not result from the vicissitudes of life but occur with apparent spontaneity.

But does not that very possibility suggest itself in the context of the argument from evil? Suppose it is pointed out that we human beings cannot come to have various virtues such as fortitude and compassion without being subject to all sorts of influences many of which result in suffering. One natural enough response to this attempt at theodicy is that God could create beings who seemed like us except they do not need "the school of hard knocks" to develop such virtues. What I am now suggesting is that the children of paradise are just such beings.

The reliance above on what is possible although highly improbable might sound far too legalistic. It is as if God had, in creating, signed a contract not to violate the natural order but now seeks a loophole so as to work some miracles. Only on those accounts in which the laws of nature are beyond even God's control does this analogy hold. But I am relying on the theocentric understanding of life-friendly laws. I should not, therefore, consider the laws as beyond control. Instead my reluctance to admit violations of the natural order was based on aesthetic considerations. I expect creation to be elegant, and this expectation is confirmed by the success of science in displaying this elegance. My judgment, here, which I invite readers to share, is that the probabilistic loophole I have mentioned is somewhat inelegant. Nonetheless it would serve as a speculation if we can think of no better.

According to an alternative speculation, God might create a brand-new universe in which it is ensured that appropriate replicas occur. That is, God fine-tunes that universe in just such a way that we have precisely one replica each. This avoids the objection I have just stated, but there is a further one. The replica, it will be objected, is a mere replica, and not the same person as the one who died. That is discussed generally in the next section, but it is worth noting that in the cases above there is no direct causal connection between the life on Earth and the afterlife. God observes what has happened on Earth and ensures that replicas occur either elsewhere in this universe or in another universe.

By modifying the first of the two speculations, we can remedy that defect and at the same time avoid resort to probabilistic "loopholes." Perhaps our brain activity leaves "fingerprints," say in patterns of rather stable states of neutrinos, and the brains of the humanlike animals develop as a result of these "fingerprints." That would ensure a direct causal connection. We must also provide a speculation about why there is only one replica of each of us. That is easy enough: the animals in this paradise could easily have evolved mechanisms to ensure diversity in their populations, and such mechanisms would prevent multiple replicas. Thus as each animal develops, it could release antibodies into the atmosphere which would cause the spontaneous abortion of any embryos that would subsequently develop in this way.

Such "fingerprinting" is much like Rupert Sheldrake's theory of morphic resonance (1985), which would provide another variation on the first speculation about an afterlife. Morphic resonance is a hypothesis intended to explain, among other things, how embryos develop their immense complexity. According to Sheldrake's theory, once a pattern has occurred it has a high chance of recurring, provided the conditions are suitable. The morphic resonance account of an afterlife is that the animals in paradise have evolved in ways that rely heavily on morphic resonance in place of ordinary heredity, and so evolved toward ever greater sensitivity to morphic influence. A by-product of this evolutionary process is the development of animals whose patterns of development are taken over by morphic resonance from the distant past. So, in addition to lowly ancestral forms, there develop replicas of all organisms there ever were, including replicas of all human beings.

In fact I think standard biochemistry suffices to explain embryonic development, and, as far as I know, there is little empirical evidence for morphic resonance. Recall, however, that I am seeking an antisupernaturalist speculation about an afterlife, not a well-confirmed theory. Let us then perform a thought experiment. Suppose there had been some fairly good empirical evidence supporting morphic resonance. Would we then have said, "But it is so implausible, there must be some other explanation," or would we have started talking of Sheldrake's law that patterns tend to recur? I submit the latter would have happened, in which case morphic resonance is an adequate speculation if we are seeking to defend the thesis that God created us for the sake of an afterlife.

A rather different account of the afterlife may be provided as a special case of a general account of divine providence and the apparently miraculous. This account is based on the idea of emergent order.[15] The incredible complexity of chemistry with its millions of compounds and complex reactions emerges from atoms composed of electrons, protons, and neutrons. And the even greater complexity of living cells emerges from the chemical properties of various large molecules. Again, the many-celled organisms have a structure that is possible because of the special features of their cells. None of this requires the violation of the natural order, but nonetheless theists are entitled

---

[15] I am indebted to Polkinghorne for the idea that emergent order is of theological significance. See, for instance, Polkinghorne 1988, especially chap. 3, where the author discusses, among other examples, the remarkably orderly arrangement of hexagonal columns of rising and falling fluid which occur in convection under controlled conditions. This order emerges spontaneously from the prior random motion of billions of molecules once the temperature difference is sufficient.

to think of it as, in a loose sense, miraculous. For we can fantasize about scientists who were shown the universe at a stage shortly after the Big Bang when no molecules had formed. What predictions would they have made about the resulting universe? Surely they would have said that but for some divine intervention no great chemical complexity would result and certainly no life. In hindsight we can, however, understand how chemical compounds and living organisms can occur. These complex and semistable systems can exist just because of the natures of their components. I call this *emergent order*. The occurrence of emergent order does not make redundant the theocentric understanding of the suitability of the universe for life. For it is astounding that there are subatomic particles that have the capacity to form atoms that form molecules that form living organisms. (In Chapter 4 I trace the occurrence of emergent order to the serendipity of mathematics.)

A feature of emergent order is that its operation can be explained and predicted more easily at its own level than by appeal to the nature of its constituents. So we can understand living organisms more easily by asking what function various components (say, the leaves of a tree or the kidneys of a vertebrate) perform than by considering how the cells interact. Even in the case of computers we understand how they will behave by considering the programming language rather than the machine language.

I now employ a speculative induction. From a few instances of emergent order we may infer the genuine epistemic possibility of other kinds of emergent order. It is an emergent order rather than any supernatural breaking of the laws of nature which provides the basis for divine providence, including that which is called miraculous. For the emergent order might be such that we could not have predicted it just by considering the components of the systems, and yet we can understand it in terms of God's intention that this order work for our benefit.[16]

But how could there be an emergent order that provided the possibility of an afterlife? One possibility would be that something like Sheldrake's morphic resonance occurs not as a basic law of nature but as an emergent feature. But here is another way, one in which there could be a "disembodied" afterlife. The dead, I suggest, might depend for their continued existence on the minds/brains of the living. Now there may be some empirical evidence for harmful ghostly parasites.[17] What I am considering, however, is a way in which

---

[16] To get the record straight I should say that there seems to me to be a Satanic emergent order as well as a providential emergent order. I would speculate that the Satanic emergent order is the unintended result of human selfishness.

[17] Hypnotherapists, from whom such empirical evidence as there is comes, cure such cases by sending the dead "off to the light." I would interpret this going to the light as a transition

the dead might live on harmlessly in an entity that is formed by the collection of all living organisms.[18] This entity would be the providential home for the dead.

This emergent order would be generated by interactions between the minds/brains of the living. Although that might seem rather far-fetched, it is worth pointing out that the issue of telepathy is still an open one, with abundant anecdotal evidence on the one hand but little by way of repeatable experiment on the other. We should be reluctant, therefore, to dismiss the idea of an emergent order formed out of all our minds/brains. For we could take telepathic communication as evidence of such an order. I would not, however, expect telepathy to turn out to be a nonphysical phenomenon. In fact I would further speculate that there is a continuum between telepathy and ordinary perception, where sensitivity to minimal cues occupies a halfway point between the two. Telepathy could well be the result of the brain's continually responding to minute variations in the overall pattern of sensory stimulation. And even if there is no telepathy, what I have just proposed as a speculative but naturalistic explanation of telepathy could still occur. So the brain's response to subtle variations in the overall pattern of sensory stimulation would still provide a possible mechanism for an emergent order.

The events of our lives would thus be recorded in patterns of collective brain activity. We would indeed live on in our descendants, but the process would be collective: no one individual needs descendants in order to live on. Quite how such physical but disembodied people could become subsequently reembodied need not here concern us. For my present purpose is not to provide a speculative understanding of all my religious beliefs but to underpin best-explanation apologetics. And for that purpose I need only an adequate motive for creation, which, it seems to me, requires an afterlife. That this afterlife is in bodily form like ours is not required.

Here is yet another speculation—one that might appeal to interpreters of quantum theory, although others might find it too bizarre. It is based on Everett's interpretation, according to which the universe continually splits (DeWitt and Graham 1973). Roughly speaking the idea is that some future event that quantum mechanics tells us now has a probability of, for example, two-thirds will occur in two out of the three universes into which the uni-

---

to a state in which the dead live on, no longer in just one of the living, but in the community of all the living.

   [18] In this connection it is worth mentioning Teilhard de Chardin, whose views have something to commend them, provided they are treated as speculations. The emergent order here being considered would seem to constitute what he calls the *noosphere*, by analogy with the *biosphere* (1959, pp. 180–83).

verse as it now is will split.[19] Shortly before or after a person's clinical death the universe splits, with the dead person living on in a fragment that is not that of us, the survivors. If you say that universe splitting is impossible, then I reply that you are probably assuming that space and time are Euclidean. But there are good reasons for accepting general relativity and so rejecting the Euclidean character of space and time.

If our universe splits, as on Everett's interpretation, then it splits into so many successor universes that even highly improbable events occur in some of them. There is no problem, then, about ensuring the survival of the dead in some of them. And notice that on this speculation spatio-temporal continuity is possible. As someone dies, the universe that person is in splits off from that of the rest of us and in that universe the person makes a "miraculous" recovery. So *strictly speaking* there is no death and hence no afterlife, just a continuation of this life. Some would consider this contrary to the Judaeo-Christian tradition, but, as I have already explained, my aim here is merely to use speculations to defend the thesis that God creates us for something better than life as we know it—my aim is not to "say it how it is."

The initial difficulty with this speculation, and it is a difficulty with the Everett interpretation generally, is that we have too many successors into which we split and some of them are not such as would suggest divine providence. There will, for instance, be universes in which we get metamorphosed in all sorts of undesirable ways. To rescue the Everett interpretation from the absurdity of the multiple splitting of all conscious beings every second, we should insist that only one of the successors of a given individual is conscious.[20] The rest are imitation persons lacking consciousness. In this way what is required to make that interpretation intellectually acceptable when considering quantum mechanics also provides an account for divine providence generally and the survival of death in particular.

Finally, I come to my least speculative and most naturalistic account of an afterlife. The "afterlife" I am inviting you to consider is extremely short, being the result of the effects of the dying brain.[21] It probably lasts about a second. But a second can seem a very long time as the brain processes slow. The experience of knowing and loving God could well be so splendid that even a moment of it would make up for a lifetime of suffering. It might also provide a sense of completion or fulfillment. Although this is in a way the most naturalistic account of an afterlife, it has the disadvantage that it lacks a social

[19] A slight modification is required if we are to consider relativistic quantum mechanics. For details of universe splitting, see McCall 1994.
[20] I leave readers to speculate about the principle governing where the conscious minds go when the universe splits. See Davis 1991 in this connection.
[21] Here I am extrapolating from reports of near-death experiences.

dimension. It would seem strange for God to create us as the social animals we are and not provide a collective fulfillment.

I have multiplied speculations because different ones might appeal to different readers. My aim, recall, is merely to offer a speculative defense of the thesis that God creates for the sake of an afterlife. Let me repeat that these speculations are intended not as assertions about what is the case but merely to show how God could have an adequate motive for creating a universe suited to embodied persons such as us. Any case for actually believing in an afterlife would, I think, have to start from the theism I am here defending and then investigate the claims of various theistic religions.

If we think of the divine motive as altruistic, it suffices that there be an afterlife in which the blessed, as I call them, experience joy and a sense of fulfillment. But I also suggested that God creates out of an overflow of joy. That explanation would seem to require something more, namely that the blessed know and love God in such a way that they can be said to *share* in the divine joy. Two questions might occur to us:

(i)   How could mere patterns of spiking frequencies in neural networks, or whatever plays the analogous role in an afterlife, result in an experience with the appropriate content to be considered a sharing in the divine joy?

(ii)   Even if the appropriate content is there, why would that not be a mere subjective experience rather than a sharing of the divine joy?

My answer to the first question is that an observer embodied in some other form than ours could just as reasonably ask how it is possible that mere neural activity results in all the wonderful things we know it does result in, for example the enjoyment of music. That observer might well be inclined toward a crude behaviorism, which denies the myriad of mental states intervening between sensation and behavior. But we know better than that observer, and we know better whether or not we identify mental states with brain processes. Because neural activity results in the array of mental states we do know of, we should not reject the suggestion that there are other mental states it could result in. In addition mystical experiences provide evidence for mental states that approximate to the ones involved in sharing the divine joy.

This leaves the second question. Would such a mental state be a sharing in the divine joy or just a blissful state? Granted that there is divine joy, and granted that the state of the blessed is also one of joy, then all we require is that the joy of the blessed depend appropriately on the joy that is God's in order for it to be described as a sharing of the divine joy. Consider, then, the following Dependence Condition:

> Had there been no divine joy to share, then the joyful state would not
> have occurred.

To illustrate that condition, suppose I am looking at the setting Sun. What
makes my experiences genuine perception? The analog of the Dependence
Condition is:

> Had the line of sight from Sun to me not been near the line of sight
> from the horizon to me, or had there been clouds between the Sun
> and me on that line of sight, I would not have had the experience I
> had.

That analog of the Dependence Condition might well be necessary, but is it
sufficient? It would seem not. Suppose I tend to hallucinate setting Suns but
I take medicine to stop hallucinations. Bright light on the retina will, however,
destroy the medicine. So if I look at the setting Sun I will tend to hallucinate
a setting Sun a minute later. That would meet the analog of the Dependence
Condition but would not be genuine perception. I therefore add a further
condition, namely:

> The Dependence Condition holds as a result of the *proper functioning* of
> the person's mind/brain.[22]

Call this the Proper Functioning Condition. In the case of the sharing of the
divine joy the Dependence Condition is satisfied, provided had there been
no divine joy, then there would have been no suitably joyful experience of
the blessed. And that is the case, because creation was partly for the purpose
of sharing the divine joy in this way with the blessed. Likewise, the Proper
Functioning Condition is satisfied because the universe was created so that,
among other things, the blessed have brains or brain analogs that will result
in the experiences being considered. Therefore the having of those experiences is no aberration but part of the proper functioning of the mind/brain.
I conclude that the joy of the blessed depends on the joy of God in a way
much like that in which a mental state depends on the perceived object in a
case of genuine perception. And I invite readers to grant that this is enough
for the blessed to be said to share in the divine joy.

---

[22] I am indebted to Plantinga for stressing the role of proper functioning. See 1993b.

5. The Afterlife and the Problem of Personal Identity

I conclude that there is no obstacle to the existence of replicas of ourselves sharing in the divine joy and that with a little ingenuity we can avoid the threat of multiple replicas. But could our replicas, existing in whatever form they do, be the very same people as us rather than *mere* replicas? For example, let us suppose Eve really existed and died at the age of eighty-three. Let us call her Eve One. There is one of the blessed who is a lot like Eve One. Call her Eve Two. I submit that Eve Two's life as one of the blessed could be related to her previous life on Earth as Eve One, much as one stage of Eve One, say the first day of her eighty-third year, was related to an immediately preceding stage, the last day of her eighty-second year.

Divine providence, we may assume, has ensured that Eve Two is psychologically continuous with Eve One, in the sense that Eve Two, on becoming conscious, is psychologically exactly like Eve One as she lay dying. To Eve Two it seems just like waking up. We can go further and speculate that Eve Two does not merely "remember" being Eve One but that her life is vividly present to her.

What more might be required for us to establish that Eve Two is the same as Eve One? Some, such as Swinburne, hold the *simple view* according to which there is a fact of the matter as to whether Eve Two is the very same person as Eve One, which fact cannot be analyzed in terms of various psychological and physical conditions. These conditions are then just taken as evidence for identity (Shoemaker and Swinburne 1984, p. 19). Perhaps that is so, but quite clearly this does not make it harder to argue that Eve Two really is the same as Eve One. Indeed, given the simple view, we are entitled to speculate that the dead survive even though not all the usual conditions hold. For it requires less evidence to establish a genuine epistemic possibility than to establish that something is the case. I therefore ignore the simple view and concentrate on the psychological and physical conditions for identity.

One plausible enough condition is that the occurrence of Eve Two with the appropriate memories and personality be no accident. So the mere fact that someone with the appropriate characteristics comes into existence is not sufficient for that person to be identical to Eve One. It is more difficult to decide if we need to strengthen that requirement. Consider two of the previously mentioned ways of ensuring an afterlife without the supernatural:

(i)   The fullest possible scientific description would be that a chance rearrangement of fundamental particles generated Eve Two, but in fact this "chance occurrence" is intended by God.

(ii)   God creates a new universe operating in accordance with different laws
           from ours in which Eve Two and the rest of the blessed come to exist.

In neither case is it an accident that a person just like Eve One comes to exist,
but many would take this as insufficient for identity, even if we assume, as
we may, that God does not produce two copies of Eve One or have one of
the blessed serve as the afterlife for two earthly lives, say Eve One and a twin
sister.

The intuition behind the claim that in neither of the circumstances above
do we have genuine identity would seem to be that genuine identity must
be the result of a direct causal connection between the successive stages (Eve
Two and Eve One). Although neither (i) nor (ii) ensures this, I have provided
various speculations that do.

Some might also require that for the continued existence of a person there
must not be a spatial discontinuity or a temporal gap between death and the
afterlife nor a sudden change in the physical constituents.[23] Three of the speculations I have provided ensure this: the continued existence in a physical but
disembodied form dependent on the activity of the brains of our descendants,
the continued existence in a branch of the splitting universe, and the "one-
second" afterlife. The others I have offered do not. Let us suppose, therefore,
that some insist that Eve Two fails to be the same as Eve One, but they grant
that this is merely because of the various discontinuities. What should my
response be? Three ranges of speculations here intersect. One is the range of
speculations about an afterlife, some of which have gaps and others do not.
The second is the range of speculations about what constitutes personal identity, for some of which spatio-temporal continuity is not required.[24]

The third range of speculations concerns the divine motive. Should we
suppose that God cares about personal identity as we humans conceive of it?
If there is some special unchanging self or soul that constitutes identity, then
that, to be sure, is a metaphysical fact God would know and presumably take
into consideration. But that metaphysical speculation would make it very easy
for there to be an afterlife. God just makes sure our replicas have our souls.
I consider souls, however, to be hypothetical entities and ones of an unfamiliar

---

[23] The referee has pointed out to me that it is rather hard both to satisfy the no-gap
requirement and to ensure there is a genuine afterlife rather than a prolongation of this life.
Fortunately the divine purpose is satisfied as much by a suitable prolongation of this life as by
a genuine afterlife.
[24] Locke, recall, distinguishes being the same person, which does not require spatio-temporal
continuity, from being the same human being, which does (*An Essay Concerning Human Understanding*, Book II, chap. XXVII).

kind. In accordance with my antisupernaturalism, therefore, I avoid positing them. In the absence of souls the facts of the case are not in dispute. There is, we are supposing, nonaccidental psychological continuity between those who live on Earth and their successors in an afterlife, but without spatio-temporal continuity. There is no further fact about whether or not we are identical to our successors, merely a verbal dispute as to whether we should be called the same persons. My judgment, which I invite readers to share, is that whether we survive or merely "survive" as these successors makes either no difference or very little difference to the motive God has in creating us.

I have defended, therefore, the thesis of anthropic theism that creation is partly for the sake of an afterlife. Those who reject that thesis on the grounds that an afterlife would be supernatural must (i) reject all speculations about the afterlife which do not result in spatio-temporal gaps; (ii) reject all speculations about our concept of personal identity which permit there being such gaps; and (iii) reject the thesis that God might well create us for the sake of our successors who are psychologically continuous with us. With what degree of confidence should this triple rejection be warranted? Not much, I say, but in any case not enough to prevent my speculation about an afterlife being a genuine epistemic possibility. And that is all I require. Notice, however, that if my account of the divine motive is no more than a genuine epistemic possibility, I have merely defended anthropic theism and have delayed establishing a decisive advantage for it over ananthropic theism until Chapter 4.

6. The "Mechanics" of Creation

I have speculated about the divine motive for creation, but I have not yet explained God's power to create. I now support the theocentric understanding of life by providing a general principle governing the power of any conscious being to act freely. I then apply it to God as a special case. To avoid supernaturalism I base this account on an account of human acts. We might ask, then, What distinguishes a human act from a piece of mere behavior?[25] One answer that deserves respect is the *causal theory*, namely that an act is a piece of behavior with a special kind of mental state as cause, such as intending to behave in a certain way (Davidson 1980a, 1980b; Bishop 1990) or trying to behave in a certain way (Armstrong 1980a, pp. 68–88; Hornsby 1980). Now the causal theory is rather controversial (see Kenny 1989, chap. 3), so I neither assume it to be correct nor assume it to be incorrect. Instead I assume some-

---

[25] In asking this question I ignore purely mental acts. That restriction is of no consequence, however, for creation is not a purely mental act. Instead it has a direct physical effect, namely the universe.

thing much less controversial: when we humans act, there is a complex physical process that begins with various brain processes, some of which might indeed be correlated to or identified with intendings or tryings. Let us call this complex causal process the *act process*. The act process begins with intendings and tryings, but it is vague just how far an act process extends. Perhaps we could introduce an artificial precision by taking all act processes to end with bodily movements.[26] But because my aim is to provide a generic account for both human beings and God, and because it would be rash to take creation as the action of an embodied God, I leave the boundary of the act processes vague. (Readers may check that this vagueness does not infect the proposed account of the power to act.)

When we humans act, some act process occurs. One obvious constraint on our powers is that the act process, and hence the act itself, should not be impossible. Moreover, no one can now do what is now impossible, such as voting differently in 1990, even though that was possible back then. The relevant sense of possibility, then, is a time-dependent one, according to which past events are no longer contingent.[27] I also assume that the laws of nature are now necessary (and have been so throughout the history of the universe).[28] We have no power, therefore, not to act in a certain way if it is determined (by earlier events and laws of nature) that a corresponding act process occurs. For example, suppose the effect of heroin on an addict is that the neurons are connected so that, in the circumstances, it is determined that no act process occurs in which the addict would refuse an offer of heroin. Then refusal is not within the addict's power.

I am considering the power of a human being to act. And I propose that a human being has the power to X only if there is an act process which is the doing of X and which is still possible. There must, however, be an extra constraint on action. For consider telekinesis. It may well be still possible for various molecules to rearrange themselves so that a spoon bends without being touched. But I, for one, cannot bend spoons that way. This extra constraint, which I investigate in the next section, seems to be something to do with either the location of the agent or what the agent is aware of.

I now speculate that there are two jointly sufficient and individually necessary conditions for any conscious being—not just a human being—to have

---

[26] This would be plausible only if we stipulate that by an action we mean a *basic* action in Arthur Danto's sense (1973, p. 28), that is, an action not performed by performing some other action.

[27] Things are more complicated if we allow backward causation, that is, the present affecting the past. See Forrest 1985a. But I ignore backward causation in this section.

[28] If instead we posit causal powers, it is not so much the laws that are necessary as the constraints on the kinds of things there are and hence on the causal powers they have.

the power to perform some act. One is that the corresponding act process is still possible. The other is the appropriate generalization of the extra constraint, whatever that turns out to be. This general principle governing powers might be misunderstood: I am not offering a theory of action according to which there is nothing more to an act than an act process that satisfies the two conditions. Rather I am providing a general principle governing the power to act freely.

Provisionally I submit that the extra constraint will not apply to God, because it is something to do with restrictions we have but God does not. In the next section, however, I digress, discussing what this extra constraint might be. The reason for this digression is caution: a more detailed investigation of the extra constraint might reveal a constraint that does, after all, apply to God.

Creation is an act whose act process is the history of the physical universe itself, at least insofar as its unfolding is determined by God. (If you like, it is the history of the universe prior to the coming into existence of other agents.) And we can understand that act by noting God's motive for creation, just as we can understand a human act, even if it is not physically determined, by noting the motives for the act.

To avoid supernaturalism I have refrained from positing special divine powers. Rather I am providing an account of the power of any conscious being. That this generic account results in so much greater power for God is largely the consequence of the fact that, prior to the creation of the universe, there are only logical and metaphysical constraints on what is possible, but none due to laws of nature. Once the universe has been created, part of what God has chosen will be those laws. Subsequently, then, the general constraint on the powers of an agent prevent even God from breaking the laws. Whether or not the initial divine power amounts to omnipotence, it is quite enough to provide the theocentric understanding of the suitability of this universe for life. For the choice of which universes to create is, in part, a choice of the laws that govern them. So God has the power to choose life-friendly laws.

7. The Extra Constraint on Action

I claim that the extra constraint on action will be trivially satisfied, and so no genuine constraint, when applied to the divine acts. But what right have I to assume this? I have two answers, each of which is of some weight by itself but which are best thought of as parts of a single answer. One is to submit that the limitations on our powers are something to do with our localized embodiment. My acts correspond to act processes that occur in my body because my body is where and what I am. We should, therefore, expect the extra constraint on action, whatever it turns out to be, to apply vacuously to God, who is not restricted as we are to one place rather than another.

The other answer to the question is to provide a speculation about the extra constraint on action, which does indeed establish its triviality when applied to God. Now we are concerned here with acts for which the agent has a motive. My speculation, then, is that an agent can act for a motive only if that agent has the appropriate kind of knowledge of the act process as satisfying, or tending to satisfy, the motive for acting. We can put this in slogan form: No power without knowledge. I further speculate that this requirement is the extra constraint on action. That is, it and the possibility constraint are the only conditions that must be satisfied for an act to be within the agent's power. Therefore God has the power to bring about anything that is still possible, provided God has the appropriate kind of knowledge of the possible ways universes might be.

Let me begin with an example that serves both to illustrate and to support this extra constraint. Consider the fantasy of a human being with special powers, who could cause others to behave in various ways by affecting their brain processes, and hence their muscles, just as they would if they acted that way. Let us call this person with special powers the Possessor. The Possessor is the telekinetic analog of the mad scientist, who features in philosophical discussions of determinism and who controls others by implanting electrodes in their brains. The Possessor, however, does not require any invasive procedure but rather exploits the way in which brain activity is, I am supposing, not fully determined.

Now the Possessor is indeed a product of fantasy. But why? What is it that in fact stops you from directly causing me to behave in various ways? Not, we are supposing, because the behavior is physically impossible. For if so, then I could not behave that way. It is because you cannot even try. Furthermore, I submit that it is lack of the appropriate knowledge which prevents you from even trying: you do not know the state of my mind the way I can know it. And it is this lack of the appropriate knowledge that prevents us meddling with the minds of others.

I am not at all sure of the precise way of characterizing the *appropriate* knowledge, but I suggest it is something to do with a direct conscious awareness of something as satisfying or tending to satisfy the motive for acting. This can be contrasted with merely knowing that it satisfies or tends to satisfy the motive. A neurophysiologist would not acquire power directly to cause me to behave in certain ways, just by monitoring my brain processes and knowing what they tend to result in. I, by contrast, do not know these brain processes as patterns of spiking frequencies in axons. Rather I am directly aware of them as filling a certain functional role, which includes their tendencies to produce various kinds of behavior.

For example, I might be directly aware of the temptation to turn off the alarm clock and go back to sleep. This temptation is either identical to or correlated with a certain pattern of spiking frequencies in my brain. Even if I knew all about such things, I would still not be aware of the temptation as a pattern of spiking frequencies. Rather I am aware of it as the tendency to turn off the alarm clock and thus as a tendency to satisfy my motive for so acting, namely the pleasure of going back to sleep.

The extra constraint on action, I speculate, is that the agent must be directly aware of something as satisfying or tending to satisfy the motive for acting, if the agent is to have the power to act. I put this speculation forward as a likely constraint, the sort of thing that, knowing what we do about humans, we would expect to hold.

How does the extra constraint on action apply to God's act of creation, an act that occurs before there is any physical basis for tendencies of any kind? It is here that it is relevant that I mentioned the satisfaction of motives as well as the tendency to satisfy them. In the case of creation, which includes the ordaining of laws, the awareness is of something that immediately satisfies the motive for creation, namely that there come to be a universe of the intended kind. (In Chapter 6 I discuss how God is aware of all things, including the possible ways universes might be.)

My speculation about the extra constraint on action was disjunctive in form, for I talked of something satisfying the motive for acting or tending to. Moreover, the human case concerns tendencies whereas the divine seems to concern immediate satisfaction. I could be accused, then, of an ad hoc addition to the account of human power serving merely my theological purposes. I plead not guilty. The disjunction "satisfying *or* tending to satisfy" is like the disjunctions "being black *or* gray" and "being certain *or* having a high degree of confidence." In each case we use the disjunctive form to describe a genuine continuum of cases. Immediate satisfaction is the limiting case of tending toward satisfaction.

To sum up: without claiming to know the precise form of the extra constraint on action, my speculation about it serves to defend the claim that God's power over the physical is constrained only by the way things that were possible can become no longer possible. In particular, God has the power to create any possible physical universe. And ascribing such a power to God is not a supernaturalist hypothesis but nothing more than the application to the divine of a general principle based on the human case and intended to apply to any conscious being whatever.

8. Is Agency Causation Redundant?

I have sketched an account of the divine power to create as a special case of a generic account that holds for all that is conscious. Our own acts are, I have been assuming, a further special case. The most serious objection to this account is that it is redundant as a way of understanding. Indeed, the objection goes, any appeal to agency causation is redundant, where by agency causation is meant the doing of an act for a reason or with a motive. To be sure, it is extremely useful to think in terms of agents having various powers to act and acting for reasons. But, the objection continues, such ways of understanding may in principle be replaced by the causal facts discoverable by science, in particular the detailed workings of the nervous system.

There are two ways of replying to this objection. The first is to concede that my proposed principle governing acts is in fact redundant in the case of human beings. Instead of relying on our knowledge of our own powers to support it, I could put it forward as a mildly supernaturalist hypothesis. In that case we leave theocentric understanding open to the charge of fatuousness, namely that the physical laws are understood only by hypothesizing some nonphysical "law" or principle governing the free acts.

A defense against the charge of fatuousness might be that some laws are intrinsically intelligible. Consider the conservation of mass, which provides a technical explication of the principle that matter does not come into or pass out of existence. I would not be so bold as to say that I know a priori that matter will not come into or pass out of existence. And indeed the conservation of mass is violated whenever energy is turned into matter or vice versa. But the conservation of mass is the sort of law or principle that—if it held— would be intrinsically intelligible. Or again, consider not the law that entropy never decreases but its popular (mis)interpretation, namely that there is an inevitable decrease in order. That is violated by such phenomena as the formation of crystals and the reproduction of life. But had it been a law it would have been intrinsically intelligible. Now compare my speculation that a conscious being can do anything that is still possible, provided the agent is directly aware of it as satisfying or tending to satisfy the motives for acting. This is likewise the sort of law or principle we might treat as intrinsically intelligible. By contrast, many of the laws scientists propose, for instance that quantum rather than classical mechanics holds, though not objectionable, lack the sort of intelligibility provided by the conservation of mass. In this way creation by God would still have considerable weight as a means of understanding the suitability of the universe for life. For it would explain laws that are not intrinsically intelligible by means of laws that are.

Such judgments of intrinsic intelligibility are, I fear, rather subjective. My preferred response, therefore, is to argue that agency causation is not redundant even in the human case. To argue for this I first consider the case in which the workings of the brain are governed by deterministic causal processes and then consider the case in which they are not. In both cases, I argue, there is room for agency causation considered as an irreducible way of understanding. And in both cases there are grounds for endorsing that way of understanding. Hence I am entitled to provide an account of free human acts, to generalize it to apply to any conscious beings, and then to use the generalization to provide an account of the divine power. So I am not positing some new principle as part of a way of understanding the physical laws. Rather I note that, even if I never considered creation, I would need to accept, as part of an antisupernaturalist account, both the physical laws and the further principle governing the powers of agents to act freely. Theocentric understanding then exploits that further principle in order to explain the physical laws. No additional law or lawlike principle has to be hypothesized.

My arguments depend heavily on the belief that we are free in our acts and the associated belief in our own moral responsibility, that is, our being blameworthy for what we have done if it is wrong. It strikes us as paradoxical to ascribe such responsibility without ascribing some sort of freedom. Now I do not suggest that we infer belief in freedom from belief in responsibility or vice versa. Rather as we mature we come to believe we are free in whatever way is required for responsibility and that we are responsible in whatever way our limited freedom permits. Moreover, we come to believe that we are in fact both free and responsible in at least some circumstances.

That naturally occurring belief in freedom and responsibility is, I take it, a properly basic belief. That is, it requires no argument in order to justify it but may be held by us provided we can defend it against objections. Assuming the objections can be met, we should retain our natural belief in the human capacity to act freely. We may then take the human capacity to act freely as a precedent for the divine power. At least we may do so if this way of understanding is not redundant.

Suppose that the natural workings of the brain are deterministic. In that case, it might be argued, only the one act that did occur was possible in the circumstances and hence noting the agent's power and motives provides no further explanation beyond a description of the workings of the brain. I discuss this case by considering a variant of Peter van Inwagen's argument (1975). The crucial premiss is the principle that whether or not we humans are morally responsible does not depend directly on events prior to our coming into existence. Let us call this principle No Direct Dependence. For example, whether or not Hitler was morally responsible for the death of millions of

Jews, and so a proper object of blame, could depend on events occurring in, say, 1800, but it could only do so indirectly. That is, his state of mind would be causally influenced by what happened in 1800 only because that influenced what happened in 1801, which in turn influenced what happened in 1802, and so on. For instance, even if Hitler had been impressed by reading a book written in 1800, his reading it in, say, 1915 depends on the book existing in 1914, which in turn depends on the book existing in 1913 and so on back to 1800.

Now suppose determinism is correct. And compare an imaginary but logically possible history with the actual one. (For the purposes of this argument bare logical possibility is enough.) These histories coincide in the way events occurring after 1850 determine what Hitler does, but they differ in that in the imaginary one events after 1850 are themselves the result of a carefully planned experiment by extraterrestrials in 1800, whereas in the actual history the events occur without interference. My basic beliefs about freedom and responsibility imply that Hitler was blameless given the imaginary history in which all he did was determined by the extraterrestrials—they get the blame instead. Therefore he could be blameworthy given the actual history, with the same chain of events from 1850 on, only if events occurring before 1850 were directly affecting his responsibility. But that is contrary to No Direct Dependence. I conclude that in the case being considered, determinism excludes responsibility.

The discussion above is based on the common-sense position that the past is quite determinate, that is, statements genuinely about the past are either true or false. But suppose this is not the case. Then we may reconcile our deterministic account of the human brain with our belief in freedom cum responsibility by supposing that the acts we now perform affect what has happened at earlier times. (See Forrest 1985a for details.) We would assume, of course, that the macroscopic details of the past were determinate and that past indeterminacy was at the scale where quantum mechanics seems to permit indeterminacy.[29] In that case, then, the appeal to an agent's powers and motives is not redundant, because, although the past determines the future, the past is not itself determinate. Hence the scientific causal explanation is incomplete.

I submit, then, that all normal human beings have a basic belief in freedom cum responsibility before they reflect critically on things, and that this can be reconciled with determinism but only by appealing to the way our present acts might in fact be affecting the past—in which case agency causation is not redundant. Basic beliefs should, however, be defended against objections, and

[29] For an interpretation of quantum theory based on backward causation, see Price 1994.

some determinists will object that they know, presumably a priori, that we cannot affect what has already occurred. They will take No Direct Dependence, therefore, as showing that determinism provides an objection to the basic belief in freedom cum responsibility and hence that determinism establishes the redundancy of agency causation as a way of understanding. My response to such tough-minded determinists is that determinism is itself highly speculative and hence does not undermine the basic belief in freedom cum responsibility.

My response requires that I consider the standard objections to the sort of freedom of action I have proposed. Fortunately many objections to freedom fail to apply to the precise thesis I require, namely that often more than one act process is still possible. For instance, it has repeatedly been objected that a free act would be unintelligible. Before replying to this objection C. A. Campbell expressed it as follows: "On your own showing no *reason* can be given . . . why . . . [someone] decides to exert rather than to withhold moral effort" (1957, p. 175). That may be an important objection to Campbell's position, but it is no objection to my belief in freedom, for I allow that in some circumstances an act may be free even if it is the only one in accordance with the balance of reasons. For instance, there may be circumstances in which the moral reasons outweigh all others and so necessitate a moral effort. If we human beings could have imitations lacking consciousness, then, even in those circumstances they would "choose" at random, like psychopaths, and so might behave in ways we could behave in but necessarily will not behave in.[30]

Again, the claim that we are determined in our actions by psychological factors such as our character is quite irrelevant as an objection to physical freedom. For in many cases a person's character influences action by supplying motives for acting. Perhaps George Washington refrained from lying because he lacked that capacity, but most honest people refrain from lying because their moral convictions provide them with motives for refraining.[31] So even if their honest character ensures the outcome, it is not an example of determinism.

Much the same goes for the threat of social determinism. Even if there were some sociological or historical explanation of why Mao Tse-tung inaugurated the Cultural Revolution in China, that explanation should surely work by showing what motives he had.

What reasons, then, could there be for assuming the brain is in fact a

---

[30] See Chapter 6 for a discussion of whether such imitations are possible. Even if they are not, the fact that they might behave differently from us saves consciousness from the threat of epiphenomenalism.

[31] The example is essentially due to Mark Twain.

deterministic system? I grant that determinism has some intellectual appeal, but only if it applies to the whole of the physical. And modern physics is not easily interpreted as deterministic. To be sure, the dynamics of a closed system is represented in quantum mechanics by a deterministic equation.[32] But if the system is complex enough to include an observer, we have reason to believe that this deterministic dynamics is an idealization. Consider, for example, the decay of a single radioactive nucleus that is being observed using a Geiger counter. The dynamics of the quantum state does not specify in any deterministic fashion the moment of decay.[33] It involves, instead, the probabilistic "collapse of the wave packet."[34]

Since physical systems are not in general deterministic, some special argument is required if it is asserted that our brain processes and hence our actions are determined. The only argument I know of is that quantum effects are negligible at the level of neurons. I think this is misguided, for so-called chaos theory has made us familiar with the idea that the magnitude of the effect need bear no relation to the magnitude of the cause. Hence quantum mechanical effects at the very small scale in the brain could indeed result in a lack of physical determinism for the brain as a whole.

I conclude, then, that (i) there is little reason for proposing determinism about the human brain as anything more than a speculation, in which case it cannot undermine our basic belief in freedom cum responsibility; and (ii) in any case determinism may be reconciled with the nonredundancy of agency causation by means of the speculation that when we act freely the whole of the past becomes more determinate.

Let us turn, then, to the case in which the workings of the human brain are granted to occur in a probabilistic fashion. The initial, and I believe correct, assessment is that the probabilistic character of the causal processes leaves much unexplained and hence agency causation is not redundant. Some philosophers, for instance J. J. C. Smart (1963, p. 123), would, however, object that probabilistic interpretations of fundamental science are of no comfort to the proponents of human freedom. For, the objection goes, there is a dilemma: determinism is a threat to human freedom, but so are probabilistic laws. This objection is based on the claim that without determinism we have mere randomness, not the free acts I require to provide an analogy for God's act of creation.

Initially this objection seems just to miss the point, because if there are

---

[32] In the nonrelativistic case this is the Schroedinger equation.

[33] For a careful discussion of whether quantum mechanics bears any deterministic interpretation, see van Fraassen 1991, chap. 2.

[34] The precise principle governing this collapse is somewhat conjectural, but it is usually taken to be Lüder's Rule. See Hughes 1989, p. 224.

motives for an act, then that act is not random. Indeed I have already conceded that the motives might be so weighty that no other act could occur, even though the act process is not determined by physical causes. There are two ways of making the objection more pressing, however, which I illustrate using the example of the decision to quit smoking. First, there is a continuity argument. Consider the chance that the smoker will in fact quit. If it is 0 percent, then there is no power to quit. What percentage chance is required if the smoker is to be free to quit? Any answer other than "Above 0 percent (or above any infinitesimal)" would seem arbitrary. We seem to be forced, then, to say that the smoker was free to quit even if the chance is negligible. But that is a peculiar sort of freedom.

My reply to this objection is that we must make sense of degrees of freedom. Then we can say of the case of near 0 percent chance that the smoker has freedom to a negligible degree. And it is not absurd to treat a negligible degree of freedom as compatible with almost certain prediction. Perhaps, following a suggestion of Graham Oddie's, we could treat the chance as a measure of how easy it is to act.[35] I do not, however, need any particular explication of the idea of degrees of freedom. It is enough that there are such degrees. Because of the intimate connection between freedom and responsibility, the notion of degrees of freedom is supported by the acceptance of degrees of responsibility, as in the widely used legal concept of diminished responsibility.

The second way of developing Smart's objection is to claim that even if the human brain is governed by probabilistic processes, the understanding of actions in terms of motives is redundant, for we could understand them by examining the chances of various acts occurring. In that case, it could be urged, we do not have a precedent for divine acts, which can be understood not in probabilistic terms but only by considering motives.

The force of that second version of the objection depends very much on how we interpret the chances involved. If we take them as propensities, meaning special causal powers that govern but do not fully determine what happens, then indeed the objection would have some force. For, it might be held, any further explanation of what actually occurs would involve a supernatural interference with the propensities. Considerations of intellectual economy, however, should stop us positing these propensities, preferring some account in which the fundamental laws result in constraints on the frequencies of various occurrences. To illustrate this, consider Everett's interpretation of quantum mechanics, in which the universe splits continually and in which an

---

[35] I have this on hearsay, so I may have misrepresented Oddie's position.

event has, say, 50 percent probability if it occurs in 50 percent of the universes into which ours will split. Moreover, suppose we treat all but one of these universes into which ours splits as fictions.[36] In that case the explanation of why an act was performed where it had, say, a 50 percent probability is just that the one actual universe is a member of a large collection of possible universes in 50 percent of which the act process occurs. No propensities need be posited. But such statistical explanations, involving fictional populations, clearly do not make redundant the understanding of the act in terms of motives.

I conclude that there is no significant objection to the project of understanding our actions partly in terms of the probabilities of various brain processes occurring but partly in terms of the reasons we have for acting. The latter way of understanding goes beyond the scientific description of things but is not incompatible with it. More important, it establishes the genuine epistemic possibility of a generic account of free acts that applies to the special case of creation as well as to our acts.

9. Two Further Objections

I now consider two further objections to the claim that God has the power to create a physical universe: the causation dilemma and the fulfillment-of-intentions problem.

The causation dilemma arises out of a debate over the Humean thesis, defended for instance by Donald Davidson (1967), that every cause/effect relation must be an instance of some law that governs the causal interactions. Now to posit an appropriate law connecting reasons with the outcomes of action would be one way of trying to understand how God creates. That results in a difficulty, namely that it is precisely the life-friendly character of the laws of nature that cannot be explained in purely scientific terms. And I have offered an obvious enough theocentric understanding of why the laws are life-friendly. This theocentric understanding requires us, however, to say that God brings about these laws by causing there to be a universe governed by them. If all causation consists of instances of laws, then there would have to be higher-order laws governing the coming into existence of the laws discovered by scientists. But now we are threatened with a fatuous explanation: to explain laws that astound us because they are life-friendly we postulate a law govern-

---

[36] This is not consistent with one of my speculations about the afterlife, in which more than one result of universe splitting contains consciousness. What I say about the case I am considering may be adapted, however, to that speculation. See Davis 1991 for details.

ing creation. The law governing creation would indeed be of a different sort—a higher-order law—but we are not, apparently, making any progress toward understanding why there are life-friendly laws.[37]

In order to retain the advantage of understanding the life-friendly character of the laws, some theists might reject the Humean thesis Davidson has defended and insist that there can be *singular* causation, that is, causation that is not an instance of a law. An example of the combination of theism with belief in singular causation is provided by G. E. M. Anscombe (1971). But it is not just theists who hold that causation can be singular. C. J. Ducasse (1969), D. M. Armstrong at one stage (1983, p. 95),[38] and Michael Tooley (1990) have all allowed the possibility of singular causation. And Tooley in particular has presented a detailed analysis of the concept of causation which shows that singular causation is at least conceivable.

We are now in a position to state the causation dilemma. On the one hand, it seems that there can be no theocentric understanding of the laws unless God is a singular cause. On the other hand, although such singular causation might be conceivable, God's power to create would be unduly mysterious or supernaturalist if we do not liken it to the power we ourselves have to affect the world around us. And that might be taken to imply that God's act cannot be a case of singular causation.

The account I have given dodges between the horns of the dilemma. God's act is *physically singular* in that it is not governed by physical laws, but it is nonetheless in accordance with a general principle governing the powers of agents. To the extent that our acts are physically free, we too are subject to that principle. This prevents divine action from being singular in a way that would indeed make it excessively mysterious. But the principle concerned is not itself a law of nature. And, moreover, it is not purely hypothetical. Rather it was based on a generalization to all conscious beings of a principle governing the acts of human beings.

Let us now turn to the fulfillment-of-intentions problem. Following Swinburne (1979, pp. 85–86), I have stressed the analogy between divine and human action. But that, it seems, leaves me open to the following objection of J. L. Mackie's (1982, pp. 79–80).[39] God's act of creation, Mackie submits, would have to be thought of as a direct connection between an intention and its fulfillment. That is, there are no events that are caused by the divine intention to create and that in turn cause there to be a universe. In our case,

---

[37] For a recent attack on the idea of creation based on just this sort of consideration, see Smith 1993.

[38] Armstrong now considers singular causation to be merely conceivable. See Heathcote and Armstrong 1991.

[39] Alan Olding (1991) makes a similar objection.

however, we know that the connection is indirect. That is, the fulfillment of our intention is caused by the operation of nerves and muscles, which are in their turn caused by the intention to act. Mackie's objection is that there is therefore no analogy between God's acts and our own. This would make theism unduly mysterious.

Mackie's fulfillment-of-intentions problem is based on the assumption that the divine/human analogy would have to be carried out by applying the human case directly to the divine. This is, I submit, a mistaken assumption, and the problem is solved by providing a generic account of which our acts and those of God are two species. Using this generic account we can explain why human acts are carried out indirectly (via brain processes) whereas those of God are indeed more direct. An example from physics might bring this out. Electricity and magnetism are two different cases of a single electromagnetic force. But the unified electromagnetic theory was not discovered merely by assuming that what was known to hold for magnetism held for electricity. (For example, although no magnetic north pole has ever been observed without an associated south pole, negative electric charge can occur without an accompanying positive charge.) Likewise, a unified account of the divine and the human power to act need not proceed by applying the human case directly to the divine. The account I have provided treats the divine power as a special case in which various constraints become vacuous.

It is worth adding to this a remark I shall have occasion to repeat in Chapter 7: how "queer," to use Mackie's idiom, it would be if the mental was restricted in its operation by some sort of metaphysical law so that, out of all the possible physical systems, only brains could be directly affected by (or be) minds. For our brains, like the rest of our bodies, do not constitute a special ontological category; they are made up of the same constituents, but more elaborately arranged, as the food we eat. But it is just such a restriction of the mental to brain activity that underlies Mackie's objection.

10. When Was This Universe Created, and Out of What?

It is traditional to think of God as creating this universe out of nothing and from eternity. Should we accept that tradition, reject it completely, or meet it halfway? In this section I show how creation need not be an event occurring some finite number of years ago and how it need not be an event in the temporal ordering as described by physicists. Likewise, I show how God can create out of nothing (or, at least, out of nothing determinate). My aim, however, is to neutralize various disputes, not to settle them. If readers prefer to think of creation as an event occurring a certain number of years ago (the

Big Bang) or to think of creation as the organization of previously chaotic matter, that would not affect the considerations of this work.

We can deny the thesis that creation occurred a finite number of years ago without being forced to embrace the difficult, although traditional, doctrine of the timelessness of God. For we may grant that there were physical events occurring any amount of time ago, however large, but nonetheless insist that creation occurred before them all. Because this might initially seem nonsensical, I provide a way of thinking of it that I find useful.[40] This is to consider a novel scale for measuring time. For ease of exposition it is convenient first to measure time in *aeons*, where I stipulate that an aeon is ten billion years, about the time since the Big Bang, if there was one. Our novel units are to be called *quaeons*. Time in quaeons is measured by dividing the time elapsed t aeons ago by the factor $(1 + t^2)$.[41] Thus one aeon ago, a year is one ten billionth of an aeon but only one twenty billionth of a quaeon. If we go back to ten aeons ago, the time elapsed is divided by 101, so ten aeons ago a year was, of course, one ten billionth of an aeon as at present, but less than one thousand billionth of a quaeon. If we measure time using quaeons, then the whole infinite past of the universe, perhaps preceding a Big Bang, would take less than two quaeons.[42]

Some might say it is only a convention that we measure time in years or aeons rather than the quaeons. If they are right, then there could be no objection whatever to thinking of God as creating the universe an infinite number of years ago, because that is only a finite number of quaeons ago. I, however, think it is not just a convention that we use years or aeons rather than quaeons. There is a fact of the matter as to which is the correct way of measuring time. What, then, is the point of talking about quaeons? It is this. Initially we might think that the claim that God creates the universe an infinite time ago is nonsense. Consideration of quaeons shows that it is not nonsense, unless, that is, it is nonsensical to think in terms of quaeons. For all I am suggesting is that creation occurred at some time less than two quaeons ago. Now whether or not aeons or quaeons are the correct way of measuring time is to be decided, if at all, by finding which results in the simpler or more elegant formulation of our scientific theories. Before we investigate this we must admit that quaeons might be the correct way. In that case talk of quaeons would not start off as nonsense. But considerations of simplicity and elegance could not turn sense into nonsense. I conclude that it makes perfectly good

[40] This is based on Edward Milne's argument as reported by Karl Popper (1978).
[41] There are infinitely many formulas that would do the trick. But dividing by $(1 + t^2)$ is one of the simplest.
[42] The exact figure is one-half pi.

sense to think of creation as occurring before the whole history of the universe, even if the universe has an infinite history. And that is my preferred way of glossing the claim that creation is not an event in time as we know it. For all I know, there is no time in the physical order of things at which the universe did not exist, yet God created the universe at the first moment.

Let us now consider what it is that God creates out of. Presumably anything that exists prior to creation is a part or aspect of God. So if there is anything physical that God uses as material for creation, it would have to be part of God, as on Jantzen's thesis that the universe is the divine body (1984). Although I myself have no objection to Jantzen's thesis, I avoid controversy by neutralizing the issue of what God created out of by showing how to defend the orthodoxy of creation out of nothing, rather than the heterodox thesis of creation out of the divine body. I also wish to neutralize the dispute over whether spacetime is itself a substance, capable of existence independently of various things in space and time.[43] If it is, and if God created by creating things in a hitherto empty space, we would have to treat spacetime as (part of) the divine body. As I have said, I do not find this objectionable, but it is controversial.

If we are to neutralize various controversial issues, we must not, therefore, think of God creating things in a hitherto empty space. Instead we may say that at the time before God created, all kinds of universes, with their more or less determinate histories and their own laws, were possible, but none actual. Hence God had the power to bring any into being. This is indeed creation out of nothing, in the sense that there was no material from which God created. But it is not the creation of things within a previously empty universe. Indeed empty universes are among the possibilities God, presumably, chose not to bring into being. And, as I have already explained, the power to create such a universe is merely a special case of a general account of the power to act freely, of which our power is another special case. So though not naturalistic, because not part of the scientific explanation of things, it is not supernatural either.

We may, therefore, defend the doctrine of creation out of nothing, by saying that prior to creation nothing physical was actual, and so there was no actual state of there being empty space. But I prefer a variant of this account according to which, prior to creation, there was something actual, namely a situation indeterminate between all the possible ways a physical universe might be. On this variant the "stuff" out of which God created was not nothing so much as a maximally indeterminate something. I call this the maximal inde-

---

[43] In fact I believe it is a substance. A good case for such "substantivalism" is to be found in Earman 1989, in spite of the author's reservations in chap. 9.

terminacy speculation, and, although I do not rely on it, I have occasion to mention it from time to time. I therefore digress in order to expound it in greater detail. Some readers may, however, prefer to omit this digression.

I hold that some but not all propositions about the future are indeterminate in that they are neither true nor false. My restriction is based on the assumption that the laws of nature that are now true hold for the whole of space and time, not just for what has already occurred. Hence any propositions entailed by a combination of the laws and those propositions about the past which are already true must themselves be already true. Now prior to creation the whole history of our universe, including its laws, was in the future and so the only propositions then true would be the metaphysically and logically necessary ones. Hence it is not as if "There is nothing physical" was true and would have remained true but for creation. Rather "There is nothing physical" was not yet either true or false but became false as a result of creation. In that sense, prior to creation the universe was in a state of maximal indeterminacy.

We may think of the maximal indeterminacy speculation as a synthesis of the Heraclitean and Parmenidean views of time. In Parmenidean fashion I consider a range of possible fully determinate four-dimensional worlds, in which every event at every point of spacetime is fully specified. (These correspond to maximal consistent sets of sentences about some universe.) What, then, are we drawing attention to with the metaphor of the passage of time? My suggestion is that the present actual world (i.e., that which is now actual) is indeterminate between a range of determinate possible worlds. Assuming the past to be now necessary, the present actual world is determinate up to the present, but its future is, I assume, indeterminate. Any world that might be actual in a year is also indeterminate but within a narrower range of determinate possible worlds. That is because much that is now still possible will cease to be still possible in a year.

On this account of time there is not the one actual determinate world of the Parmenideans but many actual indeterminate worlds ordered by increasing determinacy.[44] The "passage of time" is the correlation between the ordering of the many actual worlds, on the one hand, with the temporal ordering within the worlds, on the other. Time would cease to pass—and it would become as true Parmenideans say it always has been—if there was no further increase in determinacy, perhaps because a fully determinate actual world had been reached.

I apologize to readers for giving such a sketchy treatment of a metaphysics

---

[44] Strictly speaking this is a partial ordering because of special relativity, but we may ignore this.

of time. (See Forrest 1996a for more details.) I have said enough, however, to explain the connection between it and my account of the powers of a conscious agent. That power is the power to effect a transition from a less to a more determinate actual spatio-temporal world. Prior to the act of creation the actual world would be a state of maximal indeterminacy between all metaphysically possible worlds. Creation, like any other act, makes things more determinate.

Given this metaphysics of time, God creates out of what was there prior to creation, namely the actual world, which is maximally indeterminate between all metaphysically possible worlds. Although maximally indeterminate in this sense, it is not structureless. For its structure is described by means of all the metaphysically necessary truths, including the whole of mathematics.

If we assume, as is traditional, that prior to creation there was only God, then it follows that this initial, actual but completely indeterminate, world was part of God. We may, if that is not too misleading, follow Jantzen and think of it as the divine body. In that case necessary truths turn out to be that which is true of the divine "body," and the beauty of necessity is the beauty of God. But let me emphasize that all this is further speculation, which although relevant is not strictly required for the defense of anthropic theism.

11. Theocentric and Scientific Understanding

Is there anything in the widespread conviction that theocentric understanding is unscientific? I suspect that one source of this conviction is the assumption that God must act by directly intervening from moment to moment, deciding what to do next. The universe is far better understood if instead we suppose that God acts by means of the natural order. Thus a theist and a proponent of naturalism should give the same answer to the question, Why did the Lisbon earthquake occur? namely, "Because of plate tectonics." The theist might perhaps go on to say that without the volcanic activity responsible for plate tectonics there would be no recycling of carbon dioxide and so the Earth would become almost lifeless within a few hundred million years. But the initial answer must surely be the same.

Another source of the supposed opposition is a conflation of scientific with naturalistic understanding. The naturalistic understanding of things is an understanding that relies upon the resources of the sciences alone, or with minimal metaphysical supplement. That is a rival to theocentric understanding— a rival I respect, but which I argue against in the next chapter. But it would be dishonest to rely on the prestige of science, which is common territory between theocentric and naturalistic understanding, in order to advocate the latter.

Perhaps the supposed opposition between scientific and theocentric understanding derives from the latter's dependence on agency causation. Although I have already defended agency causation, it is worth noting the following line of thought. Our ancestors, it is said, saw agency everywhere: in the trees, the wind, the sea, as well as in animals, including other humans. But we have discovered that we no longer need think of the water *seeking* its proper place, of the tree *trying* to reach the light, or of the plant *desperately* using all its energy to set seed before winter comes. If today we say such things, we know we are speaking figuratively. The area in which we seek to understand things by appealing to the reasons of agents has contracted. So, it is thought, we might as well abandon agency even in the human context. Such "go the whole hog" reasoning has only to be made explicit for its weakness to be obvious. Our concept of agency derives in the first instance from our experience of ourselves and other humans. Our ancestors, correctly grasping that reasons do enable us to understand actions, mistakenly—but not irrationally—sought to understand the details of the universe *directly* in terms of agency. That project failed, but its failure in no way casts doubt on the appropriateness of this way of understanding. I conclude that there is no opposition between theocentric understanding and the sciences.

In this chapter I have shown how the theocentric understanding of the suitability of the universe for life may be construed as a way of understanding why matter has the power to generate life, or, equivalently, why the fundamental laws discovered by scientists are life-friendly. The motive for creation can be understood as altruistic concern for what is good or as the more spontaneous overflowing of God's own joy. In either case we need an account of the divine power to create a physical universe. Here we should rely on a generic account of both human and divine action, which implies that God is able to create any physical universe. It hardly needs pointing out that this theocentric understanding of the universe's suitability for life is tenable only if theism is a genuine epistemic possibility even prior to what it enables us to understand. For otherwise we would have removed the mystery of the universe's suitability for life only at the cost of positing a new mystery, namely that there is a God.

A theocentric understanding of the suitability of the universe for life is supported by the possibility of an afterlife and the power of human beings to act freely. Without the existence of an afterlife theists would have to claim that this life is worth living for all or that God is a utilitarian who sacrifices the well-being of some for the sake of others. I reject both those claims. And without belief in human freedom we must treat the principle governing free acts as a further hypothesis to be conjoined with theism. Adding hypotheses in this way would clearly weaken theocentric understanding.

I am defending, therefore, not just theism but a package: God plus an afterlife plus freedom. At this point I anticipate disappointment. All this is a lot of work just to understand the suitability of the universe for life. Is it worth it? Perhaps it would not be if the only thing for which there was a theocentric understanding was the suitability of the universe for life. If that were the case, then theism might have been defended as a warranted position, but I do not think atheism would be unwarranted. Nor would I have much of a case for anthropic rather than ananthropic theism. My case, however, is based not on the suitability of the universe for life alone, but on the theocentric understanding of many things. Here the cost/benefit metaphor is appropriate. Yes, theism is not without intellectual cost and it is doubtful whether it is worth it just to gain the benefit of understanding the suitability of the universe for life. But at no extra cost we can go on to explain other things as well. Now many atheists are content to leave these other things unexplained. Such contentment is, however, contrary to the principle of inference to the best explanation. For to explain additional items at no additional cost makes for a better understanding of things.

[3]
The Naturalistic
Understanding of Life

I now turn to the most common rival to theocentric understanding, namely naturalism. My aim in this chapter is fairly modest. It is to show that the naturalistic understanding of the suitability of the universe for life is no better than the theocentric understanding. In the next chapter I go on to argue for the superiority of theism over naturalism by exhibiting a range of items that have a theocentric but not a naturalistic explanation. Although of limited scope this chapter is crucial. For if theocentric understanding were significantly worse than naturalistic understanding when it came to the suitability of the universe for embodied persons, then, in spite of the advantages of the next chapter, there would be no clear overall advantage for theocentric understanding.

I am assuming that naturalists are competing with theists to see who has the better way of understanding the suitability of the universe for life. Some naturalists, as well as some theists, might refuse to enter this competition. I refer them back to Chapter 1, where I defended the project of best-explanation apologetics.

1. What Is Naturalism?

We are, then, to compare theocentric understanding with naturalistic rivals. But what is naturalism? One notable naturalist, Armstrong, characterizes it as the thesis that to be is to be in space and time (1978, pp. 126–27). The difficulty with this is that a heterodox theist, such as the theologian Jantzen (1984), may say that God is quite literally at all times and places and yet is not part of the natural order. Armstrong's thesis that to be is to be in space and time is not, therefore, a sufficient condition for naturalism. So let us try a different characterization. Naturalism, as I understand it, concerns the role of the natural sciences in our understanding. The natural sciences can be listed and comprise such disciplines as physics, astronomy, chemistry, biochemistry, and biology. Naturalists attempt to understand the universe using only these sciences. Even they might, however, grant that this ideal might be unattainable. One reason is that there may be things we cannot understand at all. Less obvious, perhaps, is how the attempt to achieve that ideal might indeed provide a way of understanding but nonetheless fail to be purely scientific, because it might require the support of some metaphysical speculation. For instance, the appeal to the sciences might be supplemented by the metaphysical principle that the universe is more likely to be simple than complex.

I mention the way naturalists tend to fall short of the ideal of a purely scientific understanding, not in order to criticize the appeal to metaphysical speculation, of which I am an enthusiast, but rather to provide a more accurate characterization of naturalism. It is, I suggest, a program rather than a thesis—the program of understanding things by going beyond the natural sciences as little as possible. This may be contrasted with theocentric understanding, in which God is central, however important scientific understanding may be as a supplement.

On the characterization above of naturalism there is no precise boundary between naturalistic and other ways of understanding, because as more and more emphasis is put on metaphysical speculations, the understanding becomes progressively less naturalistic. Some of the speculations considered in Chapter 5, metaphysical plenitude for instance, might be judged by others to be naturalistic. The demarcation is not, however, of great significance, provided I consider a representative range of rivals to theism.

The slogan, then, of naturalism is, To understand is to understand scientifically. But that represents an ideal. Naturalism is the program of adhering to this ideal as closely as possible.

2. What Is the Argument for Naturalism?

At the end of the previous chapter I defended theocentric understanding against the widespread conviction that it was unscientific. I now continue that discussion by arguing that naturalism has no advantage in being somehow especially close to the sciences. For a start we should distinguish naturalism, which I reject, from scientific realism, which I accept. I mean by scientific realism the thesis that, for the most part, scientific theories are literally true; or if they fail to be literally true, that is only because there is some undiscovered theory that is better by the standards of theory choice implicit in the scientific tradition. I am a scientific realist but not a naturalist, because I consider the sciences to tell the truth but nowhere near the whole truth.

Obviously, more is required than the premiss that, for the most part, scientific theories are literally true, in order to derive the conclusion that the sciences tell the whole truth. Is there, then, any argument for naturalism? One argument is based on Ockham's razor, or more precisely, on the presumption in favor of the intellectual economy exhibited by naturalism. I reject this argument because there is only a fairly weak presumption against *antisupernaturalist* theism, and this weak presumption is overcome by the breadth of theocentric understanding. But might there not be further arguments for naturalism that establish a presumption in favor of naturalism in addition to that derived from considerations of economy? It is rather important for my project that there be no such additional presumption, since my only complaint against naturalism is that it does not enable us to understand as much as its rivals, including theocentric understanding. And that complaint might not be enough to overcome the additional presumption.

I know of only one argument for an additional presumption in favor of naturalism, an argument I call Armstrong's dilemma. As I understand it, this dilemma requires two somewhat controversial principles. One of these, the Causal Razor, states that there is a strong presumption against positing entities that do not affect either ourselves or that which we observe. The other principle we may call the Closed Shop. It states that the universe is "a causally self-enclosed system" (Armstrong 1980b, p. 153). Now consider some entity, such as God, that is not acceptable to naturalists. Is it thought of as acting on the spatio-temporal universe or not? If not, then, by the Causal Razor, we have no reason to believe in it. If the entity in question does act on the universe, then it offends against the Closed Shop.

The failure of Armstrong's dilemma is clearest in the case of greatest interest in this book, namely God's act of creation, which has instituted the whole physical order and so cannot be a violation of it. If we interpret the phrase "act on the universe" loosely, then creation is an act on the universe by a non-natural entity, namely God, but it does not violate the Closed Shop. (That principle would be violated by supernatural divine intervention, but I am not proposing such intervention.) On the other hand, if we insist there can be no action *on* the universe until there is a universe to act on, then the first horn is blunted. For the intuition behind the Causal Razor does not discriminate between creating the universe and acting on the universe.

I conclude that Armstrong's dilemma fails, and the only argument for naturalism is that which does not mention causation but relies on the Ockhamist presumption. For that argument to succeed, naturalism must be shown to be as good as any other way of understanding. But the combination of this and the next chapter constitutes an argument for the inferiority of naturalism to various non-naturalistic ways of understanding the world around us.

3. A Proposal Derived from Hume

My general complaint about naturalism is merely that it does not enable us to understand enough. But there are some versions of naturalism I reject much more decisively than that. One such version, derived from Hume, is the claim that an infinite regress of causal explanations can explain all the events that occur, including the origin of life. By an infinite regress of explanations I mean explaining what happens at one stage by what happens at an earlier stage, explaining that in turn by what happens at even earlier stage, and so on without reaching any first event. Some followers of Hume, such as Paul Edwards,[1] boldly claim that such an infinite regress of explanations provides us with genuine understanding. Usually they make this claim in the context of the attempt to explain the existence of the universe, something I have not been emphasizing. But it might be put forward as a way of understanding the suitability of the universe for life, so it is worth discussing.

As a preliminary criticism of this Humean approach, I note that if it succeeded it would have made redundant the Darwinian explanation of evolution, except, perhaps, for vitalists. For, if we ignore vitalism, the laws of nature were believed to be those of classical mechanics and so deterministic. Hence every event would have been, in principle, explained by earlier events. So, the Humean argument would go, everything is explained in terms of the laws. Yet Darwin is rightly applauded, even by antivitalists, for a quite different style of explanation.

The appeal to an infinite regress of explanations could be criticized more incisively as the fallacy of composition, namely assuming the whole (in this case, the universe) has some characteristic (in this case, being explained) just because all the parts have that characteristic. That would, however, be a fallacy only if no case was made for the composition in question. We should therefore examine Hume's position (*Dialogues*, Part IX). Cleanthes, criticizing Demea's version of the cosmological argument, says: "Did I show you the particular causes of each individual in a collection of twenty particles of matter, I should think it very unreasonable should you afterwards ask me what was the cause

---

[1] Edwards's famous example of the five Eskimos in New York is known to many first-year philosophy students (Edwards and Pap, 1965, p. 380). My only consolation for their exposure to an oversimplified criticism of arguments for the existence of God is that other students are exposed to an equally oversimplified endorsement of the arguments.

of the whole twenty. This is sufficiently explained in explaining the cause of the parts." Hume is here drawing our attention to the supposed finite composability of explanation, namely the principle that to have explained any finite collection of items individually is to have explained the sum total of them. Now there are many situations where, intuitively, to explain the whole by explaining the parts is by no means to provide the best explanation. I have in mind those cases in which a complex system, although reducible to its components, is best understood as a whole. For example, to explain the success of a species by noting the life histories of each member would not merely be unfeasible; it would ignore the general characteristics of the species which biologists would in fact rely on to explain success.

Let us suppose, however, that finite composability of explanation did hold. Then followers of Hume would presumably be extrapolating from the case of a finite to that of an infinite number of explanations and so advocating the unrestricted composability of explanation. Like Swinburne (1979, pp. 123–24) I consider that extrapolation to be unwarranted. For there is a relevant, and rather obvious, difference between the finite and the infinite cases. In all examples of the finite composability of causal explanations at least one of the causes lies outside the collection of items to be explained as effects. But in an infinite regress of causal explanations none of the proposed causes lies outside the collection of items to be explained. Because of that crucial difference we should not assume without further discussion that the composability of explanation extends to the case of the infinite regress.

In addition it is easy to show that a totally unrestricted principle of the composability of explanation would license the explanation of something in terms of itself. For consider not just the sequence of events e_1, e_2 etc., stretching further and further into the past, but also a sequence extending into the future, f_1, f_2, etc. Suppose that f_1 explains f_2, which in turn explains f_3, etc, and that f_1 is explained by e_1, which is in turn explained by e_2, etc. Then every event in the sequence is explained by an earlier event. If unrestricted composability held, the sum of all these events (the e_n and the f_n) would explain itself, which is absurd. Therefore we should reject the unrestricted composability of explanation.

Humeans might reply that it is the *redundancy of any further explanation* that is composable. My example of the double sequence of events does not provide a clear counterexample to that claim. For Humeans might welcome the conclusion that any further explanation is redundant. Accordingly, I interpret Humeans as arguing that every stage in the history of the universe has been explained in terms of the previous stage and so any further explanation of each stage is redundant. Then, by the proposed composability principle, any further explanation of the whole history would be redundant. In particular, they say, theocentric understanding is redundant.

My criticism of the Humean position, thus interpreted, is that an absurdity results even from composability of the redundancy of further explanation. Consider a deterministic system operating in accordance with the laws of classical mechanics. The state of the system can be explained in terms of the states of the system throughout some earlier extended interval of time, however short. I assume that Humeans do not rest their composability principle on anything as contentious as time being discrete, so let us divide the last hour Zeno style. That is, consider it as composed of an infinite number of periods p_0, p_1, p_2, etc, where p_0 is the last half hour, p_1 the quarter of an hour before that, p_2 the eighth of an hour before that, etc. Then the way the system is during one of these periods is explained by the way it was during the preceding one. Hence, Humeans assure us, any further explanation would be redundant. If the composability of the redundancy of further explanation held, then any further explanation of the way the system is during the whole hour, which is the sum of all these infinitely many periods, would be redundant. But that is absurd: we are to explain what happens in the last hour in terms of what happened at least an hour ago.[2]

I conclude that understanding each stage of the universe in terms of an earlier stage fails as an attempt to understand the details of the universe, such as its suitability for life. What followers of Hume should say, instead, is that an infinite regress of explanations gives us all the understanding we shall ever get, which is thus rather limited, not that any further explanation is redundant. Several accounts, however, including some versions of naturalism, can at least provide a partial understanding of the suitability of the universe for life. And I say, You cannot win a competition you have not entered. Naturalists should, therefore, seek a naturalistic understanding of the suitability of the universe for life.

4. Anthropic Explanations

"Why is the universe suited to embodied persons?" "If it were not, then we embodied persons would not be here to ask that question." That might sound like a philosopher's joke, but we should take it quite seriously as an attempt to provide a naturalistic understanding of suitability for life. One reason for taking it seriously is that it has attracted considerable attention in

[2] I stipulate that the last hour consists of the present moment together with all moments less than an hour ago. So the moment exactly an hour ago is part of the previous hour.

recent years (Leslie 1989, chap. 6; Carter 1990). Another reason is that it provides a suitable introduction to scientific plenitude, discussed in the next section.

In the previous chapter I mentioned the "fine-tuning" required if the universe is to be suited to life in general and to embodied persons in particular. My interest in that fine-tuning was as a tempting way of emphasizing the importance of understanding why the universe is suited to life, by arguing that it is highly improbable that a universe should be thus suited. You will recall that I resisted that temptation. But there is another way of looking at the fine-tuning, in which initially we do not emphasize that it is required for a life-friendly universe but instead we note instances of fine-tuning as curious facts worth explaining if we can. How are we to explain, to take my earlier example, the (approximate) value of the weak fine structure constant? We might seek to explain it by noting that this value is required if there is to be life and then go on to remark that if the universe were not suited to life, then we would not be here to discover the fine-tuning. Such attempts at explaining fine-tuning are called *anthropic*.

As in the case of anthropic theism, the word "anthropic" here concerns not merely us humans but all embodied persons. Hence the "we" who would not be here to observe unless the universe was suited to life could have been intelligent dinosaurs living sixty million years ago as easily as mammals, or could have come from Tau Ceti Two as easily as from Earth.

Why, then, is this universe suited to life and hence to embodied persons? The anthropic reply is, If it were not, then we would not be here to ask that question. That would be entirely appropriate if we had asked, Why are we *here*, in the part of reality that is suited to life? For there is no mystery in why we are in the part that is suited to life. Where else could we be? But the anthropic reply succeeds only by taking it for granted that there is indeed *some* part of reality suited to life. And that should not be taken for granted.

As an illustration of this, consider the astounding fact that the observable part of our universe has a planet, Earth, which is the home of embodied persons, us. What is the chance of the observable part of our universe containing living organisms? Most stars are too big or too small, most planets are likewise too big or too small, or they are too far away from their sun or too near. But ours, like Baby Bear's porridge, is just right. The chance of a given star having a planet that is just right has been estimated to be about one in ten billion, or even slimmer (Hart 1982). The calculations used are so approximate that the difference between ten thousand million and, say, the Earth's human population of five thousand million is of no significance. Let us call a figure of that rough magnitude a zillion. Then the chance of finding a planet suitable for life is one in a zillion and is comparable to the chance of winning a lottery with just one prize and in which everyone on Earth has a ticket.

Once you have found a suitable planet, it is not surprising that fairly complex organic chemicals will form, including short nucleic acid molecules (DNA and RNA). But a self-replicating nucleic acid capable of further evolution is not just any nucleic acid. So just what is the chance of such a molecule arising? Here we might well decide to recycle the Epicurean hypothesis about random combinations sooner or later producing life and suppose that a mere four hundred components (nucleic pairs, as they are called) joined up *by chance* in a way that results in a molecule of DNA upon which the mechanisms of evolution can get going. If we use that as a basis for the estimates, it turns out that the chance of life arising even on a suitable planet such as Earth is the staggeringly low figure of not one in a zillion but one in a zillion cubed. (See Hart 1982, pp. 261–64.) Of course this figure could be queried, but it serves to illustrate the sort of response naturalists should make to an initially appealing line of argument for the existence of God.

Should we, then, use the staggeringly low probability of life arising on a given planet as evidence for the existence of God? The obvious objection is that there are plenty of planets in the observable universe, so it is not surprising that life arose somewhere in it. To the further question, But why on this planet? the anthropic reply would then be in order. Thus if we express surprise that we are on a planet suitable for life, it could be replied that there are a zillion squared stars in the our galaxy, and so, even given the one-in-a-zillion chance of a planet being "just right," there should be about a zillion suitable planets in our galaxy alone. And we should not express surprise at our being on one of the planets suitable to life.

The discussion need not stop there, however. For if the estimates used for the chance of life originating even on a suitable planet are at all accurate, then the observable universe, although immensely large, is far too small for life to have developed anywhere in it except as a result of an incredible chance. There are "only" a zillion suitable planets per galaxy and there are "only" a zillion galaxies in the observable universe. So the number of suitable planets is "only" a zillion squared. The chance of life arising on a suitable planet was estimated at one in a zillion cubed. So the chance of life arising somewhere in the observable universe is then one in a zillion. But that is not all that can be said. Life must not just arise; evolution must result in considerable complexity of life if it is to produce any animals who are persons like us. And who knows how likely that is? The anthropic explanation of the origin of life in the observable universe might well fail, even given that the universe as a

whole is of the right sort in various crucial respects, such as existing for long
enough and being made out of galaxies of stars with planets around them. It
might fail because the observable universe is just not large enough.

To rescue their anthropic explanation, naturalists require a small speculation. It is in fact a simple version of scientific plenitude. The whole of this
universe, it might be speculated, is zillions of times bigger than the observable
universe or it has existed for much longer than we usually estimate. However
unlikely it is that life could arise and evolve to produce embodied persons on
a given planet, it will arise in a large enough universe, provided it has positive
probability for each suitable planet. And whatever the details, we can assign
a positive probability for life to arise and to evolve into embodied persons.
To be sure, the origin of life might be a fluke involving, for all I know, just
the right combination of millions of simple chemicals at the same time. And
it might be another fluke that anything more sophisticated than some pro-
tobacterium ever evolved. For all I know, the chance of embodied persons
arising on a suitable planet might be one in a zillion to the power zillion. But
if the unobservable part of the universe is large enough, say a zillion to the
power zillion times the observable part, it is still likely to happen. Naturalists
may then give the anthropic answer to anyone who asks, But why is there
life in the observable part?

A combination, then, of the anthropic reply and the speculation that the
universe is vastly greater than its observable part preserves naturalism from any
embarrassment due merely to the extraordinarily low chance of embodied
persons coming to exist in the observable universe. But that does not show
that there is a satisfactory naturalistic explanation of the occurrence of embodied persons. For there are some factors required for life which cannot be
ensured by sheer size. The Big Bang must be of low entropy and must not
be so violent that it generates just an ever-thinning cloud of dust and gas.
Above all, the fundamental laws must be such as give rise to complex systems
such as those described by chemistry. None of that is ensured by sheer size
alone.

Before proceeding I would like to make two further comments. One is a
remark directed against those intellectual puritans who would reject any speculation and rely only on established facts. They might well find themselves
condemned to total bewilderment as to why there should be embodied persons. For the naturalistic account I have accepted as adequate requires the
speculation that the universe is vastly greater than the observable universe. I
myself find that the most innocent of speculations, but it is a speculation
nonetheless, not an established fact.

My other comment concerns the Strong Anthropic Principle, as John D.
Barrow calls it, namely the principle that there must be sentient life some-

where.[3] This could perhaps be taken as a fundamental principle governing the universe, for which no further explanation is provided. If so, it is clearly not a satisfactory answer to the question, Why is the universe suited to life? For it amounts merely to saying, The universe is suited to life because it is a fundamental principle governing the universe that there be life.

5. Scientific Plenitude

The anthropic explanation of the suitability of the observable universe for life was based on the assumption that some part of the whole of our universe is thus suited. We can, therefore, buttress it by a speculation, either scientific or metaphysical, according to which our universe is made up of an enormous number of regions that are at least as large as the observable universe.

In the previous section I considered the extraordinarily low chance of embodied persons arising in the observable universe. To explain the occurrence of embodied persons naturalistically, we required only that there were indeed many regions as large as the observable universe. That does not, however, explain the characteristics possessed by our universe without which there could not be life anywhere in it, no matter how large it is. For the sake of definiteness, let us concentrate on the value of the weak fine structure constant. Merely positing a very large universe does not explain this value if throughout the universe that "constant" is indeed constant. Naturalists may, however, speculate that the "constant" varies from region to region. The vast majority of regions of our universe would therefore have life-hostile values for the weak fine structure constant. If, however, there are enough regions, then it is likely that in some of them that "constant" has a life-friendly value. It would then be entirely appropriate to give the anthropic reply to the question, But why is the weak fine structure constant life-friendly in *our* region?

To explain the suitability of our universe for life, naturalists may resort, then, to a version of plenitude, namely that there are many regions in our universe that exhibit a suitable variety. To take another example, suppose we are thoroughly impressed by the way the Big Bang—assuming there was such an event—had to be just right to provide a universe suited to life. It must, we are supposing, be neither too violent nor too gentle. And it must have surprisingly low entropy. Now suppose there are an enormous number of big bangs, perhaps even infinitely many, and that they vary both as regards their strength and as regards their entropy. It is, then, no longer surprising that at least one big bang was just right. And the anthropic reply is appropriate to

---

[3] Stephen Hawking (1988, pp. 124–25) gives a somewhat different version of the Strong Anthropic Principle, which makes it rather like what I call metaphysical plenitude.

any who ask, Yes, but why was our big bang just right? Plenitude promises, therefore, an understanding of why the universe—or at least our part of it— is so remarkably suited to life.

This way of understanding the suitability of the universe for life is enhanced by, but does not crucially depend on, the speculation that there are many universes. Even those who deny there could be more than one spatio-temporal system should allow that the one and only Universe could contain a great diversity of regions and that everything astronomers can observe is contained in just one of these regions. (Nor need it be supposed that the regions are separated by sharp boundaries. They might or might not be.) And the diversity of these regions enables us to understand why at least one of them is suited to life.

The occurrence of many regions of this universe or even of many universes governed by the same laws as ours is somewhere on the vague border between science and metaphysics. It requires a speculative extrapolation from current science to what cannot be observed.[4] So is scientific plenitude still a naturalistic theory? Or is it a non-naturalistic nontheistic speculation? I do not quibble about whether scientific plenitude counts as naturalism. Instead I make two points. My first is that it is, in any case, a limited way of understanding, because it leaves the life-friendly character of the laws unexplained. To be sure, it explains some of the features required for life—the strength of the Big Bang, for instance. That is because it is entirely consistent with the laws to assume our universe is so large that there are many big bangs. But it is more than a mere scientific speculation to assume that there are many regions with varying laws. That would be metaphysical plenitude.

My second point is that scientific plenitude is about as speculative as my suggestions about how God might ensure an afterlife. Indeed speculations about other regions or other universes are remarkably like speculations about paradise replicas of Earth. Naturalists who seek to understand the suitability of the universe for life should not, therefore, sneer at my speculations about an afterlife.

6. Explanation by Means of Laws

By assuming that this universe is governed by life-friendly laws, naturalists can, relying on scientific plenitude as a hypothesis, explain why the (observ-able) universe is suited to life. But they have yet to explain why there are the life-friendly laws. Before I consider how they might attempt to do this, I

---

[4] By embodied persons, that is. God would know of all these life-hostile universes if they exist, but that is of no comfort to naturalists.

point out that they might not even need to treat scientific plenitude as a further hypothesis. For the laws themselves might make it highly probable that there is a universe suited to life, by showing among other things that there will be many and varied regions in the one large universe. In that way scientific plenitude would be derived from the laws rather than hypothesized. In this section I sketch two contemporary speculations along these lines. My reason for sketching them is to locate just where it is that naturalism fails to provide an understanding.

Here it is useful to distinguish *constraining laws* from *existential laws*. The former put constraints on what is the case by (i) prohibiting something as impossible (e.g., a violation of the conservation of mass energy); or by (ii) requiring one thing to occur if another occurs; or by (iii) a probabilistic weakening of (i) or (ii). And such constraining laws are what we most commonly mean by laws of nature. But we might also posit some existential law telling us that something of a certain kind exists or is likely to come into existence. For instance, at one stage Fred Hoyle proposed a law of continuous creation according to which matter comes spontaneously into existence. That would be most naturally interpreted as an existential law. The distinction is important to me, because we need to recognize that naturalistic understanding requires both constraining laws and various existential states of affairs, which may or may not have the status of laws—whatever that status is.

Traditionally the *initial conditions* have been posited as existential states of affairs. Such initial conditions fully specify the universe at its beginning, if it has a beginning. (If not, there is no obvious candidate for the posited existential states of affairs, but it does not follow that they are redundant.) The universe then develops in accordance with the constraining laws. That the existential states of affairs are rather complicated would give a significant advantage to any moderately simple hypothesis that explained them. But need the existential states of affairs be complicated? To answer this question I consider two representative naturalistic explanations of the suitability of this universe for life. For my purpose a certain amount of simplification and reconstruction is convenient. So be warned: the accounts I describe are not exactly as stated by their proponents.

My first example is based on Edward Tryon's zero mass energy speculation. Tryon has argued that there can be no true vacuum but that the nearest that is physically possible to a vacuum is a system of randomly fluctuating fields whose average mass energy is zero. Given enough time such fluctuations are almost bound to result in universe after universe. And out of this indefinitely large collection of universes some are almost bound to be suited to life (Tryon 1990). Tryon does not have to hypothesize scientific plenitude precisely because his speculation itself implies plenitude.

Clearly various constraining laws are assumed, to show for instance that a true vacuum is impossible and that the mean mass energy is zero. But what else is assumed? Apparently it is only the existential state of affairs that there is a spacetime. I am prepared to consider this an existential *law*, but the more important point is that the existence of spacetime is, like the occurrence of suitable laws, a far more economical unexplained hypothesis for naturalists than would be the occurrence of zillions of particles with specified positions and velocities.

Another scientific speculation worth noting is that of Hawking. Applying quantum mechanics to general relativity, he has been able to show how the universe could have a finite history and yet not have begun with a singularity. Here we mean by a singularity a point or region of spacetime in which the laws of nature break down (Hawking 1988, chap. 8). This suggests the following Hawking-type program. Take it as a fundamental existential law that spacetime has a structure of a certain nonspecific kind. (For example, take it as a law that spacetime is a four-dimensional manifold.) Further require it to be singularity-free. Then, relying on the constraining laws as stated by quantized general relativity, naturalists could argue that it is fairly probable that the universe is suited to life. Now the constraint that there be no singularities is just the sort of thing we should expect. So if this is all that is required to show the suitability of this universe for life, that would be especially significant.

The speculations of Tryon and of Hawking were introduced partly to give some idea of what existential laws might look like. But they also provide attempts at a naturalistic understanding of the suitability of the universe for life. An alternative, which I have already mentioned, is to hypothesize a universe that contains many large regions, among which "constants," such as the weak fine structure constant, vary. In that case we may rely on the anthropic explanation of why we inhabit a region that is suitable for life.

7. The Inevitable Limitation of Scientific Explanation

The previous two sections contain a naturalistic understanding of the occurrence of life, provided we take for granted various scientific laws (or, equivalently, take for granted the causal powers of the constituents of matter). At this point naturalists can adopt one of three strategies. The first is to stop their quest for understanding once they have explained things in terms of laws and commend such restraint to others. The second is to urge that the laws they use to explain can themselves be understood, at least partially, without further explanation. The third is to supplement their scientific understanding by means of further metaphysical speculations. Of these strategies the first requires little comment. I defended best-explanation apologetics in Chapter 1, and restraint in what you attempt to understand did not count as an intellectual virtue. The aim was to understand as much as possible with the most economical hypothesis. I grant the economy of naturalism, but what we are now examining is just how much naturalists can understand given their economical account. Here, as so often, restraint is no more than an admission of failure.

The strategy of incorporating just a little metaphysics is one I find more interesting, and I consider it in the remaining sections of this chapter. But in this section I consider the second strategy, based on the claim that there are some fundamental laws or principles that are intrinsically intelligible. Now in presenting best-explanation apologetics I avoided judgments of intrinsic intelligibility, largely because of the threat of subjectivity. Nonetheless I should allow naturalists the option of arguing that the laws are intrinsically intelligible. For that would make more attractive the naturalistic understanding of the suitability of the universe for life.

I grant that if the laws of nature were all as intelligible as the principle that nature abhors a singularity or that there is space and time, then we would have an understanding of the laws without further explanation, which, in turn, would enable us to explain the suitability of the universe for life. And, given that understanding, I doubt if my overall case against atheism would hold. Instead, because of the other features that can be given a theocentric understanding, I would claim that all three of theism, atheism, and agnosticism would be warranted positions.

What are the prospects, then, of all the laws, including the existential ones, being intrinsically intelligible? Not good, I say. But this question is complicated by the way in which there can be laws that are of intermediate intelligibility. For example, the conservation of mass energy is by no means as intelligible as the conservation of mass would have been, had that been a law. (See the appendix.) Nonetheless I concede that it might still be thought of as *fairly* intelligible.

The best prospect for intrinsically intelligible laws would seem to be some version of Tryon's zero mass energy speculation. We can hypothesize that the total mass energy of the universe is always zero, because the positive mass energy we are familiar with is canceled out by the negative energy due to the curvature of space. So there is the prospect of showing how this total zero energy state has evolved, without any violation of conservation laws, out of a state in which there is neither positive nor negative energy. It seems to follow that the existential condition required in addition to the constraining laws is merely the assertion that there was nothing. And that, surely, has intrinsic intelligibility. The big question, Why is there something rather than nothing? would be answered by saying, In the beginning there was nothing, and indeed nothing came out of nothing, so we now have nothing—in disguise.

A genuine attempt to explain the physical universe as arising out of nothing would gain us an intrinsically intelligible existential law (that in the beginning there was nothing) at the expense of constraining laws that lack the intelligibility of even the conservation laws. That is because the persistent state of there being nothing would satisfy all conservation laws, so we require more to understand why this nothing produces something. Either these constraining laws would have to establish the instability of a state in which there really is nothing, or they would have to be probabilistic laws that show that there is some probability of something evolving out of nothing.

The zero mass energy speculation is not, however, a serious attempt to explain the universe as arising out of nothing. For a start the initial state is not a true vacuum but a state in which there are already fluctuating field strengths and particles coming into and passing out of existence. Moreover, the currently most popular version of the zero mass energy speculation is inflationary expansion, first proposed by Alan Guth. According to this, the evolution of the universe from the initial state is governed by something called the Higgs field (Guth 1983; Linde 1983; Steinhardt 1983). The dynamics of the Big Bang is then like that of a boulder precariously balanced on the crest of a hill. Once it starts rolling, it will gather speed and roll down to the bottom of the valley. The required initial condition for this to occur is that the universe is in a zero total energy state but that the Higgs field provides a high potential energy. The Higgs field may well be nothing the man or woman in the street can comprehend. But that does not make it nothing at all.

In addition to the Higgs field the zero mass energy speculation relies quite heavily on quantum mechanics. And to say that quantum mechanics is highly intelligible would be to say that were classical mechanics to turn out to be correct after all, we should then seek an explanation of why quantum theory was not correct instead. Should we?

Likewise, although Hawking might propose the intrinsically intelligible law that nature abhors a singularity, and although the existence of a spacetime might also be intrinsically intelligible, that is not all he needs. He also requires, at very least, the combination of quantum mechanics and general relativity, and it would be a bold person who argued that quantized general relativity was intrinsically intelligible.

8. The Appeal to Simplicity

I have argued for the inevitable limits to a purely scientific understanding. It follows that the sciences must be given a metaphysical supplement if naturalists are to find some way of understanding the life-friendly character of the laws. One metaphysical supplement that remains in the spirit of naturalism is the appeal to simplicity. It is preferable to accept without further understanding laws that are simple rather than those that are complicated or messy.

This appeal to simplicity requires that there be an objective distinction between more and less natural classifications, because what seems simple given one classification seems complex given another. It also requires that we have some knowledge of that classification. These requirements may pose problems for naturalism. Nonetheless I concede the objectivity of simplicity. And I further concede that the laws that have been discovered are fairly simple, even though not intrinsically intelligible. Naturalists may attempt, therefore, to understand the suitability of the universe for life by appealing to the simplicity of the fundamental laws of nature. I have, however, a serious objection to this attempt. There are many other systems of law which could have held, which are even simpler but not life-friendly. Hence the life-friendly character of the laws cannot be understood by the appeal to simplicity. Initially this claim might seem puzzling. For do we not choose between theories largely on the grounds of simplicity? So if there are simpler laws, why do we not believe in them rather than in the ones we have chosen? But that would be to ignore the other constraints on theory choice, in particular the empirical constraint. A theory, however simple, must be adequate to the data if it is to be accepted. To be sure, there can be a great deal of discussion of what that adequacy amounts to. But a total disregard for observation is a form of insanity.

This objection can be pressed home by a consideration of all those possible universes in which nothing interesting happens but nonetheless the laws are remarkably simple. Classical mechanics provides us with some excellent examples of these boring universes. Suppose the only force is gravity and the universe always has been and always will be filled with a uniform dense homogeneous fluid. It just stays that way. It surely is simple, but dull. Another classical mechanical universe that is far simpler than ours but not suited to life is a "billiard ball" universe in which there are lumps of incompressible matter traveling through a vacuum and interacting only in accordance with the laws of Newtonian mechanics. There is little physics and no chemistry in such a universe. Now it is quite preposterous to suggest that the laws scientists discover are as simple as those in such boring universes. So simplicity alone cannot be used to explain the laws that actually occur.

Perhaps it is not their simplicity but their elegance or some other aesthetic quality that enables us to understand the laws. Thus some might hold that the combination of fundamental simplicity with richness of detail is of aesthetic value and that it is precisely this aesthetic value that enables us to understand why the laws are as they are. There is much to be said for that, but it is beyond naturalism and I defer consideration of it until the next chapter. Here, though, I insist that a purely naturalistic appeal to simplicity fails as a way of understanding why this universe is suited to life. It fails because there are many simpler systems of laws that are hostile to life.

9. Necessitarianism

The appeal to simplicity has failed, but I consider one last attempt to provide a largely naturalistic understanding of the life-friendly character of the laws. This is necessitarianism, which is the thesis that the laws of nature are necessary. It is initially plausible that to explain things in terms of necessary truths is the very best way of explaining. Hence if necessitarianism is correct, it seems the naturalistic understanding of life in terms of laws is of this very best kind.

It might have seemed so obvious that the laws are necessary that many naturalists could well have assumed their work was over once they had noted that there is a scientific explanation of something in terms of the laws. But even if the laws are necessary in some sense—and so deserving to be called laws rather than mere regularities—this necessity might "merely" be that they are essential for this universe. That is, *this* universe could not exist unless there were *these* laws (Bigelow 1990; Bigelow, Ellis, and Lierse 1994). In that case we cannot understand why there are the laws there are by arguing that they are necessary. For this amounts merely to understanding that there are these laws if there is this universe. It is far from obvious, therefore, that the laws are necessary in a stronger sense, which could be likened to the necessity of mathematical truths. Nonetheless, provided that is put forward as a speculation, necessitarianism is a development of naturalism worth considering.

The aim of necessitarianism, therefore, is to understand various truths, in particular that the universe is suited to life, by hypothesizing that the laws that explain these truths are not merely essential but necessary. My objection to necessitarianism is that discovering necessity can do no more to help us understand than discovering truth. And if it be replied that necessity is the mark of intrinsic intelligibility, my retort is that the most I would concede is that the combination of necessity and simplicity is good evidence for intrinsic intelligibility. But I have already argued that the laws of nature, especially those of quantized general relativity, are just not simple enough to be intrinsically intelligible. If naturalists truly seek a simple necessary being as the terminus of all our explanations, I commend to them the God of classical theism. To support my claim that necessity by itself provides little evidence for intrinsic intelligibility, I tell an anachronistic story about lazy Pythagoreans. (For the purposes of this story I assume that space is Euclidean.) The Pythagoreans notice that for many different right-angled triangles the square on the hypotenuse equals the sum of the squares on the other two sides. They also find no counterexample. Because of this inductive evidence they are convinced that Pythagoras's theorem is true. Nonetheless they do not consider that they have yet understood why it is true. By now, however, they have done a hard day's work, so they postpone the further task of proving it. While they are eating their bean-free dinner, one of them does the philosophical thing and asks why they think they could understand it even if they could show Pythagoras's theorem followed from various axioms. The others reply that axioms are necessary and if they prove it they have, therefore, shown Pythagoras's theorem is also necessary. That, they say, is why proving it results in understanding. At that point the lazy Pythagoreans realize that they do need proof in order to understand. For (i) they are convinced of the truth of the theorem, and (ii) because it is a geometric result, if it is true then it is necessarily true.

I invite readers to agree with me that something has gone wrong. But if so, I submit that the same thing has gone wrong with necessitarianism. Even if, as I doubt, the *demonstration* of necessity always provides understanding, the mere *warranted belief* in necessity does not.

In the discussion above I might have missed the necessitarians' point. Perhaps they are not hypothesising necessities but really do want to claim that we could *prove* the laws, much as we prove mathematical theorems. Thus Hume makes Philo speculate that "could we penetrate into the intimate nature of bodies, we should clearly see why it is absolutely impossible . . . they could ever admit of any other disposition" (*Dialogues*, Part IX). Philo likens this to the rule for deciding if a number is divisible by nine, a rule that can be understood by proving it. It would not, therefore, be necessity that has a special role in explanation but provability.[5]

In the absence of any such proof the suggestion amounts to no more than a version of the threat of the unknown hypothesis. To say that if we only

[5] If we interpret proof as meaning a demonstration from "self-evident" principles, then Hume's suggestion is best interpreted as a joke at the expense of those such as Demea in the *Dialogues* who attempted to prove the existence of God in that way. The suggestion that the laws are provable should, if we are to take it seriously, be interpreted as saying that they can be derived from some intrinsically intelligible principles governing the universe. My response to the suggestion applies, however, whichever way we interpret it.

knew, we might be able to prove the laws is like saying that if we only knew, we could find a better nontheistic explanation than any yet proposed. That was one reason why I am arguing against atheism and why I am defending theism rather than arguing against agnosticism. Conversely if we only knew, we might be able to demonstrate theism a priori. None of those suggestions about what might be the case, however, contributes anything toward an actual understanding of the suitability of the universe for life.

10. The Comparison of Theocentric with Naturalistic Understanding

There is a great deal that can be explained scientifically which theists cannot in fact explain in terms of the divine purpose in creating. For example, the fact that the gases helium, argon, neon, krypton, and xenon arc all chemically inert and nonradioactive has a scientific explanation in terms of their structure. But it would be hard to argue that God has some special purpose in providing five chemically inert nonradioactive gases rather than three or four. And such examples could be multiplied. If we had to choose, then, between a theocentric and a scientific understanding, it would be an uphill struggle to defend the superiority of the theocentric. But that is not the contest. For there is no incompatibility between scientific and theocentric understanding. Rather the competition we are here concerned with is between naturalism and theocentric understanding. Both parties take scientific explanation for granted.

In the next chapter I provide a theocentric understanding of some other things. But here we have concentrated on one striking feature of the universe, namely its suitability for life and for embodied persons in particular. I have argued that the naturalistic understanding of this striking feature requires that the life-friendly character of the laws must be accepted without understanding. That there are life-friendly laws can, however, be understood in a theocentric manner as follows. The laws scientists aim to discover are brought about by God in the initial act of creating a physical universe. There is a universe with life-friendly laws precisely because it is part of the divine plan that there be embodied persons. The only law—if indeed it should be called a law—that is left unexplained on the theocentric account is that which governs the power of any conscious being to act freely. That "law," like the principle that nature abhors a singularity, might well be considered an intrinsically intelligible one. More important, it is already required for an account of free human actions. So it is not something we have to hypothesize in order to explain the oc-currence of life-friendly laws.

Theocentric understanding achieves more than naturalism, then. But it might be objected that we have understood more only at the cost of positing more. How should we decide which is the better way of understanding the suitability of the universe for life? I argue later in this work that God is a genuine epistemic possibility even prior to the consideration of what can be given a theocentric understanding. That reduces the cost of "positing" the existence of God so that it is no greater than the cost of there being unexplained laws. I also provide a defense against the argument from evil. Given that God is a genuine epistemic possibility and given the defense against the argument from evil, I invite readers to judge that theocentric understanding and naturalism are about as successful as ways of understanding the suitability of the universe for life. Theocentric understanding shows its superiority only because, as I argue in the next chapter, it explains more.

When, therefore, I have shown what else can be understood in a theocentric manner, when I have argued for the genuine epistemic possibility of theism, when I have defended it against the argument from evil, then I shall say to the naturalists, "La Place was wrong; you have need of that hypothesis."

Appendix : The Conservation of Mass Energy

Conservation laws are especially appealing, and naturalism would be in a stronger position if all laws were as intelligible as the conservation laws. It is important, however, not to think that the currently accepted conservation of mass energy is as intelligible as the conservation of mass would have been if that had been a law. The latter would have expressed the idea that the physical stuff of which the universe is made never comes into existence or passes out of existence. And that would have been intrinsically intelligible. Indeed we could then compare the following two children's questions: Where does all the stuff come from? and Where does God come from? In both cases part of the answer might be that what has always been there does not need a cause to come into existence. (This is only part of the answer in both cases, because we can always seek, although not demand, a further explanation.)

I claim, however, that the conservation of mass energy is not as intelligible as the conservation of mass would have been. It is not enough merely to say that mass and energy are just two forms of stuff. We must look more closely at what energy is. Energy takes two different forms, kinetic energy, due to motion, and potential energy, which is stored in a field. Consider kinetic energy. It is entirely due to the motion of the particle concerned. So the convertibility of mass and energy tells us that the mass of a particle depends on how fast it is moving. This is not the intrinsically intelligible principle that stuff is conserved. Initially it seems like a rather magical proposal that the stuff of which things are made increases in quantity just because that thing is moving.

Now consider potential energy. If a piece of elastic is stretched, it accumulates potential energy, so it becomes slightly more massive as a result. Whatever this potential energy is, it would seem to be something quite different from kinetic energy. The most obvious interpretation of potential energy, at least before the acceptance of special relativity, was that it was indeed a *potential* energy and not actual energy at all.

A further peculiarity of potential energy is that it can be negative. To illustrate this I consider the case of electrostatic attraction. Consider a universe with just two particles in it of opposite charges, say an electron and a positron. As they fall toward each other, they gain in speed and hence kinetic energy, so they must be losing potential energy. Therefore a state in which the particles were distant must have a significantly higher potential energy than the state in which they are near. But a state in which they are distant is one in which the effect of electrostatic attraction should be considered negligible. So it should be thought of as having a potential energy very near zero. Hence the state in which the particles are close together has a significantly lower potential energy than the near-zero figure. Hence it has negative potential energy. A similar assignment of negative energy to gravity is precisely what is relied on in the zero mass energy speculation. I have no objection to negative energy provided it is not combined with the idea that energy is a form of stuff.

It could be objected that the potential energy is arbitrary up to a constant. That is, adding a constant to the potential energy of electrostatic attraction at all points would leave unaltered the dynamics of the two particles, for it is only the difference between potential energies at different places which is significant. In that case, it could be said, we can ensure that the potential energy is always positive.

If that objection succeeded, it would, it should be noted, entirely undermine the zero mass energy speculation. But I do not think it succeeds. First, if space is continuous, as it is widely thought to be, and if we are considering point particles, there is no limit to just how large and negative the potential energy could be, as the particles get closer and closer together. (The energy is inversely proportional to the distance between the particles.) So adding some fixed value to the potential energy will not prevent negative values occurring. Second, even if it is insisted that space is discrete or there could be no point particles, the negative energy is taken to affect the overall mass. Thus in the case of an electron/positron pair, the overall mass of the pair is increased by the kinetic energy of the particles but decreased by the negative potential energy. Adding a constant to the potential energy would amount to saying that the overall mass is greater than it is usually taken to be. This undermines the claim that we can add a constant to the potential energy without affecting the dynamics. For there might be some third, electrically neutral, particle orbiting the electron/positron pair—its dynamics would be affected by the addition of the constant to the potential energy.

Indeed there is a situation in which physicists really do make use of the way energy can be negative. It occurs when they are discussing the evaporation of black holes. No particle can escape a black hole, but the mass of a black hole can decrease because of a flow of negative energy into it (Davies 1981, p. 124).

I conclude that the conservation of mass energy is best thought of as merely an elegant enough law rather than being intrinsically intelligible.

[4]
The Breadth of
Theocentric Understanding

In the previous chapter I granted that naturalism is about as good as theism if we seek to understand only the suitability of the universe for life. In this chapter I continue the debate by considering what else we might understand. I begin with two items that are very much in the spirit of scientific realism and hence especially likely to be granted by naturalists: the fact that the universe is governed by regularities, and the progress of science toward the truth. I then turn to the theocentric understanding of moral supremacy, of the beauty of the physical world, and of the serendipity of mathematics.

I would like to emphasize that I am not proposing a series of different arguments for the conclusion that there is a God, one from the suitability of the universe for life, another from the regularity of the universe, and so on. If I were, then each argument would be vulnerable to the charge that the cost exceeds the benefit. For it is not worth positing God in order to explain just one feature of the world around us. No, my argument is, as Mitchell (1973) put it, a *cumulative* one. Belief in God enables us to understand many different features of the world. The benefit on each occasion might perhaps be less than the cost. But there is just the one cost, whereas the benefits accumulate. I consider none of the benefits to be negligible, but the one I personally consider the greatest, although not the easiest to articulate, is the theocentric understanding of beauty.

1. The Regularity of the Universe

The observable universe is orderly, with fairly simple generalizations holding not just in a certain region but everywhere. Often I call these generalizations *laws of nature*, without worrying about whether they really deserve that title. In this section, however, I refer to them as *regularities*, leaving it open for the moment whether or not they should be called laws. This assumption that there are such ubiquitous regularities has a priori appeal. Furthermore, many successful scientific explanations are based on that assumption. In particular, physics has been fruitfully applied to astronomy and to history. This provides empirical confirmation that the regularities are ubiquitous, at least in the restricted sense of holding throughout the *observable* universe. For example, most of the easily observed stars belong to what is called the main sequence. Now there is a physical explanation both of the correlation between the mass and the color of stars in the main sequence, and of the occurrence of stars not in the main sequence. The explanation is that, for most of their active life, stars release energy by converting four protons into one helium nucleus. For as long as that nuclear reaction continues, the star belongs to the main sequence. But after the free protons have been consumed, stars can continue releasing energy only by means of a different nuclear reaction. The point of the example is not in the details but in the assumption that the same nuclear reactions occur in far distant stars, and hence many millions of years ago, as occur in the Sun or in our laboratories. Again, if we turn from astronomy to history, the fact that dating using carbon 14 is corroborated by traditional historical methods strongly supports the unchanging character of the processes of radioactive decay.

It is widely assumed that the most fundamental regularities are ubiquitous in the sense of holding throughout this universe, that is, everywhere that is a finite distance from us in space or time. Perhaps, though, this assumption is incorrect and the most fundamental regularities vary from region to region. For instance, mass energy might be conserved not on 100 percent of occasions but on some variable percentage. I grant that possibility and so seek to explain only the ubiquity of the regularities in the observable universe.

Swinburne (1979, chap. 8) has argued that such ubiquitous regularities are improbable on the supposition that there is no God but far more probable on the supposition that there is a God. This forms the basis of a piece of Bayesian apologetics. Unfortunately it is hard to make sense of these probabilities except the way Swinburne does (1979, p. 28n), namely as epistemic ones. (The alternative construal of probability as statistical involves proportions of universes with and without regularities—a topic on which, to understate matters, we lack knowledge.) And to say that the regularities have low epistemic probability on the supposition that there is no God is just to say that, in the absence of other evidence, if we suppose there is no God, we would infer that there would not be regularities. But the occurrence of regularities seems to be just the sort of thing we believe a priori, that is, in the absence of evidence. For that reason I do not argue that regularity is improbable given naturalism. Rather I argue that the theocentric understanding of the regularities is superior to the naturalistic understanding.

What, then, is the theocentric understanding of regularity? Some regularity, but not all, can be understood in terms of the need for us to be able to predict, to a limited extent, the effects of our action. If the generalizations that held up to 1900 had ceased to hold in 1901, it would not have been possible for humans in 1901 to have affected one another and their environment in the ways they intended. Indeed, after a while, failure of regularity would prevent any rational formation of intentions and turn us into mere observers of a world beyond all control. It is part of the divine plan, we may assume, that our lives have the sort of meaning that requires that our intentions are sometimes fulfilled. (See Swinburne 1979, p. 146.) That explanation does not, however, hold for the distant past before there were any animals capable of intention, or in regions far removed from all life. There the regularity would be explained primarily in aesthetic terms: assuming God has reason to create, God will create beautifully, and beauty requires order. (See Swinburne 1979, p. 146.)

In addition to the ubiquity of the regularities, we may note that the regularities are in some sense necessary, contrary to the Humean position according to which they are mere generalizations. Now it is not clear in what sense they are necessary. But at least we may assert this much: the regularities that actually hold here and now would still hold here and now if we were to decide to act in ways other than we do. And because of their ubiquity we may drop the "here and now" qualification. For example, the regularities are not just such that flour, eggs, chocolate, and other ingredients combined in the appropriate way have in fact resulted in chocolate cakes, but such that they would have resulted in a chocolate cake, and not scrambled eggs on toast with chocolate sauce, if they had been put together on another occasion in the same way.[1] Interpreted this way, then, the necessity of those regularities we call laws is not a highly debatable metaphysical thesis but rather a presupposition of our having the powers we all assume we do have—and of our not having supernatural powers.

The theocentric explanation of the necessity of those regularities we call laws is that their holding at a given place and time, even in the future, has already been brought about by God as part of the initial act of creation.[2]

---

[1] Or, if the laws of nature are probabilistic, then the probability of a chocolate cake rather than scrambled eggs resulting from the recipe would be the same had we decided to bake a cake.

[2] This does not exclude the suggestion, discussed below, that the laws are essential characteristics of the kind of universe we inhabit. God might well ordain these laws in creating a universe of this kind.

Therefore they are necessary in the same way that everything that is past is commonly taken to be necessary. In particular, they are both beyond our power to alter and such as we can rely on in order to exercise our powers. Moreover, just as we take for granted all events before 1945, but not events after 1945, when discussing what would have happened if the atom bombs had not been dropped on Japan, we always take for granted those regularities we call laws when discussing what would have happened, because those laws are fixed before any physical events at all.[3]

Some might hold that all events have been brought about by God in creating the universe, not just these ubiquitous regularities. I disagree, but I would say that in that case all events hold of necessity. Others might find it puzzling how God would have the power to cause regularities to hold in the distant future. I reply that such a power is not supernatural. Rather it follows from my general account of the powers of free agents.

We have, then, a theocentric understanding of the necessity and ubiquity of the laws. There are five responses naturalists could make to this. The first is to accept necessity and ubiquity without any attempt at an explanation, but to do so would be to concede that, in this respect at least, theocentric understanding is superior to the naturalistic.

The second naturalistic response is to deny the necessity, and perhaps even the ubiquity, of the regularities we call laws. This is, I submit, the Humean position that the "laws" are merely those regularities toward which we have a certain kind of attitude. (They might be the regularities we are prepared to rely on when making predictions or indulging in speculations about what might have happened in other circumstances.) I hold that Humeans should be bold enough to refuse to call them *laws*, but that is a minor point. More important, we have good reason to believe in both the ubiquity and the necessity of various regularities, and so I find the Humean position unduly skeptical. For, as I have already mentioned, their ubiquity has been confirmed by the successful application of physics and chemistry to astronomy and history, and we should believe in their necessity because that is a presupposition of the belief that we have various powers to affect the world around us. I therefore reject the Humean account.

The third response is to explain the ubiquity and necessity of regularities by means of a naturalistic metaphysics of laws. For example, there is the Dretske Tooley Armstrong theory that laws of nature are relations between properties. Thus Newton's law of gravitational attraction would be explained as a relation of necessitation between two complex structural properties:

---

[3] On the maximal indeterminacy speculation the event of creation is a restriction of the actual to a world indeterminate between all those in which the regularities hold.

(i) the property of consisting of two parts a specified distance, r, apart and with specified masses, m_1 and m_2; and (ii) the property of consisting of two parts exerting a force on each other in accordance with Newton's formula, Gm_1m_2/r^2.

I offer some criticism of this and other metaphysical explanations of the necessity and ubiquity of the regularities in the next section. But even apart from those criticisms I am confident that any such naturalistic understanding of laws will involve a substantial metaphysical hypothesis, of which the positing of relations between properties is an example. Naturalists might claim that these metaphysical hypotheses are less extravagant than belief in God. No doubt that would be the case if we aimed to explain nothing more than the ubiquity and necessity of the regularities. But we should be concerned with the *marginal* cost of understanding. My claim at the end of the previous chapter was that consideration of the suitability of the universe for life left theocentric and naturalistic understanding roughly on a par. To decide between them we should ask what extra hypotheses are required in each case to explain further data, in this case the ubiquity and necessity of laws. In the theocentric case we have only to make some rather plausible assumptions about the aesthetics of creation. In the rival naturalistic case we have to make a more substantial hypothesis, such as a relation of necessitation between properties.

The fourth response by naturalists is to insist that the occurrence of necessary and ubiquitous regularities is intrinsically intelligible. That is, we would seek explanations for any supposed cases in which there were no such laws, rather than seeking explanations as to why they do hold. I have considerable sympathy with that claim. I have already conceded that the conservation of mass, if it had been true, would have had intrinsic intelligibility. Another example I gave was the principle that nature abhors a singularity. Perhaps the existence of space and time could be added to the list. In general, however, it is not the laws themselves that are intelligible but, it is here being submitted, the higher-order principle that the most fundamental nature of things is, of necessity, the same everywhere and at all times.

To say a truth is intrinsically intelligible is to say we would seek an explanation of its not holding with more zeal than we seek an explanation of its holding. It is not to say it is totally intelligible, in the sense that any further explanation is fatuous. On the subjective issue of what we seek to understand I can only invite readers to share my judgment, which is that the occurrence of ubiquitous and necessary laws is not totally intelligible. There is some intellectual gain, therefore, in a theocentric explanation of the ubiquity and necessity of laws. We have explained something that, perhaps, we did not especially seek to explain but was still worthwhile explaining. This response, then, like the previous one, illustrates a definite, though not spectacular, advantage of a theocentric understanding of the ubiquity and necessity of the fundamental regularities scientists seek to discover.

Finally, naturalists might argue that the ubiquity and necessity of various regularities is required for there to be life, so the naturalistic explanations of the suitability of the universe for life hold here too. I disagree: the necessity of laws is borne out by considerations of what we have and have not the power to do, even if we do not do it, not what has in fact happened. All that is required for life to evolve is that the regularities do, for the most part, hold. Again, life could have evolved even if the laws were not ubiquitous but varied even within the observable universe.

2. Naturalistic Accounts of Laws of Nature

In the previous section I referred to various naturalistic accounts of laws of nature. There I merely made the point that any such account would require a substantial further metaphysical hypothesis, whereas the theocentric understanding of ubiquity and necessity requires nothing more than the elaboration of the account already given. In fact I consider that available naturalistic accounts of laws of nature are even less satisfactory than those remarks might suggest. In this section I consider three initially promising accounts of laws of nature and argue that none of them explains both ubiquity and necessity.

First, consider the Dretske Tooley Armstrong theory that laws are relations between properties (Armstrong 1983). Consider, for instance, a law stating the tendency of a physical system in a certain state to come to be in a different state. Then being a system of a certain kind in a certain state is a property of the system, call it F-ness, and its tendency to come to be in a different state shortly afterward is another property of the system, call it G-ness. The Dretske Tooley Armstrong theory requires the (to my mind plausible) assumption that the properties F-ness and G-ness are universals, that is, the very same in all their many instances. The theory then states that there is a special relation of *necessitation* between F-ness and G-ness. That relation would be primarily a relation between universals and only in some derived or secondary sense a relation between the particular systems. It is thus a *higher-order* relation. This serves to explain the ubiquity of the law, for universals are not restricted to some times or places rather than others, so a relation between universals would hold in all places and at all times.

As an aside, let me say that this naturalistic account of the ubiquity of laws provides a reason to reject the speculation that other universes are governed by other laws. According to that speculation, it is not surprising that there are life-friendly laws in some universe and, of course, not surprising that we are in one of the life-friendly ones. The reason for rejecting that speculation is that a universal is the very same in all its instances, not just in this universe but in all universes. Hence, on the naturalistic accounts of laws being considered, all universes must be governed by the same laws. Therefore this account of regularity would succeed only at the cost of obstructing one of the naturalistic attempts to explain the life-friendly character of our laws.

More significant as a criticism is the way the Dretske Tooley Armstrong theory fails to explain the necessity of laws. For, as David Lewis points out, we cannot explain necessity just by calling a higher-order relation one of necessitation (Lewis 1983, p. 366). That does not make the theory fatuous, for it still serves a purpose in explaining the ubiquity of the regularities, given this unexplained relation of necessitation. Even so, it is at a disadvantage compared with the theocentric understanding, which provides an explanation both of ubiquity and of necessity.

Another promising naturalistic account of the laws is to explain laws in terms of essential causal powers (Harré and Madden 1975, chap. 7). We might well agree that electronish behavior is essential to being an electron, in that nothing could be an electron unless it behaved in the electronish way. Nonetheless tracing necessity and ubiquity back to essences in this fashion merely results in a rephrasing of the request for explanation. Initially we asked why electrons and protons behave as they do necessarily and at all times and places. The reply was that otherwise they would not be electrons and protons. But now the question becomes, Why is it necessarily the case that the fundamental constituents of the physical universe at all times and places include electrons and protons rather than *selectrons* and *sprotons*, which are just like electrons and protons except that they lapse from their proper behavior when in certain neighborhoods? Thus the essential property theory of laws does not result in genuine progress toward an understanding of necessity and ubiquity.

The third and last account I consider is that the laws are essential not to individual particles but to the kind of universe we inhabit (Bigelow, Ellis, and Lierse 1994). On this account the universe could not belong to the kind it does unless it was governed by the laws that do in fact govern it. That is plausible enough. What we are seeking to explain, however, is why we inhabit a universe governed by ubiquitous and necessary regularities. And to be told that it would not be our kind of universe if it was not thus governed is singularly unhelpful as an explanation.

I conclude that whatever merits these various accounts have as competing speculations within the program of naturalism, they fail as explanations of both the ubiquity and the necessity of the regularities to be found in our universe.

3. Our Capacity for Intellectual Progress

We have many capacities that are difficult to understand naturalistically. In accordance with my emphasis on science in this work, I concentrate on how we have, collectively and with considerable labor, made progress with scientific theories.[4] Suppose you are some sort of angel or god and you visit Earth at five-thousand-year intervals. Ten or more visits ago you noticed the presence of modern human beings and, among other things, you delighted at the theories they formulate in order to try to understand things. On your most recent visit, five thousand years ago, you noticed the increasing complexity of society and the resultant change to some of the theories. You had, however, no reason to suppose that humans would make any significant intellectual progress beyond the stage of self-serving theories. (They were self-serving in that they seemed to be confirmed by observation but that was just because the content of observation was so very theory-laden—we saw what we expected to see.) When you come back this time, how astounded you will be! After some sixty thousand years wandering around in intellectual circles, we humans have started making progress. (In ethics and religion as well as science, I say. But for the purposes of this discussion I restrict my attention to scientific progress.) Although we should be careful here, as elsewhere, not to *demand* an explanation, there is an advantage to those theories that provide one.

I begin by noting that there are two different things we might try to explain concerning our intellectual capacities. The first is why we come to believe the theories we do believe. The second is why these theories are, for the most part, either true or near the truth. I have no objection to the evolutionary by-product account of why we form the theories we do. We rely, for instance, on inference to the best explanation (or some variant) because doing so enabled our ancestors to achieve the limited success of survival and reproduction. Having that tendency, we humans now come to have beliefs about all sorts of things, including scientific theories, for which the direct survival value explanation would fail.

Thus far, the naturalistic account is not inferior to the theocentric one, which is that God wants us to achieve by our own efforts various good things, including an understanding of what has been created. But I now ask the further question of why the methods used to arrive at scientific theories have, for the most part, arrived at or near the truth. And here the naturalistic understanding would have to go like this:

---

[4] I owe to Plantinga the general point that it is hard to provide a naturalistic understanding of our capacity to know. See especially Plantinga 1993b, chap. 12.

The explanation of our having various belief-forming tendencies is that
those of our ancestors who had them tended to form beliefs that were
useful (to survival and reproduction) because true. If they had not been
for the most part true, then our ancestors would not have survived and
we would not have inherited the tendency.

The naturalistic explanation of the truthfulness (for the most part) of the beliefs
we acquire using such methods as inference to the best explanation is based
on the value of having true beliefs for survival and reproduction. It is an
excellent explanation, therefore, of the truth of those beliefs that are indeed
useful for survival and reproduction, and these are just the true beliefs we
already had tens of thousands of years ago, when our protoscientific theories
were, for the most part, myths. But something extra is required if we are to
explain our ability to arrive at the truth of various scientific theories, including,
ironically, the theory of evolution used in the naturalistic explanation itself.

What is this something extra?[5] It is the assumption that there are general
principles or methods for inquiry that will tend to lead to the truth regardless
of topic. Let us call this the assumption of the *topic-neutrality* of method.
Granted that assumption, we have indeed an evolutionary explanation of our
ability to arrive at scientific truth. For if there are topic-neutral methods of
inquiry, then there is survival value in coming to use them. And it does not
undermine this evolutionary account that this survival value attaches to the
less theoretical instances of the methods.

How, then, might naturalists explain the topic-neutrality of method? They
might say that we discover precisely those truths that the methods selected
for by evolution enable us to discover. That response would be fine provided
we had some independent way of checking the theories derived using our
methods. We are seeking to explain, however, not why it is that we came to
produce the theories we have, but why those theories are true or near the
truth. So that response just shifts our attention to those general methods, such
as inference to the best explanation, that we use for checking the truth of
theories. In fact it is precisely such general methods that are the plausible
candidates for topic-neutrality. For each discipline will tend to develop its
own special methods, which will be subject to such checks, and these special
methods will change from time to time. Thus some sciences, such as physics,
require repeatable experimental confirmation of theories, whereas others, such
as geology, are confirmed by observations that are not experimental.

Again, naturalists might claim that the occurrence of ubiquitous and fairly

---

[5] Here I would like to acknowledge a debt to Alison Manion. Any clarity I have achieved
on this matter is due to discussions with her.

simple regularities itself explains the topic-neutrality of method.[6] For it is just the detection of fairly simple and recurring patterns of one sort or another, especially the sounds emitted by those around us when we were learning to speak, which was conducive to survival.

That naturalistic response would have been adequate had the *Greek program* succeeded, namely inferring the fundamental regularities directly from naked-eye observations of the world around us. It is instructive to consider an area where the Greek program eventually produced apparent success, namely astronomy in the hands of Kepler. The planets were eventually shown to move in accordance with simple laws in simple (elliptical) orbits. Newton, however, by giving a further explanation in terms of a more fundamental, and not directly observable, pattern rendered the Greek program outmoded. The success of our methods in arriving at the truth can be seen in hindsight to be due to what I describe as God's paper chase. There are enough simple patterns in what is observable without special equipment, for us to discover enough science to discover more patterns and develop technologies, which in turn enable us to discover more patterns, and so on. The proposed naturalistic understanding of our success requires not merely that the fundamental laws be suitably simple (something which we might find intrinsically intelligible) but that there are enough simple regularities at intermediate levels. That is something we have discovered on the supposition that our methods of inquiry lead to the truth. And it can be explained precisely by appealing to God's intention that eventually we discover the truth. But it can be neither explained naturalistically nor treated as intrinsically intelligible.

Instead of appealing to our belief in simple regularities, naturalists could appeal to the intrinsic intelligibility of the thesis that the methods are topic-neutral. As always, I am prepared to consider such claims, while trying to avoid them myself. What might be intrinsically intelligible, I grant, is the topic-neutrality of deductive reasoning represented by traditional syllogisms. And I further grant that before the consideration of evolutionary theories we might, in spite of Hume's analysis of induction, have considered intrinsically intelligible the topic-neutrality of all our reasoning. Darwin, however, altered this. For once we have given an evolutionary explanation of the success of our methods of reasoning on matters concerning survival, we then find puzzling, and so seek an explanation for, their success on matters not concerning survival.[7]

---

[6] I am indebted to Cornell University Press's referee for suggesting that this is a line naturalists might well take.

[7] See Plantinga, 1993b, pp. 219–37, for a development of this sort of point. Unlike Plantinga, I am not, however, arguing that naturalists should be agnostic about our intellectual powers. All I need at this point in the discussion is to resist a claim that would have been appropriate

I am now in a position to state more precisely the superiority of the theocentric over the evolutionary understanding of our ability to discover scientific truth. Naturalists who rely on evolution must assume the topic-neutrality of our methods of inquiry; they cannot provide a satisfactory explanation of that topic-neutrality; and their own reliance on evolutionary explanations prevents it being intrinsically intelligible. To that extent the evolutionary account makes a mystery of scientific progress. I should say, though, that it does not follow that the naturalistic account undermines our reliance on inference to the best explanation to arrive at, say, the theory of evolution. For the ability to understand why a method tends to arrive at the truth is not required for that method to be warranted. (Something can have a high a priori probability even though it is beyond our understanding.)

Now it might be objected that the theocentric understanding of our capacity to arrive at scientific theories progressing toward the truth is defeated by the prevalence of error, itself demonstrated by disagreement. I could assimilate this to the argument from evil discussed in Chapter 8. But there is no need to rely on a more general discussion of evil. For although there is value in individual achievement, there is also value in collective achievement, spread out over thousands of years. And we have no reason to expect God to arrange for the former in place of the latter. Again, there is no reason to expect God to arrange for sudden rather than gradual progress. Likewise, it is quite compatible with the theocentric understanding of our truth-acquiring capacities that there be many sincere atheists. What would undermine this piece of theocentric understanding would be lack of large-scale progress in a community that devotes significant resources to the pursuit of truth.

I have made a case, then, for the superiority of a theocentric over a naturalistic understanding of our capacity to arrive at the truth, or more precisely, of the progressive character of the collective efforts of sincere truth-seekers as illustrated by the history of science. There is, however, an alternative way in which a naturalistic account of the truthfulness of our beliefs might be attempted without recourse to evolutionary theory. It is to take the ways we tend to form belief as partly constitutive of the truth. There are several such accounts, the most famous being Kant's, although Kant discussed knowledge rather than truth. Likewise, according to Hilary Putnam's *Peircean Realism* (1978), for a belief to be true just is for it to be in accordance with the ideal theory. Again, Brian Ellis (1990) argues that the true beliefs are precisely the ones that are formed in accordance with what he calls the epistemic virtues,

---

before Darwin, namely that it is intrinsically intelligible that our methods of reasoning are topic-neutral.

which, on his naturalistic understanding of them, are just the ways we humans happen to form beliefs in normal cases. There is, then, a family of accounts of truth, often called antirealist, according to which beliefs are true in part because they are arrived at by various methods we could list, including, we may assume, inference to the best explanation. Such antirealist accounts make it look as if there is no mystery whatever in the topic-neutrality of our methods of arriving at the truth. For, it is said, the way human beings extend those methods from practical to theoretical questions constrains what the truth is on theoretical matters and so guarantees the suitability of those methods for arriving at the truth.

I am convinced that the truth is transcendent in the sense that it is not merely whatever belief is arrived at in the appropriate fashion. Rather the truth is a goal we seek but might or might not attain. And that is why I am astounded that science has achieved so much. The proposed antirealist understanding of the progress of science toward the truth is quite contrary to the transcendence of truth and should therefore be rejected. But I concede that this part of theocentric understanding is audience-specific. Nonetheless there is apologetic value in it. For many atheists who are scientific realists would grant the transcendence of truth. Moreover, I argue in Section 5 that naturalists must either concede the superiority of the theocentric understanding of moral supremacy or reject that supremacy out of devotion to transcendent truth. Obviously naturalists who reject the transcendence of truth are especially vulnerable to this argument.

4. Understanding Moral Supremacy

Not every position on morality is an attempt to understand. We might well decide to accept the moral order as something that is experienced without understanding. That is a position I respect, provided it is recognized for what it is and not thought of as itself a way of understanding. Let me further stress that I am not attempting to establish some incoherence in moral practice without theism. Nor am I arguing that theism makes people morally upright. My thesis is rather that there is something to do with morality for which there is a theocentric but not a naturalistic understanding. There may well be several such features. (See Forrest 1989c, 1994b.) Here I concentrate, however, on just one, namely *moral supremacy*.[8]

I begin with a statement of moral supremacy:

---

[8] A somewhat similar argument based on epistemology rather than morality could be developed. See Devine 1989, chap. 6.

> That something is morally wrong provides a reason for not doing it
> which outweighs any reasons based on special interests, even though
> these interests are highly significant in the person's life.

Moral supremacy might seem a rather harsh claim. For it might suggest that
we should ignore all ties of love or loyalty in the pursuit of duty. But those
suggestions are not genuine implications of moral supremacy. For what is
morally wrong may itself be influenced by special interests and need not, in
all cases, be derivable from easily stated rules. For example, suppose some
criminals are hidden by friends from the police. That is not obviously a case
of the friends ignoring moral duty for the sake of personal interests. It could
be interpreted as showing that we have different moral obligations toward
friends and strangers. What moral supremacy states is that *if* you believe that
the morally right thing is to give up your friends to the police, *then* your
moral reason for not protecting them outweighs any reasons you have for
protecting them.

It is hard to characterize in what way moral reasoning outweighs various
other considerations. For it lies somewhere between saying that one morally
ought to be persuaded by moral reasoning, which is trivially weak, and saying
that it is irrational not to be persuaded by moral reasoning, which is implau-
sibly strong. Because of this difficulty I concentrate on an example. The members of ARM (the Aesthetic Resistance Movement) have discovered a way
of creaming off a significant portion of state revenue and, without any risk of
discovery, can direct it to encourage the arts. Neither they nor their families
and friends will be personally enriched as a result. Some of them claim a moral
intuition that embezzlement is wrong and that this redirection of funds is
embezzlement. The others, who settle moral issues by examining the consequences rather than appealing to intuitions, take more persuading that it is
wrong but eventually decide that, for reasons quite beyond their control, the
resulting burden of extra taxation will fall on the poor. On balance, then,
people will be worse off.

All the members of ARM conclude that their splendid plan is morally
wrong and so they do not carry it out. I now ask why the members of ARM
decided not to go on with their scheme. I am not asking why members of
ARM should, in general, be moral, still less why they should not be thorough
egoists. Members of ARM are, it is to be assumed, generally morally upright.
However, it is the prospect of directing millions of dollars to the arts which
appeals to these honest citizens. They are tempted. But, the story goes, they
reluctantly resist the temptation. Why?

It could be objected that often moral reasoning does not in fact outweigh
other considerations. Members of ARM might have succumbed to the temp-

tation to embezzle for the sake of the things they hold dear. My reply is that moral considerations are *experienced* as outweighing others even in those cases in which temptation is not resisted. Otherwise we would not speak of temptation.

An initial explanation of moral supremacy is that moral convictions are experienced as outweighing others precisely because they are experienced as prohibitions. This explanation does not, by itself, require that there is a God. For at this stage in the argument, the "God" whom we are obeying might, it could be suggested, be no more than a social construct. Indeed the "God" who is being obeyed might not even be thought of as God. Consider all those atheists in ARM who experience the moral as outweighing other reasons. For them this overriding character of morality is still a matter of its being like a command, only they do not believe in anyone who commands.

For this initial explanation of the overriding character of moral reasoning to be at all convincing, we have to note that the experience of moral convictions as like commands need not be discursive or articulate. Consider the analogy with perception. There is a process of putting something into words, which when applied to perception results in perceptual beliefs. The beliefs are no doubt expressed in a language, or at least in a languagelike system of thought. But the perception that leads to them is not itself a belief. Likewise, the overriding character of morality might derive from an experience that may naturally enough be put into words by saying it is like a command of God, but until then is not put into words.

Now some people do seem to experience moral convictions as commands, and for the sake of presentation I continue my discussion on the basis that this is how they are experienced. However, many others who grant that moral reasons outweigh other considerations lack any experience of being commanded.[9] That is why I do not totally endorse the initial explanation of moral supremacy. Fortunately this does not significantly affect the subsequent discussion. For there is an alternative theocentric understanding of moral supremacy, in which we say God commands us precisely by means of the sense of the overriding character of morality. That is, God ensures that we shall have this sense in order to affect us in a way that resembles the way we are affected by the command of someone we are willing to obey.

If we ignore this complication, my proposed theocentric understanding of moral supremacy is that the inarticulate experience of the moral as outweighing other considerations may be interpreted as the experience of the divine prohibition. The members of ARM who resist temptation have indeed obeyed a prohibition by God even if they do not know that this is what they

---

[9] I am indebted to James Franklin and to Barry Miller for pressing this point home.

have done. This theocentric understanding of moral supremacy requires that a divine command does give us a reason to act and one that outweighs other considerations. That claim is supported by the assumption I made, when considering the motive for creation, that God creates for the sake of every individual and not just for the general good. Therefore I interpret moral convictions not merely as the experience of being commanded by God but as the experience of being commanded by one who should be trusted "though the Heavens fall." For obedience to the divine commands will result in what is good for oneself, those one loves, and everyone else. Hence it is foolish to think that we could plan better than God has, even if the divine plan is not the best possible (perhaps because there is no best possible).

We have, therefore, reason to obey God's commands, insofar as we know them. What reason might conceivably outweigh this? Hatred might motivate an action of great harm to the one hated but far worse for the one hating. The Bible story of Cain and Abel may be used to illustrate this. Abel's virtue shows up Cain's moral mediocrity. Cain, as a result, hates Abel with such intensity that he is prepared to kill Abel even though he knows God will punish him. We may modify the Bible story so that Cain believes in an afterlife and the possibility of damnation. To kill Abel is not therefore sufficient. Cain in his hatred corrupts Abel, making him, to all appearances, even more damnable than himself. "See you in Hell, brother!" he thinks, and he means it. We can, in a fashion, understand such hatred. Perhaps it is even minimally rational. We can even understand a sequel in which Abel, although corrupted, is eventually saved and, in spite of all, pleads to God for Cain. In this sequel Cain rejects the grace God would give him for Abel's sake, precisely out of hatred for Abel.

The point of this example is to show how the search for reasons that might outweigh the divine command merely comes up with ones that are recognizable as ignoring all the intuitively overriding character of morality. So however hard it is to say in just what sense morality is supreme, I claim the divine commands are supreme in just that sense.

One objection to my proposed explanation of moral supremacy is based on the diversity of moral convictions. How can I say that God prohibits all the different things people have taken to be wrong? It would be possible to be a vegetarian who treats Friday, Saturday, and Sunday as days of rest. But it would not be possible both to embrace total nonviolence and to fight a holy war. My reply to this is that God ordains, sustains, and works through the natural order, rather than disturbing that order. The quality of moral experience, like any other experience, is most immediately caused by the workings of the brain, which in turn can be explained partly in terms of neo-Darwinian evolution and partly in terms of the dynamics by which societies change. That all this can be taken as a veridical experience of moral convictions of the kind I have been describing is due not to direct divine intervention but rather to God's intention in bringing about a universe in which these evolutionary and social forces operate as they do. In this way we can explain the overriding character of moral reasoning without having to claim that all moral intuitions are correct. There is an analogy here with ordinary perception. Illusions can be explained as due to the processes connecting the objects with our mental states without our having to deny that we perceive the objects themselves. (Perhaps illusion shows that perception is indirect. If so, moral experience should not be considered a direct experience of God.)

It could be further objected that God, in setting up the natural order, should have prevented moral error. For moral error is especially serious, the objection goes, because of moral supremacy. There is considerable weight to that further objection, but it is recognizably a variant of the argument from evil, which is discussed in Chapter 8. So it requires no detailed discussion here. I note, though, that some version of the free will defense could be especially appropriate. It is rather more likely that our (cultural) ancestors freely doing what they knew to be wrong resulted in widespread moral error than that it resulted in earthquakes and infectious diseases.

The theocentric understanding of moral supremacy is that the process by which we come to feel the over-riding character of moral reasoning is a process intended by God as a prohibition of various kinds of act. Initially this piece of theocentric understanding looks extraordinarily vulnerable. For why not just leave God out of the picture? Our brains being as they are, we find ourselves with moral convictions that seem to have this overriding character. Unless I, the theist, concede that naturalistic account as far as it goes, I cannot plausibly square my account with the prevalence of moral error. For if God were to act directly, bypassing the natural order, in giving moral reasoning its overriding character, then God would not merely be tolerating moral error but endorsing it. Given, however, that there is this naturalistic explanation, why seek a further, non-naturalistic one?

Alternatively, the naturalist could attempt a more detailed explanation of the overriding character of morality, using Freudian, Marxist, or Durkheimian accounts. I consider the last of these, because I find it the least implausible. But readers will have no trouble substituting the Freudian or Marxist accounts. Moral supremacy might be explained, in Durkheimian fashion, as a sense of being commanded by a "God" who is in fact just the society to which you belong and without which you could not have been the person you are. (See

Durkheim, chap. 7, sect 2.) This sense of being commanded would not usually be articulated. Indeed it would be expected to evaporate once we do articulate it as a command by society. Obviously the details would have to be filled in, but this looks a promising naturalistic explanation.

Simpler still, the naturalist could argue with some plausibility that the over-riding character of morality is historically derived from divine command theories. Had our culture never been dominated by the Judaeo-Christian tradition, had we remained "happy" pagans, then morality would have been important but never supreme. We have yet, therefore, to show the superiority of the theocentric understanding of belief in moral supremacy. I argue for that in the next section.

5. The Resilience of Moral Supremacy

Why do I claim that the theocentric understanding of moral supremacy is superior to the readily available naturalistic substitutes? Because they are *deflationary* whereas theocentric understanding is not. To see what I mean by a deflationary explanation here, let us return to ARM. Some members hold the theocentric understanding of moral supremacy. That, if anything, confirms them in their resolve not to embezzle. Others, however, hold one of the naturalistic explanations I have sketched, perhaps the Durkheimian one. We might expect them now to consider moral supremacy to be an illusion. To be sure, something remains of the consequentialist line of thought. It is still the case that the embezzlement of public funds would do more harm overall than good, and that indeed provides some reason for not embezzling. But it is also the case that the embezzlement will foster the things ARM holds dear, and that provides some reason for embezzling. What is now missing is the sense that the moral reason outweighs the other one, and the related sense that the desire to embezzle is a temptation to be resisted rather than merely another way their minds could be made up. Still less could moral intuitions not based on thought of consequences outweigh other reasons. Indeed it is hard to see how they could survive at all.

Naturalistic explanations of moral supremacy are deflationary in the sense that they do not really explain it but rather *explain it away*. More precisely, a deflationary explanation of the occurrence of a belief is not an explanation of what is believed but rather an explanation of our having the belief, which, if accepted as a correct explanation, provides a good reason for ceasing to have that belief. My claim, then, is that naturalistic explanations of moral supremacy are deflationary. Thus, if members of ARM really believe that its being as if commanded not to embezzle is merely their experience of society personified protecting the general good, they will surely ignore that as-if command, saying they have already given society its due in recognizing the consequentialist reasons as of some weight. Hence they would be entirely warranted in favoring their own special interests over the consequentialist considerations, which, they might reasonably claim, have less weight for them.

I have yet to argue that being deflationary is a weakness in the explanation. Before I do so I should say something about the prospects of a nondeflationary naturalistic explanation of moral supremacy. I think the prospects of such an explanation are slight, and I challenge naturalists to try to provide one. To supplement that challenge I distinguish what I am talking about from other tasks that present less difficulty for naturalists. One such task is to show the irrationality of egoism if accepted as a general policy. It may well be to the advantage of any human being to become the sort of person who is habitually unselfish and who has a general policy of avoiding egoism. (See Parfit 1984, pp. 1–24.) I grant this, but it has nothing to do with my example of the members of ARM—they are far from egoistic. But I cannot see any overall advantage in becoming the sort of person who would *always* put the interests of humanity at large above various special interests. For a start the energetic pursuit of special interests results in a more efficient use of time and resources than a dilute general humanitarianism. Again, although people who care equally for all might well count as secular saints, would we really want to live with them?

The other task that might be easy enough is that of showing there is nothing irrational in doing what is in fact morally required. This is easiest if we assume a consequentialist account of right and wrong. The value and disvalue of consequences surely provides some reason for acting as consequentialists say we ought. In the absence of any principle adjudicating between moral and other reasons for acting, there is, therefore, nothing irrational about acting as consequentialists say we ought. I grant that, but it does not even begin to enable us to understand moral supremacy. For there would likewise be nothing irrational about letting other reasons outweigh the examination of consequences. So this concession has little to do with my project, which is to understand moral *supremacy*. I am not arguing that without belief in God morally right actions are unjustified. Rather I am arguing that theism provides the only satisfactory way of understanding moral supremacy.

It remains, then, to discuss the deflationary naturalistic explanation. For those who, in the manner of Nietzsche, are indeed prepared to reject moral supremacy as illusory, the naturalistic explanations are in perfectly good order. But not all naturalists will be as ruthless as Nietzsche. Many naturalists who are members of ARM will continue to believe in moral supremacy even

though the only naturalistic explanations are deflationary. I am not saying they
are irrational. What I am saying is that moral supremacy is a mystery to them.[10]

Moral supremacy has, then, a certain *resiliency*, in that we are reluctant to
follow Nietzsche and instead tend to continue accepting moral supremacy
even in the face of plausible naturalistic accounts that explain it away. It is in
the resilience of moral supremacy that theism has an advantage over naturalism. This is important not merely as providing a further piece of evidence for
theism but as a reason for preferring anthropic to ananthropic theism and
indeed as a reason for preferring the version of anthropic theism according to
which God cares for us as individuals rather than engaging in a utilitarian
calculus. For if it is not to be explained away, moral supremacy is best explained by supposing that part of the moral experience is that we may trust
the one who commands "though the Heavens fall." And such complete trust
is most obviously reasonable if the one I trust cares for me, and those I care
for, not just for humanity as a whole.

It might be objected that naturalists could understand the resilience of moral
supremacy much as someone can understand a phobia or compulsion. I reply
that there is a significant difference. Knowing about a phobia enables the
sufferer to understand unconsidered remarks and unplanned behavior. But to
the extent that the phobia influences considered remarks or planned actions,
its influence must be hidden from the sufferer. Suppose, for example, that a
boy with the unfortunate name of Jack Frost grows up with a phobia about
the cold. Knowing he has it might enable him to understand his instinctive
reaction of dismay when it snows. But suppose further that Jack, after reflection and with his phobia recognized for what it was, advised a friend, who
he knew liked the cold, not to move to Montreal on the grounds that it was
too cold there in winter. That would be something he could not at the time
understand just by noting his own phobia. He would presumably rationalize
it somehow. Contrast this with the naturalists who *even on reflection* urge fellow
members of ARM not to embezzle. That calm reflective judgment must, I
say, be taken as a reaffirmation of moral supremacy and hence a refusal to
explain it away.

I have assumed we are reluctant to abandon moral supremacy. But should
not those who do not already believe in God be Nietzschean about the topic,
recognizing indeed that moral considerations are of some weight but freeing
themselves from the tyranny of the ghost of God which makes the moral
seem supreme? I ask in turn, What is the force of the assertion that we *should*

---

[10] Probably some naturalists have divided minds about moral supremacy. In that case they
find it a mystery insofar as they accept it.

be Nietzschean? Obviously it cannot be thought of as an overriding moral obligation, on pain of gross inconsistency. More likely, the objection is that unless you already believe in God, the acceptance of moral supremacy is unwarranted. My reply is that both naturalists and theists who believe in moral supremacy may take this to be a properly basic belief grounded in moral experience. That implies not that it may be held dogmatically against objections but merely that being unable to explain something is no objection to it. Moral supremacy, if accepted, is best explained by means of anthropic theism, and the most charitable thing to say about Nietzscheans who insist we should reject it because it cannot be understood naturalistically is that they are probably relying on something very like classical foundationalism and so will not grant that moral supremacy could be properly basic even for those naturalists who treat it as a mystery.

I have yet to consider those naturalists who do not in fact find moral supremacy resilient—the members of ARM who embezzle without scruple—and who are, therefore, in a position to explain away their colleagues' acceptance of moral supremacy. Let us divide these into those who eagerly abandon moral supremacy and those who do so with reluctance. The former group I consider to be morally defective. But the latter are in a more tragic situation. They have abandoned something of great importance for the sake of something else of importance, namely what they take to be devotion to the truth. Here I remark that if the truth is merely the reflection of our modes of thought, then it is not worth abandoning moral supremacy out of devotion to it. And the transcendence of truth was just what I required in order to exhibit another respect in which theocentric understanding was superior to naturalistic understanding, namely in the capacity to explain intellectual progress.

To sum up, I can divide naturalists into three groups: those who are not even drawn toward a continued acceptance of moral supremacy, those who are drawn to it but reject it out of devotion to what they take to be the truth, and those who continue to accept moral supremacy even though it is beyond all naturalistic understanding. My discussion is not directed at members of the first group, whom I find repugnant. I refer the second group back to the section on intellectual progress, and to members of the third group I make the point that they have conceded the superiority of theocentric understanding, which does enable us to understand moral supremacy.

6. Further Discussion of Moral Supremacy

Philosophical discussions never die; they just degenerate into rejoinders to replies to objections to arguments—all embroidered with footnotes. I now

consider some further objections that might be raised to the theocentric understanding of moral supremacy. Newman's argument from conscience could
be loosely interpreted as a piece of best-explanation apologetics based on the
articulation of an often implicit understanding of moral supremacy as due to
a divine command. I therefore consider Mackie's objection to Newman's
argument (Mackie 1982, chap. 6) and discuss whether it holds against the
theocentric understanding of moral supremacy. Again, the theocentric understanding of moral supremacy implies the divine command theory, namely
that wrong acts are wrong because they are prohibited by God, not prohibited
by God because they are wrong. I therefore consider the well-known objections to the divine command theory.

First, let us consider Mackie's objection to Newman's argument. Either
you trust the phenomenology of conscience or you do not. If you do, then
you should accept the autonomy of conscience, namely that it is a source of
moral insight dependent on nothing outside itself. But, in that case, conscience
cannot, Mackie says, be the command of God. On the other hand, if you do
not trust the phenomenology of conscience, you have no reason to prefer a
theocentric to a naturalistic understanding of it. Now I have not been considering conscience—the concept strikes me as tainted with misconception.[11]
But Mackie's dilemma is relevant to my discussion of moral supremacy.
Mackie is, in effect, submitting that the supremacy of moral reasoning is part
of a package and that it stands or falls with moral autonomy.

In discussing this objection it is important to distinguish moral autonomy,
which forms the basis of Mackie's objection, from the autonomy of the moral
agent, namely the thesis that it is up to each agent to decide individually what
is right or wrong rather than accept the judgments of others. That thesis is
about how to discover what is right and so is quite compatible with the
theocentric understanding of moral supremacy. (Presumably the autonomous
moral agent's judgment may be guided, but should not be coerced, by God.)

I ask, then, why moral autonomy and moral supremacy are thought of as
a package. Perhaps it is just that we have two prima facie claims, both of
which have some intuitive or phenomenological basis, and that Mackie thinks
it is arbitrary to accept one claim but not the other, by insisting on moral
supremacy but denying moral autonomy. That would be a very weak argument. For assigning equal *prima facie* weight to two considerations does not
make it arbitrary to attach more weight *ultima facie* to one rather than another.

---

[11] Concerning conscience, I have profited greatly both from reading *Newman on Conscience*
(Grave, 1989) and from conversations with Ya-wei Huang. My own position is that our current
conception of conscience is the result of an improper "modern" restriction to one's own acts
of a faculty of making emotionally laden judgments of the moral character of various acts,
whether one's own or others'.

The reply above is, I think, a little shallow. The link between moral supremacy and moral autonomy is probably intended as a conceptual one. Indeed it might be urged that supremacy implies autonomy. For if morality is not autonomous, in particular if some acts are wrong because prohibited by God, then there are reasons, namely ones based on religious convictions, which would, so it seems, outweigh moral reasons. Kierkegaard, on one reading, endorses such a failure of moral supremacy when he presents with approval the story of Abraham, who violates the moral order by intending to sacrifice his son, Isaac. Perhaps Mackie's point, translated into the terminology I am employing, is that there can be no moral supremacy without moral autonomy.

My criticism of that line of thought is that moral autonomy is perfectly compatible with, indeed implied by, the divine command theory. To think otherwise would be like accusing the author of *Waverley* of plagiarizing from Scott. If an act's being wrong just is its being prohibited by God, then the autonomy of morality is not independence from divine prohibition. It is, rather, the autonomy of the divine prohibition. I conclude that Mackie's objection to Newman's argument from conscience holds, if at all, only if we already reject the divine command theory.

Perhaps it is further objected that an autonomous divine judgment would be arbitrary and hence God might have commanded the most heinous acts, as William of Ockham seems to have held. In reply to this I insist that the phenomenology from which moral autonomy derives its plausibility does not support an unrestrained moral autonomy according to which moral prohibitions are quite independent of consequences. Rather, even if strict consequentialism (namely that the moral rightness of an act depends *entirely* on its consequences) is rejected, the autonomy of conscience would be constrained by the requirement that proper attention be paid to the consequences. Likewise, an autonomous divine command need not be arbitrary but could be constrained by proper attention to the consequences. Autonomy is not the same as arbitrariness.

A slightly different Mackie-style objection concerns not the autonomy of the content of moral judgments so much as the supposed autonomy of moral motivation.[12] Moral supremacy, it could be objected, derives from the sense we have of our own worth. To do what is wrong is to be false to what we hold dearest about ourselves. It is to treat ourselves as of no worth. My objection to that account of moral motivation is that it is dependent on, and so

---

[12] I am indebted to James Franklin for drawing my attention to this. Presumably Dostoevsky in *Brothers Karamazov* was, among other things, contrasting autonomous and theonomous moral motivations.

cannot itself explain, moral supremacy. Consider the case of a fictionalized Gauguin who took aesthetic considerations to outweigh moral ones and so abandoned all his normal obligations because only so could he pursue his artistic career. For this fictionalized Gauguin, to do what was morally right, and so sacrifice his artistic career, would be to be untrue to himself and contrary to his sense of self-worth. It is only those who already accept moral supremacy who would think of moral failure as being untrue to themselves.

I conclude that the Mackie-style objections fail, and I turn to the divine command theory. I refer the reader elsewhere for sustained defenses of that theory (Forrest 1989c), but I should discuss two of the most important objections. First, there is the Euthyphro dilemma. Does God prohibit acts because they are wrong or are they wrong because prohibited? Objectors assume that on any version of the divine command theory the latter is intended. But in that case, it is said, there is no reason for God to prohibit *these* rather than *those* acts.

Neither horn of the Euthyphro dilemma is sharp if the divine command theory is introduced solely to understand moral supremacy. We could say that God prohibits acts because they are wrong but that the overriding character of their wrongness (namely that it outweighs other considerations) then derives from the divine prohibition. That reply is coherent because in the divine case, unlike ours, there might well be no nonmoral reasons in conflict with the moral ones when deciding what to prohibit. (God, unlike us, would not have reasons based on greater affection for some than others.)

I prefer, however, to take the second horn of the dilemma: wrong acts are wrong because prohibited by God. I go on to say that they are prohibited because God values various things for us. The mistake in the Euthyphro dilemma is the Kantian assumption that the only good reason for a divine prohibition would be a moral reason. But not all values are moral values, and, for example, to alleviate suffering because you realize what it is like to suffer and so assign (nonmoral) disvalue to suffering is as commendable a reason as alleviating suffering because it is wrong not to.

Another widespread objection to the divine command theory is that it implies the Karamazov Principle that if there were no God then no act would be morally wrong, which is said to be absurd. One possible response is to restrict the theory to the explanation of moral supremacy. If there were no God then some acts would still be morally better than others, and being one of the worse acts would provide us with some reason for not performing an act. What would be lacking would be any moral reason that would outweigh other reasons. But this is a mere detail. The Karamazov Principle is correct, except in detail, but it suggests something incorrect, namely that if I cease to be a theist then I should reject (the overriding character of) morality. Here is an analogy: I believe that everything material is created, so that if there were no God then there would be nothing material. It does not follow that if I cease to be a theist I should cease to believe in matter. Of course not. Rather I should cease to believe that everything material is created. Or, to take an analogy that does not mention God, water is H_2O; therefore if there were no hydrogen, there would be no water. It does not follow that if I cease to believe in hydrogen I should cease to believe in water. Rather I should cease to believe that water is H_2O. I submit that it is what the Karamazov Principle suggests that is absurd, not the principle itself.

Some readers might prefer to state the Karamazov Principle as the indicative conditional "If there is no God then no act is morally wrong" rather than as the counterfactual conditional "If there were no God then no act would be morally wrong." In that case it is parallel to "If there is no God then there is no matter" and "If there is no hydrogen then there is no water," and is defective in exactly the same way, namely that belief in its antecedent fails to support belief in its consequent.[13]

A further consideration here is that if I *meant* the same by "morally wrong" and "prohibited by God," then I should indeed reject morality if I ceased to be a theist. (Likewise, if I meant the same by "H_2O" as "water," then if I ceased to believe in hydrogen I should cease to believe in water.) Perhaps some advocates of the divine command theory have proposed it as an analysis of the meaning of moral terms. But I do not. I am proposing it as an account of the real nature of moral wrong, just as I believe H_2O to be the real nature of water.

7. The Understanding of Beauty

> How ugly the stars are tonight! How trivial the pounding of the waves on the beach! And is it not crass to be thrilled by mountains? The rain forest and the wild-flowers are quite repulsive. And as for sunsets. . . .[14]

If a full-blown relativism in aesthetics was correct, then those responses would be unusual but not in any way improper. But my reaction is that anyone who fails to appreciate the beauty of this universe is defective. Natural beauty has

---

[13] On one account all three indicative conditionals would be true. Their defective character would just be a failure of assertibility. See Jackson 1987.

[14] I am indebted to A. B. Palma for pointing out just how silly it sounds to say, "How ugly the stars are tonight!"

as much claim to be an objective feature of this universe as do the colors, sounds, and so forth on which it is based.

Now it could be objected that colors, sounds, and other so-called secondary qualities are experienced differently by different species. Hence the beauty that depends on them would be species-relative. I do not know whether dogs are capable of aesthetic appreciation, but if they are, then they are more likely to be impressed by the olfactory symphony of an unpolluted environment than by anything visual. This is not, however, a serious objection to the theocentric understanding of beauty. For we may distinguish between the sensuous beauty of things, which is perhaps species-relative, and the nonsensuous ordered beauty that any intellectual being could appreciate. The sensuous beauty of this universe can be understood as a *gift* from God to us, dogs and other animals, and extraterrestrials, if there are any. And it is proper that gifts are for those to whom they are given. To dogs God gives perhaps wonderful combinations of scents. To us God gives the sky at night, the beauty of the plants and animals and scenery. From a rather narrow point of view such gifts are unnecessary. But they immensely enrich our lives.[15]

The nonsensuous beauty of this universe is, if anything, still more impressive. And here I note a curious feature of the history of the sciences. Scientists, guided by the intuition that the fundamental laws of nature must be beautiful ones, posited laws that were later discovered not to be fundamental. So in fact they discovered nonfundamental laws that were beautiful. Therefore we cannot explain the nonsensuous beauty of the universe by insisting that laws must be beautiful if they are to be fundamental. For example, classical mechanics still describes, in an approximate fashion, some austerely elegant aspects of the physical world, even though its (approximate) laws are now considered to depend on the laws of quantum mechanics.

Nonsensuous beauty can be understood in two, complementary, ways. The first is that God, recognizing the value of such beauty, would not create a world that lacked it. That is, creation is guided by aesthetic motives as well as being for the sake of the sentient beings who are created. (Alternatively, the beauty of creation is an expression of the divine beauty rather than a deliberately chosen feature.) The second is that just as sensuous beauty can be understood as a gift to us, likewise nonsensuous beauty can be seen as a sharing of that which God appreciates.[16] This way of understanding both sensuous

---

[15] Why do I omit the beauty of human beings themselves? The human form is beautiful for humans. But I omit those things for which there is an obvious rival explanation in terms of evolution. Any social animals capable of aesthetic appreciation would no doubt find their own kind beautiful—even mole rats.

[16] Can God not then appreciate sensuous beauty? I have been arguing ad hominem against

and nonsensuous beauty as a gift provides us with a reason for preferring anthropic over ananthropic theism.

There is a further element to the theocentric understanding of beauty as a gift. It enables us to understand the significance of beauty. The beautiful (not here distinguished from the sublime) is not merely pleasing; it is *transcendent*. That is, it points beyond itself. The theocentric understanding of this transcendent character to the beautiful may be expressed, somewhat opaquely, by saying that the beauty of this universe reveals to us the infinitely greater beauty of God, on whom it depends. Beautiful things and people suggest to us that there is something infinitely more beautiful. To simplify the discussion, suppose the transcendent character of the beautiful was entirely due to this suggestion. In that case to dismiss the suggestion as misleading is to *deflate* the transcendent character of beauty. If, however, we do take the beauty of things and people as pointers to the infinitely greater beauty of God, then we can understand the transcendent character of beauty in a nondeflationary fashion. Hence a resilient "sense" of the transcendent character of beautiful things lends itself to a theocentric understanding in exactly the same way as does resilient moral supremacy.

When I was discussing moral supremacy, I conceded that a naturalistic explanation was satisfactory apart from its deflationary character. But, with the exception of the beauty of members of one's own species, it is far more difficult to find a social or psychological function played by the appreciation of natural beauty than it is, say, to explain the role of song and dance. I suspect that naturalists will have to say that the appreciation of beauty is a by-product of something else for which there is a more direct naturalistic explanation, such as the ability to see something as a whole and not just as a collection of parts. But such an explanation cannot begin to explain the special quality of the appreciation of beauty or why there is such an abundance of both sensuous and nonsensuous beauty. Moreover, as I have already suggested, we may well have a resilient "sense" of the transcendent character of beautiful things. It is likely that any naturalistic explanation of the appreciation of beauty will be incompatible with this resilience, because it will tend to assimilate the beautiful to the pretty or the pleasing.

---

those who would insist that the appreciation of beauty is species-relative because dependent on secondary qualities. If so, then we would have no reason to believe that what is sensuously beautiful for us is so for God. I have myself, however, no objection to the claim that the "secondary" qualities are genuine qualities of the objects, and that different species—or even different individuals—are aware of different selections from the range of secondary qualities. In that case God would appreciate all the sensuous beauty of this universe, not merely that of light and color and shape, not merely that of scent and of sound, but that of other modes we cannot comprehend.

8. The Serendipity of Mathematics

According to the standard calculus of probabilities, all mathematical theorems have a probability of 100 percent. So there is little scope for taking mathematics as a datum for Bayesian apologetics. The situation is different, however, with best-explanation apologetics. How is it, I ask, that a handful of necessary constraints can result in surprisingly beautiful mathematical theorems? For example, with the exception of 2, all prime numbers, being odd, must have either remainder 1 or remainder 3 when divided by 4. That is just the sort of triviality we expect to find among our stock of necessary truths. And, before doing mathematics, we had no reason to expect results of much greater interest. Likewise, it is trivial that some odd prime numbers can be expressed as the sum of two squares and others cannot, and it is obvious that those that can must have remainder 1 when divided by 4. But now there is a result we could not have anticipated: any prime number with remainder 1 when divided by 4 is the sum of two squares.

A single example of mathematical serendipity would not be that impressive, but it keeps occurring in many branches of mathematics in a way that someone ignorant of the subject would not have anticipated. Furthermore, it is the unexpected constraints on necessary truths that underlie the emergent order which I have had occasion to mention in connection with divine providence and the afterlife. Hence all emergent order is in fact an instance of the surprising character of mathematics. For example, we say that the elaborate variety of distinct and stable chemical compounds is the result of nothing more than the comparatively simple physical constraints on the (outer) electrons of the atoms that make them up. Mathematics is the magician that pulls the rabbit of chemistry out of the hat of physics. If God could break the laws of mathematical necessity and, moreover, had no motive for obeying them, then the physical constraints would not have resulted in chemistry as we know it.

As elsewhere, we may request, although not demand, an explanation. Why should mathematics be like that? The obvious answer is that by proving a theorem, you come to understand why it is true. There are, I suggest, two things wrong with this obvious answer. The first is that many mathematical proofs are indirect in the sense that they require results from another area of mathematics. For instance, many theorems about the integers have been obtained only by using the theory of complex numbers. It is intuitive, however, that results about the integers must hold because of what they are, and so the detour through the theory of complex numbers provides total conviction that the results are true but not a sense of having understood.

The other thing wrong with the understanding-by-proving suggestion is that it provides an explanation of mathematics theorem by theorem but leaves the serendipity of mathematics quite mysterious. The Humean rejoinder would be that to understand each part (each theorem) is to understand the whole (and hence the serendipity of mathematics). In the previous chapter I mentioned the occurrence of emergent order as a counterexample to the Humean principle of the composability of explanation. Here again I deny that understanding components one by one is always the best way of understanding features of the system as a whole.

Another attempt at understanding mathematical necessity is the Kantian hypothesis that all necessary truths are mind-dependent: either they are true because of our concepts (if they are analytic) or they are true because of the preconceptual workings of our minds. Although the Kantian hypothesis explains the occurrence of some necessary truths, it fails to explain the serendipity of mathematics. For why should we discover hidden riches in what is simply the result of our imposing order upon reality?

There is little prospect, then, of a satisfactory naturalistic understanding of the serendipity of mathematics. And here, as in some other cases, the naturalist should decline to offer an explanation. But by doing so the naturalist concedes an advantage to theists, provided there is a theocentric understanding of mathematical serendipity.

Although Descartes held that God could have ensured that there were different mathematical truths, the majority opinion is that they hold of a necessity that not even God has power over. We should not, therefore, explain mathematical serendipity in the same way as we explain the beauty of the natural order. Rather we should explain the serendipity of mathematics as due to its being (i) objective, and so likely to surprise us; and (ii) of aesthetic value. (That surprise is a mark of objective discovery forms the basis of my rejection of idealist ways of understanding in the next chapter.) These features may in turn be explained by theists if they grant that objective metaphysically necessary truths, over which God has no power, describe the divine nature. For in that case the beauty of mathematics is one component of the beauty of God.[17] Thus the serendipity of mathematics is explained by means of the thesis of the divine beauty.[18] That, in turn, may be proposed as a plausible enough expansion of theism. Or it could be supported by the claim that God is a perfect being.[19]

[17] Georg Cantor, I have been told, investigated the infinite partly for theological reasons. I am submitting, though, that the study of the whole of mathematics, not just the infinite, is to "the greater glory of God." Plantinga (1980, p. 144) has more recently drawn to our attention the theological significance of mathematics. Christopher Menzel (1987) has provided a theocentric understanding of mathematical necessity, but in terms of divine "creative" activity rather than as reflecting the divine beauty.

[18] Moreover, the mathematical form of the natural sciences goes some way toward explaining how the beauty of creation reflects the beauty of God.

[19] For a presentation and defense of perfect-being theology, see Morris 1987, chap. 1. For a discussion of the dependence even of necessary beings on God, see Morris 1987, chap. 9.

9. The Case Against Naturalism

The case against naturalism is that it does not enable us to understand as much as its theocentric rival. Even those tough-minded naturalists who are prepared to accept various deflationary explanations of moral supremacy and the "sense" of the transcendence of beauty, and who reject the project of understanding the serendipity of mathematics, should be impressed by the theocentric understanding of three items in addition to the suitability of the universe for life. These are the ubiquitous and necessary regularities that govern the natural order, our surprising success in learning about that order, and the nonsensuous beauty exhibited by it.

Let me repeat that this case depends on some of the results of future chapters. I need to argue for the genuine epistemic possibility of God if theocentric understanding is to be taken seriously. And I have yet to reply to the argument from evil. But before I turn my attention to those matters, I need to consider various attempts at understanding that are neither naturalistic nor based on anthropic theism. That is the topic of my next chapter.

[5]
Non-naturalistic Rivals
to Anthropic Theism

I have presented a case for the superiority of anthropic theism over naturalism. These two are not, however, the only attempts at understanding such features of the universe as its suitability for life, moral supremacy, and the beauty of things. In this chapter I examine various rivals to anthropic theism that I do not consider to be naturalistic. My aim is to argue that they also are inferior to theocentric understanding, insofar as they are genuine rivals. I shall also consider some versions of ananthropic theism, arguing that these are inferior to anthropic theism.

1. A Survey of the Rivals to Anthropic Theism

I cannot hope to survey all possible rivals to anthropic theism. Indeed, if I could, then I would not be worried by the threat of the unknown hypothesis. In this chapter I consider all the rivals I can think of, other than naturalism itself, which I have already discussed. Let us begin, then, toward the naturalistic end of the spectrum, with pantheism.

There are several versions of pantheism. One is the having of an attitude of reverence and awe to the natural order or to the universe as a whole. That may well be commendable, but reverence and awe are not the same as understanding. More interesting as an attempt at understanding is the idea that the large-scale physical processes that occur in the universe either are the same as or give rise to various mental states, which could then be identified with a god. Such a god could influence the detailed development of the universe, but there would be nothing like the traditional doctrine of creation by which God causes the whole universe to exist. We may contrast this with the speculation, reminiscent of process theology and quite compatible with theocentric understanding, that God is, to some extent, a self-determining being, where the self-determination is enacted via the physical universe, which might even be thought of as embodying God. (Compare the maximal indeterminacy speculation.) This position could be considered pantheism in a generic sense, although panentheism would be more specific.[1] The important point, though, is that I reject pantheism only insofar as it is a rival to anthropic theism. Likewise, polytheism is rejected only if interpreted as a rival to anthropic theism.

After rejecting pantheism and polytheism, I turn to metaphysical plenitude, by which I mean belief in a variety of physical universes that do not all obey the same laws. (I have already discussed scientific plenitude in Chapter 3.) One version of metaphysical plenitude is that the variety of universes is sufficiently great for any possibility to be represented in some universe or other. If this is otherwise acceptable, then it promises us a way of understanding why this universe has life-friendly laws, as follows:

> Given a sufficient variety of laws in different universes, it is to be expected that our laws, which are life-friendly, will occur in some universe. We may then give the anthropic answer to the question, But why this one?

Still fairly close to naturalism is aesthetic understanding. We understand, I once suggested, by noting the fittingness or harmony of things (Forrest 1991b). I still take this idea quite seriously, and I think there is indeed a way of using it to understand why the universe is suited to life. For living organisms and the ecological systems they make up have their own aesthetic value. To be sure, there is aesthetic value in nonliving systems as well, but that would not prevent us understanding the occurrence of life aesthetically as having its own special kind of beauty.

Aesthetic understanding can be considered a special case of what I call evaluative understanding, namely the thesis that what happens is ultimately to be explained by what is valuable. A better-known case of evaluative understanding is provided by Leslie's extreme axiarchism (1979), the position that *ethical requiredness*—what ought to be the case—causes things to come to be as they ought to be. Evaluative understanding mimics the theocentric: whatever reason God has for bringing about a situation, we can attempt to un-

---

[1] Panentheists stress the immanence of God in the Universe while not denying that God is more than the Universe. See Hartshorne 1987.

derstand the same situation without God just by saying that it is good that this situation occurs.

I next consider idealism. Fortunately the discussion of whether any version of idealism is correct is not necessary for our purposes. It is far easier to show that idealism fails as a rival way of understanding to the theocentric than to refute idealism itself. In fact some sort of theistic idealism might well provide an answer to one of the questions not discussed in this work: How is the physical universe even a possibility?

Finally, I consider two versions of ananthropic theism, arguing that both are inferior to anthropic theism: that nightmare topic, the all-powerful but malicious God; and the aesthetically motivated but amoral God.

2. Pantheism and Polytheism

Pantheism, treated as a genuine attempt at understanding, is faced with a dilemma. On the one hand, if the God of pantheism is an impersonal deity, then pantheism provides little advance over naturalism. Perhaps an impersonal pantheism offers us an explanation of those mystical experiences in which everything is experienced as a unity. For if there is an emergent order in our universe as a whole, it is plausible enough that some interaction between it and the complex order of our brains would result in an appropriate sense of all things being one. Such an impersonal pantheism would, however, explain neither resilient moral supremacy nor our capacity to make intellectual progress. Nor can it explain those aspects of the beauty of things which I interpret as a gift from God to us.

On the other hand, if pantheism amounts to belief in a personal deity, a god, then it is a rival to theism only if this god is not powerful or knowledgeable enough to count as God. Now I have no objection to the speculation that there are such gods (or angels) in addition to God, and they might be embodied in large-scale physical processes. Belief in a god of restricted power is, however, inferior to theism if put forward as a rival. I have three arguments for this. The first is based on the premiss that, for the sake of simplicity, we should avoid arbitrary restrictions to divine power, such as denying the power to create universes with more than eleven spatial dimensions. From this non-arbitrariness assumption it follows that the only plausible god of restricted power would be one with no control over *any* of the most fundamental characteristics of the universe, such as its quantum mechanical and relativistic character or its number of spatial dimensions. These fundamental characteristics are such as to make our universe suited to life. So, I claim, belief in a god of restricted power does not enable us to understand the suitability of the universe for life and is thus inferior to anthropic theism.

We could overcome this difficulty by combining belief in one or more such gods with belief in many universes. This god, or these gods, make the best they can out of universes that are not entirely within their control. In most cases the best is purely aesthetic, but because the universes differ there are some in which a god can produce life. These many universes, however, would not be created by God. Rather they would be there waiting to be molded. Hence positing more than one of them clearly complicates the theory, which is, once again, inferior to theism.

It has been suggested (by the referee) that even gods of restricted power could ensure the suitability of a universe for life by altering the laws of nature. There are two ways of interpreting this suggestion. One is to say that the fundamental laws were altered. But it is simpler, and so preferable, to suppose that the fundamental laws are unchanging. Hence this interpretation should be rejected. The other interpretation is to deny that the fundamental laws were altered but to suppose that various physical constants vary and the god has the power to fine-tune their values, so as to ensure the universe's suitability for life. In that case what we usually think of as the laws, with various precise values for constants, could have been altered. I grant that as a possibility but insist it is not merely the fine-tuning of constants that is required for life. The fundamental laws must be appropriate also.

I conclude that the hypothesis of a god of restricted power either explains less or requires the additional posit of many universes. In either case it is inferior to theism. And this leads to my second argument. I have recorded, but without emphasis, the theocentric understanding of why there is a physical universe. That becomes rather important in the context of a decision between belief in a god of restricted power and belief in a god of unrestricted power. In both cases we posit a personal deity, but in the former we have to posit (fairly determinate) uncreated universes as well, which is a disadvantage.

My third argument against a god of restricted power is to propose a dilemma. Are these gods dependent on physical bodies or not? If they are—for instance, if they are patterns of extragalactic plasma—then both their existence and their power to influence the universe depend on there being suitable laws of nature. So we would be assuming, not explaining, the suitability of the universe for life. On the other hand, if they are disembodied, then the fact that they are of restricted power and knowledge becomes more puzzling. For in the absence of any detailed mechanism explaining their power and knowledge, the only plausible hypotheses are either that they could have no power at all or that it is unlimited.

Polytheism, which might even be implied by pantheism,[2] deserves more respect than it is usually given, provided it is not restricted to myths about

---

[2] If the universe has expanded sufficiently rapidly to prevent any network of causal relations

gods afflicted with perpetual adolescence. And I have already made a concession to polytheism by stipulating that theism is to be construed as the belief
that there is a God, rather than that there is precisely one God.[3] For example,
there might be any number of Gods each with the power to create any
number of universes of any kind. The only restriction to their power would
be noninterference with the creations of another God, but that would, I
submit, be no different in kind from the inability of any agent to alter what
is already the case.[4]

Nor, as I have already said, do I object to the speculation that there are
one or more gods in addition to God. Polytheism as a rival to theism must
therefore be interpreted as the belief that the universe was not created and
that there are gods of restricted power. I have already argued against that
position when discussing pantheism. My conclusion concerning both pantheism and polytheism is, therefore, that they need not be rivals to theism, but
if they are rivals, then they are inferior.

3. The Rejection of Metaphysical Plenitude

In Chapter 3, I considered the combination of anthropic replies with scientific plenitude. The idea was that a purely scientific account of things might
well show that there are different universes or different regions in this universe, which vary in many respects. It would not, then, be puzzling that this
universe is suited to life, for nothing capable of puzzlement could inhabit a
universe unsuited to life. The chief defect with scientific plenitude was that
it could not enable us to understand why the laws themselves were life-
friendly. That was because all the universes would be governed by the same
laws as ours. The obvious way of remedying that defect is to postulate universes with different laws. The resulting hypothesis of metaphysical plenitude
promises us a way of understanding why this universe is suited to life in,
among other respects, its laws. Given sufficient variety, *some* universe must be
suited to life, and it is no surprise that we are in one of those that are thus
suited.

I myself have no objection to a multitude of universes obeying different

---

across the whole universe, a deity dependent on the physical universe might well have undergone fission as the universe expanded. See Longair 1993, pp. 166–71.

[3] There would be many Gods, not just many gods, if each of them would be considered
God were there no others.

[4] There are, nonetheless, objections to this sort of polytheism. First, there is the general
worry about what would make two disembodied minds two rather than one. This worry is
exacerbated if we identify God with unrestricted consciousness. More important, perhaps, is
the intellectual pressure toward thinking of all created things as dependent on just one uncreated thing, and identifying this one uncreated thing with God. See Wainwright 1986.

laws from our own, although in the previous chapter I noted one promising naturalistic understanding of laws of nature that excludes this hypothesis. Indeed, on the assumption of theism, it would seem ad hoc to deny that God could create many universes. I argue, however, that positing this variety fails if it is intended as a rival to the theocentric understanding of the suitability of this universe for life. Let us consider the most extreme case first, that in which all consistently describable physical universes are posited, varying in the laws, if any, on which they operate and in their number of dimensions. Let us call this unrestricted plenitude. A version of this is implied by Lewis's *modal realism*, according to which the other universes I am considering are the possible worlds (Lewis 1973). On Lewis's theory they are not actual but nonetheless real. I am not, however, discussing possibility and actuality, so whether or not these universes are thought of as parts of the actual world or as nonactual worlds need not concern us.

I have two criticisms of unrestricted plenitude as an attempt at understanding. The first, which is less conclusive, is that far from being a simple or elegant hypothesis, unrestricted plenitude offends grievously against Ockham's razor.[5] The second is that it cannot explain the suitability of the universe for life.

I now develop the first criticism: Is unrestricted plenitude a simple hypothesis? The simplest answer to the question of what exists would be "Nothing," but that is obviously incorrect. Is the next simplest answer "Everything," meaning "Everything possible"? Or is that in fact the most complicated answer, because it includes worlds of indefinitely great complexity? Initially there seem to be two opposed considerations here. On the one hand, the brevity of the phrase "everything possible" suggests that it is a very simple hypothesis. On the other hand, it appears to be the worst of all possible violations of Ockham's razor. I now argue that unrestricted plenitude is in fact an excessively complicated hypothesis. I argue for this by criticizing the apparent simplicity of the answer "Everything possible" and by endorsing Ockham's razor.

Here it is relevant to consider Berry's Paradox, generated by the phrase "the least integer not nameable in under nineteen syllables." The paradox is that the phrase itself contains fewer than nineteen syllables, so the integer named by the phrase both is and is not nameable in under nineteen syllables. This paradox may be avoided if we distinguish first-order from higher-order descriptions. First-order descriptions do not themselves have recourse to naming, reference, description, or any semantic relation as part of the description itself. And the phrase "the least integer not nameable in under thirty syllables, using a first-order description" is not paradoxical, although no doubt it suffers from ambiguity until we have standardized the language of arithmetic.

---

[5] This is Swinburne's chief criticism. See Swinburne 1990, pp. 154–73.

Berry's Paradox is instructive in the context of giving "Everything possible" as an answer to the question, What exists? For Berry's phrase is short, but it is not a straightforward way of describing an integer. Moreover, if for some purpose we needed to order the integers in terms of the number of bits of information in a standardized description, then it would be highly eccentric to include Berry's phrase among the standardized descriptions. The moral is that simplicity can be measured, roughly, by the ease of comprehension of some selected set of *allowable* or *standardized* descriptions. As a result it is far from obvious that the answer "Everything possible" is especially simple. For it might well fail to be an allowed description. If it does fail, then the hypothesis of unrestricted plenitude has to be described by means of the infinitely long list of all kinds of possible universes. So the mere fact that the phrase "everything possible" is short does not establish the simplicity of unrestricted plenitude. Further discussion is required.

I now turn to the opposing consideration, namely Ockham's razor. If stated in the form "Entities are not to be multiplied more than is necessary," then it is misleading in two ways. The first is that multiplying entities should be thought of as hypothesizing them without further explanation. Ockham's razor should not be used to reject a multiplicity that is derived from other hypotheses. In particular, it should not be used to reject metaphysical plenitude if that is supported by the argument that whatever reasons God has to create this universe, it is likely there are similar reasons for creating other universes. The second way in which Ockham's razor might be misleading is that the sheer number of entities of a given kind should not worry us. Indeed, given that we accept entities of a given kind, say electrons, perhaps the simplest hypothesis is that there are infinitely many of them. Ockham's razor should, I submit, be expressed as follows: *Kinds* of entity are not to be hypothesized more than is necessary.

Scientific plenitude, which posits many universes made of matter obeying the same fundamental laws as ours, does not offend against this version of Ockham's razor and could be considered fairly simple. But unrestricted plenitude offends grievously. For any possible kind of entity, however unlike anything we know of, would exist. The magnitude of the offense is hard to grasp since our imagination is so limited. Two feeble examples have to suffice. One concerns the number of spatial dimensions. Any number of dimensions is, presumably, possible, so according to unrestricted plenitude, there are universes of every dimension. The second example concerns two rival hypotheses, that of homogeneous matter versus that of point particles in empty space. There will be possible universes superficially resembling ours made up of homogeneous matter, and possible universes superficially resembling ours made up of point particles in empty space. Surely we should not posit two kinds of matter when one would be enough. So the hypothesis that there are universes of both kinds offends against Ockham's razor. Even worse, though, are all those universes parts of which are made up of homogeneous matter and parts of which are made up of point particles.

The situation, then, is that the argument in favor of the simplicity of un-restricted plenitude depends on an assumption that is far from obvious, whereas the argument against its simplicity is a straightforward application of Ockham's razor. I conclude, therefore, that there is a presumption against it.

That is a minor objection, for perhaps the presumption could be over-come by Lewis's use of unrestricted plenitude to provide the semantics for modal logic (Lewis 1973), by the Nozick-inspired suggestion that it is self-explanatory (Nozick 1981, pp. 116–21), or for some other reason. I turn, therefore, to a more serious complaint.[6] It is that unrestricted plenitude cannot explain why the universe has been suited to life for millions of years. All it explains is why there is life *now*. So it is at a great disadvantage when compared to the theocentric understanding not merely of there being life now but of there having been life in the past (and, for that matter, of its likely continuance into the future). The reason unrestricted plenitude cannot enable us to un-derstand why the universe has been suited to life for millions of years—or even for the time taken to read this paragraph—is that this continued suitabil-ity is understood by appealing to the orderly character of the universe. But unrestricted plenitude allows there to be universes that either are irregular or operate in accordance with regularities so complicated that they exhibit no order we could notice.

In order to expand on this I ask two questions: (i) Why is there life here and now? and (ii) Why was there life here one minute ago? Unrestricted plenitude indeed implies that there will be universes in which life lasts at least a minute, or for that matter, at least a billion years. But merely noting that some situation X occurs does not explain why it occurs within the region of which we have experience. Consider, for example, the case in which we have witnessed a human being apparently levitating. From unrestricted plenitude we could infer that beings like us will witness others like us levitating in many universes. Surely that would not explain the apparent levitation. We should seek alternative explanations, such as the interaction of brain processes with gravity, or fraud. Some extra condition or conditions are required, then, if the unrestricted plenitude is taken to explain the occurrence of X. The most straightforward extra condition is that X occurs in a fairly high proportion of

[6] For objections of this general kind, see Leslie 1989, pp. 97–98, and Forrest 1982. Lewis himself refers to similar objections by Schlesinger, Adams, and Smart (Lewis 1986, p. 116). Because of Lewis's response (1986, pp. 116–23), I now think these arguments succeed only in showing that there are styles of inference (e.g., reliance on Ockham's razor) whose reliability Lewis cannot explain.

cases. But by means of the anthropic reply we may weaken this to, X occurs in a fairly high proportion of cases in which there could have been persons to wonder at the occurrence of X.

Now let X be the fact that the universe has been suited to life, by which I mean not merely that there happens to be life here and now but that it has been suited to life for at least a minute—and, presumably, far longer. This is a fact that has a theocentric understanding and may also be partly understood using scientific plenitude. But when we use unrestricted plenitude, we find that we have no reason to suppose that a high proportion of universes that are like ours here and now have been suited to life for even as long as one minute. Of course they must contain life for a few seconds if there are to be question-askers, but the presence of question-askers at one time in no way requires life a minute earlier. (It takes less than a minute to ask the question, Why has there been life for at least a minute?) Ordinarily we would assume that the only way the question-askers could come into existence would require that there had been a long development of life. That assumption is not, however, warranted on unrestricted plenitude, precisely because all coherently describable kinds of universe occur, including those irregular and disorderly universes in which apparently random motions of atoms in the void just happen to produce a region of the universe just like ours for thirty seconds, only for it to dissolve again into chaos.

In reply to this objection we might be tempted to say that although it is logically possible, it is exceedingly unlikely that this universe be formed in some way, such as random combination of atoms in the void, that allows momentary life but does not amount to any continued suitability. That is not, however, a relevant objection. For at most it shows that among all logically possible universes an exceedingly small proportion are momentarily inhabited even though of no continued suitability. It does not follow that only a small proportion of the inhabited universes have come into existence in this chance fashion. For that further conclusion to be warranted, we would have to show that the universes that are genuinely suited to life for some length of time outnumber those that are momentarily inhabited even though of no continued suitability. And this would have to be argued without resorting to the premiss that the universes being considered are governed by fairly simple laws such as ours. Given any orderly regular universe like ours, there will be infinitely many possible variants that start off life-hostile then mimic ours for a minute, even to all the apparent traces of past life, before dissolving back into chaos. That prevents us showing that the possible universes that are suited to life for some length of time outnumber those that are only momentarily inhabited. It might even be possible to argue that the proportion is the other way round, but I suspect that we have here the common failure of proportions to be defined in infinite populations.

I am not arguing, though, that if you believe in unrestricted plenitude you should suspend judgment as to the suitability of the universe for life for any extended period of time. Rather, if you believe in unrestricted plenitude, you should just accept the suitability of the universe for life as a mystery. In comparing explanatory accounts it is a matter of some weight if one of the accounts explains less than the others. And I have argued that unrestricted plenitude is in that unfortunate position, when compared to theocentric understanding. So I recommend that it be rejected as a way of understanding this universe.

That is my argument against unrestricted plenitude, but our topic is the broader one of metaphysical plenitude. Might we not posit just enough universes to be able to understand why we are in one with life-friendly laws, without positing so many that we cease to understand why ours is governed by fairly simple laws at all, and so cease to understand its suitability for life for some length of time? One suggestion here is a combination of the appeal to simplicity with metaphysical plenitude. Perhaps the principle is that all universes governed by simple enough laws exist. Or perhaps the principle is that the simpler the universe, the greater the chance of its existing, or the more copies it has.

These versions of metaphysical plenitude suffer from two minor defects. The first is that there will be some arbitrariness in the mathematical explication of such principles. The second is that even when explicated they would still be more complicated than unrestricted plenitude. Those defects do not, by themselves, exclude metaphysical plenitude, but they lessen its appeal. Theocentric understanding will, therefore, be superior—assuming, of course, that God is a genuine epistemic possibility and that I give a reply to the argument from evil. The superiority derives from a combination of the minor defects mentioned above with the breadth of theocentric understanding, presented in the previous chapter. For no version of metaphysical plenitude can explain intellectual progress, resilient moral supremacy, or the beauty of the universe.

Let me repeat that although I reject unrestricted plenitude I am not criticizing other versions of metaphysical plenitude, except as ways of understanding. I am quite happy, for instance, with the suggestion that God has created an array of different universes obeying different laws. My criticism is of the attempt to use metaphysical plenitude to understand why there are life-friendly laws governing our universe. And my criticism is partly that its prima facie most appealing form, namely unrestricted plenitude, cannot explain the suitability of the universe for life, except for a few seconds, and that, in any case, metaphysical plenitude lacks the breadth of theocentric understanding.

4. Evaluative Understanding

In the chapter before last I considered the metaphysical thesis that things are more likely to be simple than complicated. I argued that this did not provide a way of understanding the life-friendly character of the laws. That was because there are many universes simpler than ours which could not contain life. Simplicity, however, is, as often as not, invoked as an aesthetic consideration. I turn, therefore, to a more general aesthetic understanding of things, which goes back at least to the Pythagoreans. Perhaps we can understand why things are as they are by noting their ordered beauty or some other aesthetic value. Here we would be appealing to the Aesthetic Principle, namely that the universe exhibits aesthetic value. Advocates of this way of understanding might claim that this principle was intrinsically intelligible. Explanations based on it would, therefore, lead to considerable understanding.

It is a difficult task to articulate the basis for the aesthetic value of the universe. It suffices, however, to note one feature that lends itself to aesthetic value. Following Descartes we could emphasize the aesthetic value that occurs when richness of detail is combined with fundamental simplicity. An example of this is to be found in urban aesthetics. Neither the drab uniformity characteristic of totalitarian regimes nor the individualistic suburb composed of totally different styles of house has as much appeal as a street of houses each with individual character in the details but all of basically the same style and proportions. This combination of richness of detail with underlying simplicity and order is something we might expect an aesthetically valuable universe to manifest. Living organisms and the ecosystems they make up exhibit this combination to a high degree. So the Aesthetic Principle goes some way toward an understanding of the suitability of the universe for life.

Before proceeding I should mention some related ways of understanding. For the criticisms I provide apply quite generally to them. Aesthetic understanding is based on the recognition of aesthetic value. We might generalize and suggest that the recognition of any value, not just aesthetic value, provides a way of understanding. Let us call this *evaluative* understanding. In place of the Aesthetic Principle we would have the Value Principle, namely that the universe is valuable. We could then explain many of its features, including its suitability to life, by appealing to its value, including its aesthetic value.

A well-known version of evaluative understanding is Leslie's extreme axiarchism (1979). According to Leslie it is a fundamental principle that things are as they are ethically required to be. On the assumption that it is ethically required that there be life, this explains why the universe is suited to life. Or if life is valuable but not ethically required, we may nonetheless rely on the Value Principle to explain the suitability of the universe for life. Instead we could propose the Principle of Perfection, namely that whatever is perfect must be the case. That principle might be used as a premiss in an Anselmian argument for the conclusion that there is a God. But it has been suggested to me that what is perfect is not God so much as a universe with life.[7] So this principle could be used as a rival to the theocentric understanding of the suitability of the universe for life.

Somewhat different, because not explicitly evaluative, is the Hegelian way of understanding, in which the large-scale processes are governed by "Reason" even though there may be no personal God to have the reasons. Although in Hegel this is conjoined with idealism, its power to explain is separable from that position. (I consider the Hegelian attempt at an idealist understanding of things in the next section.)

One reason for rejecting aesthetic or Hegelian ways of understanding is that they fail to explain resilient moral supremacy. I grant that proponents of aesthetic or Hegelian ways of understanding may find reasons for doing what is morally required. But then I grant that even naturalists have reasons for doing what is morally required. That is not, however, enough for resilient moral supremacy. Recall that anthropic theism explains resilient moral supremacy by noting the perversity of any reason for disobeying God. That, in turn, was based on the assumption that God creates the universe not just for the general good but for the good of each individual. Evaluative or Hegelian understanding can compete with theocentric understanding only if it can parallel this providential concern for the individual's well-being. It is hard to see how aesthetic or Hegelian understanding could achieve this. But Leslie's extreme axiarchism would, provided it is assumed that what is ethically required implies the good of all those who themselves seek to do what is ethically required. Much the same holds for the project of understanding things in terms of the Principle of Perfection, provided perfection has itself a moral component.

Thus some but not other versions of evaluative understanding fail to explain resilient moral supremacy. In addition I have a general objection to them, based on one of Mackie's criticisms (1982, p. 237). Mackie says that Leslie's extreme axiarchism is open to a criticism similar to the one he has already given of Swinburne's attempt to explain things in terms of personal explanation. (Here by *personal explanation* is meant understanding of the way the universe is by appealing to an agent, God, who acts in much the way we humans are usually thought of as acting.) Mackie's criticism is that both extreme axiarchism and belief in God as a nonphysical agent are based on a misunderstanding of examples.

---

[7] I am indebted to Julie Körner for drawing to my attention the possibility of a nontheistic use of the Principle of Perfection.

In spite of Mackie's overall position, his criticism of Leslie's extreme axiarchism could be adopted by theists. The criticism, which I endorse only in part, is that all familiar cases in which things occur because they are ethically required are cases that can be understood in terms of agency. It is the belief that something ought to be the case, not the fact that it ought to, which brings it about. Moreover, if that belief brings something about, then it does so because someone has the belief. Much the same criticism can be made of the other variants on evaluative understanding. Works of art do not come spontaneously into existence created by the need of beauty to exist; artists create them. Again, contrary to the Hegelian suggestion, we humans are not the pawns of Reason but agents who, for our own often misguided reasons, act on one another and on our environment.

I suspect that Mackie's criticism is based on the empiricist assumption that fundamental principles must be extrapolations from what is experienced using ordinary observations. This is not the place for an extended objection to that form of empiricism. It suffices to say that it is not the method of physics, the fundamental theories of which are by no means mere extrapolations from what is observed. I further suspect that Mackie is partly guided by the common-sense views on these questions, and common sense is no doubt on the side of agency as a way of understanding. But in this case common sense amounts merely to folk metaphysics and has little weight as an authority.

Nonetheless I think Mackie's criticism has considerable force. First, any prima facie intrinsic intelligibility of the various evaluative principles totally evaporates when we remind ourselves of the familiar facts. Yes, what is ethically required does tend to get done, but only because there are good people around. Yes, what is beautiful does tend to come into existence, but only because people seek beauty. Although I have not emphasized considerations of intrinsic intelligibility, I consider this to be a significant disadvantage.

Pressing Mackie's criticism a little harder, I note that we are able to understand everything that might seem to need evaluative understanding by appealing to the way agents act for reasons. (Mackie would go on to say that in turn this can be understood naturalistically. I refer readers back to Chapter 2 for my defense of theism against this charge.) In particular, anything we can understand by pointing to the beauty, goodness, or reasonableness of the universe could also be understood by appealing to the motives God has for creating it. Assume, for a while, that the fundamental principles governing our understanding of things should not be multiplied. In that case proponents of evaluative understanding should not treat the way agents act for reasons as a way of understanding things *additional* to their evaluative understanding.

I now propose a dilemma: either free acts performed for good reasons are exempt from the constraint of the Value Principle or whatever an agent does,

freely or otherwise, is in accordance with it. If proponents of evaluative understanding agree that there are free acts exempt from the Value Principle,
then there is much that their position fails to explain but that can be explained
on Swinburne's account, and hence on mine. On the other hand, if all apparently free acts are to be explained as instances of the Value Principle, then
we are not, I would say, responsible for our actions. Or, as others would say,
we are responsible even though what we do is not understood in terms of
our reasons. Either way some basic belief about human responsibility is rejected. Now I grant that basic beliefs can, and should, be overcome if there
are good theoretical reasons for doing so. But what we are considering in this
case is the choice between two non-naturalistic accounts, only one of which
requires us to reject the basic beliefs about responsibility.

In this way proponents of evaluative and Hegelian understanding must either concede something mysterious in their account or reject basic beliefs
about freedom and responsibility—beliefs that need not be rejected on the
theocentric account. It turns out, then, that the belief in freedom and responsibility, which played an important role in defending theocentric understanding from Mackie's criticism, can also be used to endorse his criticism of
evaluative understanding.

A possible objection to this criticism of evaluative understanding is that the
supposed fundamental principle that fundamental principles should not be
multiplied is self-defeating, because in proposing it I am violating it. Or, more
plausibly, it might just strike us as too strict. Perhaps I should not have assumed
it but should rather tolerate a pluralism of ways of understanding things. In
that case we might understand some things in terms of the reasons agents have
for acting but understand others in terms of the value they have. There are
two rather different ways of developing this pluralist suggestion. The first is
to link it with one of my proposed versions of the apologetics of understanding, mentioned in Chapter 1, according to which *any* good enough way of
understanding provides at least an approximation to the truth. In that case
theocentric understanding and evaluative understanding would both be near
the truth.[8] A more demanding way of developing the pluralist suggestion
would be to integrate the evaluative understanding with the way of understanding actions as being performed for reasons by agents.

---

[8] We can begin to see how this might be the case by considering the widespread thesis
that, necessarily, there can be no values without consciousness of the value. Combining this
with the speculative identification of God with unrestricted consciousness (developed in Chapters 6 and 7), we find that the two rival theses have come quite close together. Anthropic
theism now states that things are to be explained as a result of consciousness of their value,
whereas extreme axiarchism states that things are to be explained as a result of their value, of
which necessarily there is consciousness.

This integrated approach requires some further discussion. Given the Value Principle, or some variant, it might be puzzling why there are any agents, who, sometimes at least, bring about what is good. Why does not what is good just come about anyway? One answer to this question is that it does just come about anyway, because agency causation is redundant. I have already rejected this as contrary to the belief in the freedom required for responsibility. Advocates of the integrated approach should, therefore, give the only other answer, namely that the production of what is good by someone acting for reasons is itself better than the spontaneous coming into existence of what is good. For example, they might claim that it is better that stone be carved into shape than that suitably shaped stones form naturally. I have no objection to that claim. But if agency is valuable in this way, it follows that it is better that there be a God who creates this universe than that this universe comes into existence spontaneously. In this way the Value Principle would limit its own application, so that it was restricted to an explanation of God and of those events, if there are any, that God has left up to chance.[9] Indeed the result of retaining both evaluative understanding and personal explanation would be to endorse theocentric understanding, with the bonus that we may now give A. C. Ewing's answer to the question, Why is there a God? namely, "Because it is good that there is a God." (See Ewing 1973, chap. 7.) If instead of the Value Principle we rely on the Principle of Perfection, the answer would sound more familiar: "There is a God because God is a perfect being."

To sum up my comparison of evaluative understanding and theocentric understanding:

(i)   If, like me, you initially have a basic belief that you have the freedom required for responsibility, then any choice between evaluative and theocentric understanding should be in favor of the latter. For evaluative understanding, unlike theocentric understanding, either multiplies mysteries or requires the abandonment of that basic belief.

(ii) If, however, you do not, even initially, have a basic belief in the freedom required for responsibility, and if you consider it necessary to choose between evaluative and theocentric understanding, then the superiority of theocentric understanding lies mostly in its greater intrinsic intelligibility.

(iii) Perhaps we do not have to choose between fundamental ways of understanding things. In that case we could claim that both evaluative and theocentric understanding approximate the truth.

(iv) Finally, we might propose combining our fundamental ways of under-

---

[9] For a defense of the initially startling thesis that God would leave things up to chance, I refer readers again to van Inwagen 1988.

standing. That results in an endorsement of theocentric understanding
with the bonus that we can answer the question, Why is there a God?

In different ways and to different degrees, then, I have argued for the superiority of theocentric over evaluative understanding. I grant, however, that
this superiority is not so great as to exclude as unwarranted an agnostic indifference between the two.

5. Against Idealistic Understanding

I now criticize the idealistic understanding of the order and beauty of this
universe and its suitability to embodied persons. Let us first consider the version of idealism in which reality depends on us, either individually or collectively. Here the explanation is based on the Kant-inspired thesis that we find
order and beauty, including the requirements for life, because we ourselves
have imposed that order and beauty. Whether the ordering is that which any
rational being would have to impose so as to give some meaning to phenomena (as in Kant's account) or whether it is some kind of social construct is,
for present purposes, a mere detail. It is important, however, to remember
that the rival to the theocentric understanding of things is the imposition-of-
order thesis, not the more general thesis that all things are spiritual or mental.
That thesis by itself neither explains order and beauty nor is a rival to theism.

The imposition-of-order thesis has considerable plausibility at the phenomenal level: the perceived world may to some degree be a construct. But, I
claim, the order described by the sciences is not imposed or constructed.
Rather it is discovered. This claim is based on the failure of the Idealist Prediction. Idealism can explain why there is some order among phenomena,
but merely saying that the order is imposed does not explain which order is
imposed. What we require is a prediction about the kind of order that would
be imposed. And in fact there is an entirely reasonable prediction. It is that
the order imposed should be one that we do not find surprising, or, at least,
that is no longer surprising once various psychological or sociological studies
have revealed the true nature of that which does the imposing of order. We,
in this century, are especially able to appreciate, however, the important fact
that the order described by scientists is surprising and that it remains surprising
even after we investigate the hidden forces operating in the mind and in
society. Why should we be surprised at an order we ourselves—as opposed
to God—have imposed? I am not saying it is impossible that we impose, for
instance, curved space on "things in themselves" and are then surprised to
discover that space is curved. But what I am saying is that such surprise is

itself surprising, and without an adequate explanation of it the imposition-of-order thesis fails as an attempt at understanding.

This argument from the failure of the Idealist Prediction may be reinforced by comparing cases where the imposition-of-order thesis enables us to understand with cases where it does not. Suppose we were initially puzzled by the fact that human beings go through sharply separated developmental phases, such as infancy, childhood, adolescence, and adulthood. Why are there longish periods in which a human being remains much the same, for example as an adolescent, and then suddenly "settles down" and becomes an adult? In that case the imposition-of-order thesis would be extremely attractive. It is not really that there are these sudden changes; it is just that we selectively attend to those changes that fit that picture and ignore others. And this imposition-of-order thesis is attractive precisely because the order we "discover" is so far from surprising.

By contrast, now suppose we were living in a society in which the conventional wisdom, accepted by men and women alike, was that women were not fit to make important decisions. Suppose, however, we discovered that the men were given to making only the "really important" decisions such as who should buy the next round of drinks. In fact decision making is left to the women, who are far better at it. Nonetheless men and women uniformly treat decision making by women as exceptional. In that case it is surely the "fact" that men make decisions which is to be explained as a social construct, not the truth that women are better at making them. Precisely because the truth is startling in that society, it is not the result of an imposition of order. At least, before we would be warranted in saying that it was, we would need to have discovered some hidden forces operating in society or in the minds of individuals, such as the continuing influence of a suppressed matriarchal order.

In the case of the order discovered by scientists, Kant's account of the Euclidean character of space was a fairly promising imposition-of-order explanation. Why is space Euclidean? Because we make it so. That would have been fine, just because we always expected space to be Euclidean. Most now believe, though, that space is non-Euclidean, which is not what we expected. In this way, then, the failure of the Idealist Prediction provides reasons for rejecting the idealist attempt at understanding.

I anticipate three objections to this argument from the failure of the Idealist Prediction. First, it might be objected that although the order we actually find is surprising, it is not surprising that we find some order in this universe. This objection, however, concedes too much to be serious. For it allows that we are restricted in the order we impose, so there is still some nonimposed orderability in one way or another prior to our imposition of order. In that case we may still ask why this universe is suited to life, meaning, Why is this universe so *orderable* as to be suited to embodied persons? There is not a satisfactory imposition-of-order answer to that question even if there is an imposition-of-order answer to the question, Why is the universe *orderly*?

It might be further objected that it cannot be surprising that we find an order suitable for life, because, as living organisms, we could not live in a universe that was not suited to life. Hence, even if the particular way in which the universe is suited to life cannot be explained by idealism, that it is in some way or another suited to life can be. I have two replies to this objection. The first is that living organisms could easily impose an order unsuited to life. For the order we impose cannot in fact be a true explanation of how we come to exist—that would be circular. Rather the imposition-of-order thesis tells us that our best efforts at understanding why, among other things, we came to exist merely reveal the ways we impose order. Living organisms might, therefore, have imposed an order quite unsuited to life. For any order or system actually capable of generating life would probably be far more subtle than anything we might be expected to impose. My second reply is that in fact the imposed order used to be a vitalist one. What we expected to find, I submit, was that the universe was suited to life, but only because there were special laws operating for living organisms which were not those governing inanimate objects. I conclude that the imposition-of-order explanation of the suitability of the universe for life has been outmoded by biochemistry. This provides another instance of the failure of the Idealist Prediction.

Finally, it might be objected that one, central, scientific theory actually supports idealism, namely quantum mechanics, which is often interpreted as merely describing how physical systems generate, in orderly but baffling ways, various observations. I am in fact resolutely opposed to such idealistic interpretations of quantum mechanics (see Forrest 1989a), but fortunately I need not debate the issue here. For it is not part of such interpretations that we impose the order on the observations. Quantum mechanics, thus interpreted, supports idealism only in the sense in which idealism asserts the mental or spiritual nature of reality, not in the sense in which it competes with theocentric understanding. Indeed the chief reason for adopting this idealistic interpretation of quantum mechanics is that the order in the observations is said to defy realist interpretation. Thus it is definitely not just what scientists expected.

According to a more Hegelian idealism, the mental or spiritual character of reality does not require that we humans impose order. Hence it is not open to the argument from the failure of the Idealist Prediction. If the mental or spiritual is here to be thought of as a personal God, then this is either no rival to theism or it is pantheism, which we have already discussed. Hegelians provide a novel way of understanding only if they replace the physical laws by dialectical principles governing the evolution of Reason. These dialectical principles are then treated as laws of progress from the less to the more organized, harmonious, and beautiful. Hence this universe will be suited at some stage to embodied persons, because we represent an important stage in this development. That would explain why the laws are now life-friendly.

My criticism of this version of idealistic understanding is that it shares the same defect as the previous Hegelian explanation I considered. For Hegelians are not merely extrapolating from the known tendency of humans to impose order on the world around them. Nor, unless they are Hegelian theists, are they extrapolating the laws of thought and spiritual development that hold in the human case. Rather they are positing novel fundamental principles governing spiritual development. There is, then, a contest between the Hegelian way of understanding and personal explanations. Everything I said about the contest between evaluative understanding and personal explanation now holds of this contest. And, unlike Leslie's extreme axiarchism or the Principle of Perfection, Hegelianism cannot, as far as I can see, provide a satisfactory explanation of resilient moral supremacy.

One obvious reply to my criticisms of idealistic understanding is that idealists might well not be interested in scientific understanding in general and the laws of nature in particular, so the question why there are beautiful and life-friendly laws lapses. But that reply is inadequate. For we are considering idealism as a way of understanding. And, I say, there just is no alternative to understanding the details of this universe except by means of, among other things, the sciences. If, therefore, idealists abandon scientific understanding, then they are just not proposing a rival to the theocentric-cum-scientific understanding I am endorsing. Although I have not argued against idealism as such, I conclude that any attempt at an idealistic understanding of things fails to achieve even equality with theocentric understanding.

6. A God of Malice?

Consideration of the evils around us might lead to the thought that the universe was created by a malicious God, just to torment us. The issue here is not whether we can *prove* the universe was not created out of malice. I fear we cannot—only the actual experience of the love of God can completely save us from that nightmare. No, the issue is whether this version of ananthropic theism is as good a way of understanding things as anthropic theism.

Let us consider, then, a God who creates out of malice. This indeed explains why the universe is suited to life, for presumably there has to be life if there is to be suffering. But it does not explain some of the other things that can be explained by the belief in God. For instance, it explains neither the beauty of the world, with its power to console, nor our capacity to make progress toward the truth. To this it could reasonably be replied that I have merely expounded the mirror image of the argument from evil, and that a God of malice explains precisely what is problematic for a loving God and vice versa. The difference in explanatory power, then, is not brought out in those things that can be understood as gifts from God. This still leaves, however, one important consideration against belief in a God of malice. Because it is unreasonable to have faith, hope, or love in a God of malice, belief in such a God cannot explain resilient moral supremacy. For it is not even especially prudent to obey a thoroughly malicious being, who is as likely to take pleasure in tormenting loyally evil servants as in venting anger on the righteous. Hence those who believe the universe is ruled by a God of malice cannot understand the resilience of their own moral righteousness. Indeed their predicament is far worse than that of naturalists. For they must take seriously the possibility that the moral rules they conform to are indeed the commands of God, but of a God who ensures that the actions thus commanded turn out, contrary to human expectations, to have the worst of consequences.

Resilient moral supremacy might, then, tip the balance in favor of a good over an evil God. But the chief advantage of anthropic theism over its Satanic mirror image lies in the motive for creation. The intention to do harm, unlike the intention to secure the well-being of others, or, for that matter, the intention to produce what is beautiful, "refers," in Hume's words, to our "state and situation." As my earlier example of Cain and Abel illustrates, malice arises from such sources as envy or frustration, which would be absurd in a God powerful enough to ensure life-friendly laws. On the other hand, as I have argued in Chapter 2, God, having no unsatisfied needs, would be far more likely than we are to act for the good of others.

This point about motives may be supported by considering, instead of a God of malice, a God who really did create out of "an inordinate fondness for beetles," as J. B. S. Haldane facetiously suggested, with all other sentient life as a by-product. We should grant that this fails, among other reasons, just because the motive is so implausible. Likewise, the hypothesis of a God of malice fails because malice is not, on reflection, judged to be an appropriate motive.

I have suggested two, compatible, accounts of the divine motive: the recognition of what is good and the spontaneous overflow of joy. Could these motives be adapted to a God of malice? The recognition of disvalue does not provide a motive by itself; there has to be some further explanation of why disvalue is perversely sought. The overflow of suffering or self-hatred might, however, explain creation. Let us therefore examine the possibility that a God powerful enough to create a universe should lead a hellish life and so create a hellish world. One difficulty with this suggestion is that we obtain more economical hypotheses if we extrapolate as far as we can from our own human experience to that of God. And it is our experience that just being conscious is in itself rather pleasant, as is attested by both joie de vivre and the state of meditation. Suffering comes about, all too readily, from external stimuli or by contemplating things that are not as they should be. It is likely therefore that, prior to creation, the divine state would be one of bliss and most unlikely that it would be one of suffering. In addition, if the divine state of consciousness is one of suffering, it is totally mysterious why we do not all suffer in the same way as such a God would, by having this intrinsically horrible conscious state from which we could obtain partial relief only by distraction. I doubt if anyone is really like that; I know I am not.

7. Art for Art's Sake?

There is a strong case, then, although not as conclusive as I would like, for rejecting the hypothesis that the universe was created out of malice. The case for rejecting a God who is motivated by aesthetics alone is rather different. For I acknowledge that someone free from all needs might well be motivated aesthetically. Moreover, we should take seriously the frivolous-sounding speculation that God creates neither for the sake of what is good and beautiful nor out of malice but simply out of boredom. That has much the same implications as an aesthetically motivated but amoral God.

To begin my criticism of the aesthetically motivated God, I ask whether among aesthetic motives we need to include the appreciation of the dramatic and poetic qualities that only the personal can provide. Or is a "cold" impersonal aesthetic motivation enough? If we include only the impersonally beautiful, then we can indeed understand why the physical universe is governed by elegant fundamental laws and, of course, why it is beautiful. We can understand why there is life, for living organisms and the ecosystems they make up excel as systems of great complexity arising out of fundamentally simple laws. We can appreciate, say, the marvels of biochemistry not just because it is necessary for life but because it is so fascinating as chemistry. On this view, then, God creates a world with life simply because it is beautiful in a rather narrow and impersonal way, and as a by-product there are embodied persons. God does not value us as persons, although God may find our brains fascinatingly baroque.

An aesthetically motivated God explains a great deal and is not going to be troubled by the argument from evil. Why then should we reject it? First, if God is aesthetically motivated in this narrow fashion, God can have no reason to issue commands that are for the sake of our well-being.[10] Therefore we cannot avail ourselves of the theocentric understanding of resilient moral supremacy, which I expounded in the previous chapter.

A further objection is that a narrowly aesthetic motivation requires no physical universe at all. God could be a conceptual artist, deriving aesthetic satisfaction, or perhaps just relief from boredom, just by thinking about beautiful structures. Unlike us, God has no need to aid imagination by means of perception and no need to cooperate with others for the sake of greater aesthetic satisfaction. The obvious rejoinder to this is that the aesthetic motive is not a self-directed seeking of aesthetic experience but rather the production of what is beautiful because the beautiful is good. Thus the deaf composer or the blind painter might create neither for the sake of self nor for the sake of others. I grant this, but that motivation assimilates aesthetic creation to the production of what is good just because it is good. And that leads us back to the account of the divine motive for creation given in Chapter 2. In the context of creation for the sake of what is good it would be ad hoc to restrict the motive to the aesthetic. That this universe is beautiful cannot, therefore, be explained by means of a God whose motives are narrowly aesthetic.

In reply to these objections it could be suggested that God is aesthetically motivated in a broader fashion and that embodied persons exist because we make for good drama, or at least provide the sort of aesthetic value we might find in poetry rather than severely abstract art. For the dramatic interest that the personal provides requires real people, not just imaginary ones. That is partly because God should have genuine empathy with those taking part in a drama and partly because, for good drama, there should be the sense that people could have chosen otherwise. Because of our limited knowledge, these requirements can be satisfied in the human case by acting. But God would require the real thing.

Belief in a God who is motivated in ways that are broadly as well as narrowly aesthetic, or for whom boredom is best relieved by drama, is, therefore, a more tenable speculation than a God interested only in a narrow aesthetics of patterns and structures. I have, however, two objections to it, one straightforward, the other less so. The straightforward objection is that in deciding between anthropic theism and an aesthetically motivated or bored God, we are choosing between attributing to God all the motives that do not refer to

---

[10] As James Franklin has pointed out to me, an aesthetically motivated God could well issue commands for aesthetic reasons, including the command not to destroy ecosystems or make species extinct, and God might punish us if we do not obey them. Such commands would not, however, cover all of any normal system of moral obligations.

our "state and situation" or just some of them. And it is somewhat arbitrary to suppose God would be motivated by some but not others.

The less straightforward objection is that once the aesthetic motive is broadened, it becomes more than purely aesthetic. (I leave readers to make the adaptation to the speculation that God creates out of boredom.) Before I state this objection, let us consider a borderline case between the narrow and the broad aesthetic motivation. Tourists often go to religious shrines, such as Lourdes or Varanasi, and take in the scene, without much concern for the people involved and without sharing their faith. The scene includes its fair share of petty crime, poor taste in religious ornaments, beggars, and so on. But they all add to the atmosphere. I am interested in this case because it illustrates how the broadly aesthetic becomes entwined with the moral. If our tourists had no empathy at all with the faithful, then the scene would become a mere spectacle. But as a mere spectacle it would be quite second-rate. The faithful are inelegantly dressed and not especially attractive, there are long pauses in which nothing happens, the singing is flat and slow, and so on. No, the tourists are entertained precisely because it is more than mere entertainment. There is a suppressed involvement. With parts of themselves they do care for the mutilated and the destitute, and they do resonate with the faith of the faithful. But unless the tourists are also believers, this involvement is suppressed, which is why we may consider it to be primarily an aesthetic experience.

Examples such as the one above, as well as examples of great works of drama, show that in the human case broad aesthetic motivation requires a capacity for concern for the people involved in the dramatic events. This concern is suppressed if the response is primarily aesthetic, but it must be there. It may be suppressed for excellent reasons. ("They *are* only actors.") Or the reasons may not be so good. ("If I get involved I have blown my chances of promotion.") And this leads to my objection to the idea of a God whose motives are broadly aesthetic but not altruistic or in some other way moral. It is that the capacity for concern is necessarily, not contingently, required for broad aesthetic motivation. Hence God, like us, must have a capacity for altruistic concern or something like it, if the divine motives are (broadly) aesthetic. But we have no reason to believe that the divine concern would be suppressed. Therefore the speculation that God's motives are purely aesthetic is less satisfactory than the speculation that the motive is both aesthetic and altruistic.

The considerations above are somewhat inconclusive by themselves, but we can add to them the superiority of anthropic theism in its capacity to explain intellectual progress and resilient moral supremacy. In both cases belief in an untrustworthy God renders mysterious that which can be explained by belief in a trustworthy one. And, I take it, an amoral but aesthetically motivated God, or a God who creates solely out of boredom, is not to be trusted.

8. The Conditional Superiority of Theocentric Understanding

The discussion of the last four chapters can be summed up in a number of claims I ask readers to judge.

(i)   There are several features of the universe, including the life-friendly character of the laws discovered by scientists, resilient moral supremacy, the beauty around us, the progress of science toward the truth, and the serendipity of mathematics, which cannot be given a naturalistic understanding but can be given a theocentric understanding.

(ii)   The only rivals that come close to theocentric understanding in the range of features they explain are some versions of evaluative understanding, such as Leslie's extreme axiarchism or the Principle of Perfection.

(iii)   Evaluative understanding might turn out not to be a rival to theocentric understanding at all. But if they are rivals, belief in freedom cum responsibility decides the issue in favor of theocentric understanding.

(iv)   Belief in an aesthetically motivated God comes close to anthropic theism in its explanatory power, but anthropic theism provides a more plausible account of the divine motive. In addition it provides an explanation of resilient moral supremacy.

(v)   Because of its advantages, anthropic theism (supplemented by scientific realism) should be judged to be the best available way of understanding the universe, provided some prima facie disadvantages can be overcome.

(vi)   The most striking prima facie disadvantage is that provided by the amount and kinds of evil there are. Unless this disadvantage can be removed, belief in an aesthetically motivated God might well be the best overall way of understanding things.

(vii)   Another prima facie disadvantage is that theism might seem an outlandish hypothesis, which could be accepted only if it explained even more than in fact it does.

Removing these prima facie disadvantages is the task of the remainder of the book.

[6]
The Theoretical
Niche Argument

1. The Analogy between God and the Mind

I have presented a case for the superiority of theocentric over rival ways of understanding and for the superiority of anthropic over ananthropic theism. That case is, however, subject to two provisos. One is that I reply satisfactorily to the argument from evil. That is the task for Chapter 8. The other proviso is that I succeed in showing that theism is a genuine epistemic possibility. In the language of probabilities this amounts to showing that there is a non-negligible probability that there is a God even prior to the consideration of such features as the suitability of the universe for life. Or, without resorting to the language of probabilities, it amounts to defending theism against the accusation that it is antecedently just too implausible.

My case for the antecedent plausibility of theism generally, and anthropic theism in particular, is based on the precedent set by those respects in which we humans cannot be understood in purely physical terms. And these respects in which we cannot be understood in purely physical terms are ones we are quite familiar with. Hence that which we are familiar with does indeed set a precedent for God, which shows how theism does not require the supernatural. For instance, Cartesian dualists should initially propose that God and the human soul are two species of the same genus. And if they recoil from that initial proposal, perhaps as a result of religious experience, they should nonetheless treat such Cartesian theism as the best available explanation of various features of the world around them. They could then claim that the best available explanation is not so much true as near the truth.

For those who reject dualism but nonetheless deny the completeness of the physical understanding of human beings, the precedent is not so clear. They might incline toward the following instrumentalism about souls:

> It is convenient to reify the respects in which we humans cannot be understood physically and say that it is *as if* we have a non physical component, the mind or soul, even though there is no such thing.

The analogy would then suggest that God is not strictly speaking a thing but that it is convenient to think of God this way. That would be a version of nonobjectual theism, which was mentioned in Chapter 1 and which is developed in the next chapter.

Unless we investigate further the gaps in our understanding left by physicalism and model our account of God on those gaps, this instrumentalism about souls would suggest an instrumentalism about God, according to which it is merely as if the universe was created by a personal God for the sake of, among other things, our well-being. That is not a position I wish to defend. Instead I explore in greater detail the analogy between God and the respects in which we humans cannot be understood in physical terms.

2. The Idea of a Theoretical Niche

The respects in which human beings are not purely physical provide, I have claimed, a precedent for God. To make this more precise I rely on what I call the Theoretical Niche Argument:

1. Physicalism is incomplete as a way of understanding human beings.
2. So the aspects of human nature that cannot be understood in purely physical terms establish a theoretical niche for what I call unrestricted consciousness.
3. Hence there is a genuine epistemic possibility that there is unrestricted consciousness.
4. Unrestricted consciousness may be identified with God.
5. Therefore there is a genuine epistemic possibility that there is a God.

The details of this argument take up the rest of this chapter and overflow into the next. Let me stress that my goal in these two chapters is merely the genuine epistemic possibility of theism. Let me also stress that the gaps in understanding need not correspond to missing entities. For example, the fail-

ure of physicalism as a way of understanding appearances does not imply that
there are nonphysical "qualia" or "sensa."

The idea of a theoretical niche may be introduced by considering its role
in scientific speculation. For instance, some paleontologists tell us that five or
six hundred million years ago there were many basic patterns of animal organization (phyla) quite unlike those now in existence (Gould 1989). It would
surely be an abuse of Ockham's razor to insist that there is a strong presumption against the positing of such novel kinds of animal. Rather we should
grant that the theory of evolution provides a theoretical niche for such novelty
without actually predicting it.

The idea of a theoretical niche is broader, however, than that of a subkind
of a kind we already know of. Suppose, for instance, that black holes do exist.
They are not stars or galaxies or any other kind we already know of. Nonetheless general relativity has provided a niche for them. In much the same
way, I submit, the gaps in the physicalist understanding of human beings leaves
a niche for God even if we are reluctant to think of God as of the same kind
as a human mind.

Although I have already given two actual examples of theoretical niches, I
now consider a more fanciful one that presents a closer analogy with the case
of God. Imagine a universe made up of "little gritty granules," like the atoms
of Democritus only lacking the hooks. And suppose scientists in that universe
learn about the shapes of the atoms and how their interaction depends on the
shape. In fact it turns out that all the atoms they know of are regular convex
polyhedra (tetrahedra, cubes, octahedra, dodecahedra, and icosahedra). But
there remain some as yet unexplained phenomena. As a result, two rival heterodox theories are developed in which "atoms of the sixth kind" are posited
which are not regular polyhedra. On one it is posited that these atoms are
prism-shaped, with two triangular and three square faces. On the other they
are spherical. Orthodox scientists reject both on Ockhamist grounds. Now I
sympathize with their rejection of the prisms—asymmetry has been introduced for the first time—but I would judge the Ockhamist rejection of spherical atoms to be unfair. Spherical atoms, however, being curved, are of a more
novel kind than prism-shaped atoms, which are still polyhedra and could be
thought of as between tetrahedra (with four triangular faces) and cubes (with
six square faces). My defense of the spherical atoms as more plausible than
prism-shaped atoms is that the underlying theory of these atoms is that they
be highly symmetrical regular shapes. That leaves a niche for the most symmetrical and regular shape of all, the sphere. In much the same way the gaps
in physicalist understanding leave a niche for God as a special and limiting
case of the way in which we are not entirely understood in physicalist terms.

My program for this chapter, then, is to argue that there are gaps in the physicalist understanding of human beings and, exploiting these gaps, to argue for the genuine epistemic possibility of unrestricted consciousness, which is then identified with God.

3. Physicalism as an Attempt at Understanding

I construe physicalism as a thesis about human beings, with the assumption that it will extend to other animals. And I take it as the thesis that necessarily there could not be what, following Keith Campbell (1970, pp. 100–101), I call imitation human beings, namely molecule-for-molecule replicas of ourselves that lack consciousness. Notice that physicalism in this sense is incompatible with one of my speculations about the afterlife, in which universes split but with conscious versions of our replicas in only one of the many subuniverses.

I have several reasons for characterizing physicalism by considering physical replicas of individual human beings rather than as the popular supervenience thesis that no two "possible worlds" are exactly similar in all physical respects but not exactly similar in all respects. The chief reason is that I am relying on the antisupernaturalist strategy of likening God to that about ourselves which cannot be understood in purely scientific terms. In the context of that strategy it is helpful to discuss our own natures first and so consider physicalism to be, as I have characterized it, a thesis about human beings, not entailing anything about God.

Physicalism does not coincide with naturalism. For in one respect physicalism is stronger, because naturalists could be dualists who insisted that psychology was one of the natural sciences and that it ought to discover psychophysical laws. But in another respect physicalism is weaker. For, as I have characterized it, it is obviously compatible with theism.[1]

My characterization of physicalism raises the further question of what sort of necessity we are considering when we say that necessarily there could not be an imitation human being. It could not just be the sort of necessity the laws of nature have. For that would make physicalists out of any dualists who held that the mental depended on the physical in accordance with psycho-

---

[1] It is not quite so obvious that the supervenience thesis is compatible with theism. Suppose, though, that God is noncontingent. Then no two possible worlds could differ in that one contains God and the other does not, so the existence of a noncontingent God is quite compatible with the supervenience thesis. As, however, the referee pointed out to me, theists might well hold, contrary to the supervenience thesis but without any supernaturalism, that God could have had a different attitude toward the universe without there being any physical difference to show for it.

physical laws. We can give a name to the sort of necessity required by calling it metaphysical necessity. I assume that not everything that is metaphysically necessary is true by definition and that laws of nature are not obviously metaphysically necessary. But, beyond that, I know of no neutral characterization. In the context of theism I suggest a truth is metaphysically necessary if either (i) God had no power to make a world in which it was not the truth, even if God had wanted to; or (ii) the truth in question is logically entailed by truths such that (i).[2] For a theist, then, physicalism amounts, roughly, to saying it neither now is nor ever was within the divine power to create imitation human beings.

My aim is not to reject physicalism but to show its limitation as a way of understanding. I am, however, committed to rejecting what I call *reductive physicalism*.[3] This is the thesis that the description of the mental states follows of analytic necessity from a description of the physical states. Here by *analytic necessity* I mean a necessity similar to that which is true by definition. To those who endorse Quine's critique of the analytic/synthetic distinction (1953b), I am tempted to remark that in that case I am saved the task of refuting reductive physicalism. But I think it is fairer to adopt the "Hold on to Nurse, for fear of worse" strategy. As Frank Jackson points out, even a flawed analytic/synthetic distinction is useful until we have something better (1977, pp. 2–3).

My case for the genuine epistemic possibility of theism requires that I either refute or at least cast significant doubt on reductive physicalism. For to know that a truth is analytic confers understanding of why it is true. So if reductive physicalism were correct, then to understand the physical would confer understanding of all there is to be understood about us humans. There would be no residue, as it were. But it is this residue—that about us for which there is no understanding in physical terms—that provides the precedent or analogy for God.

It is enough for me to cast significant doubt on reductive physicalism, rather than refute it, because, in this part of the book, I am aiming only to establish theism as a genuine epistemic possibility. That could be granted even by those who initially considered reductive physicalism to be rather more likely than

[2] The reason for this complicated way of putting it is that if God is necessarily good, then some things that are within God's power might well be impossible, because not such as a good God would do even though a good God could do them.

[3] Reductive physicalism in this sense could be called *strong* reductive physicalism to contrast it with *weak* reductive physicalism, which would be the thesis that in the human case mental properties are identical to physical properties, but by an identity that is metaphysically necessary without being analytic. Weak reductive physicalism coheres quite well with classical theism, but that coherence is beyond the scope of this work. See Forrest 1996b.

not. Numerical probabilities are of heuristic value in illustrating what is going on here. If initially I thought there was, say, an 80 percent probability that reductive physicalism was correct, the remaining 20 percent might establish, using the Theoretical Niche Argument, a 1 percent probability for theism even prior to examination of the further evidence for it. This could then rise to, say, 90 percent on examination of further evidence. Assuming that reductive physicalism is incompatible with theism, this would then lower the probability of reductive physicalism to 10 percent. In that way the evidence for theism would greatly reduce the initially high probability of reductive physicalism from 80 percent to 10 percent. For simplicity of exposition, however, I present my case against reductive physicalism as a reason for rejecting it even before we consider the power of theocentric understanding.

In sum, the Theoretical Niche Argument depends on the incompleteness of the physical understanding of us human beings. Hence it requires a case against reductive physicalism. Over the next five sections I provide such a case, and, in doing so, I also argue that the physicalist understanding of human beings is indeed incomplete. But I do not argue against physicalism as such.

4. The Functionalist Characterization of Mental States

Reductive physicalism would be easily refuted if physicalists were restricted to describing mental states and processes using only the language of neurophysiology. For it cannot be true by definition that a certain pattern of neuronal activity is, on a given occasion, the desire for yet another cup of coffee. Nor could we ever understand desires merely by describing these patterns of neuronal activity. For if these patterns are just considered as spiking frequencies and synapse firings, we have no reason whatever to suppose that a given pattern of neuronal activity is even something we could be aware of, let alone a desire. Physicalists are, however, free to describe human beings using causal or, more generally, functional vocabulary. To simplify matters, physicalists could claim that a state of a human being which is, as Armstrong (1968) put it, "apt to cause" the drinking of coffee would be the desire for a cup of coffee. What else, they might ask, could a state apt to cause the drinking of coffee be but such a desire? Philosophers are notorious for answering rhetorical questions, and one answer might be that a desire to drink cold gravy together with the false belief that the cup in front of you is a cup of cold gravy would tend to cause the drinking of a cup of coffee. But that is no objection to functionalism. It merely illustrates the simplification involved in the characterization provided above. A more detailed functionalist characterization would be able to distinguish various states that on a given occasion result in the same behavior, by showing how they interact differently with other mental states.

My aim in the next three sections is to exhibit the gap in the physicalist understanding of human beings, a gap that cannot be filled even if physicalists rely on the functional characterization of mental states as (i) tending to cause behavior of various kinds, (ii) tending to be caused by stimuli of various kinds, and (iii) interacting in complex ways with other mental states. To exhibit this gap we could rely on many arguments. The following come to mind: that from our capacity to refer to distant objects, that from appearances, that from personal identity over time, that from the unity of the mental, that from consciousness, and that from introspective understanding. The first argument suffers, however, from the possibility of a skeptical reaction. For it could be said that we cannot refer to distant objects and even that we should ignore reference completely. So I do not here rely on it. (But see Forrest 1992.) And considerations of personal identity are rather similar to those governing the unity of the mental at just one time. So I do not consider both of them. Again, I take the fact that things appear to us and the fact that we are conscious to be the same fact. This leaves me with three arguments against reductive physicalism: the Argument from Appearances, the Argument from the Unity of the Mental, and the Argument from Introspective Understanding.

5. Appearances

Physicalism does not enable us to understand the fact that things appear to us rather than not appearing at all. But what is this fact? That things appear to us is, I am assuming, the same fact as that we are conscious of things and the same fact as that there is, in Thomas Nagel's phrase, "something it is like to be" us. Here, then, we have the most obvious gap in physicalist understanding. And by the Theoretical Niche Argument an unrestricted consciousness—roughly speaking a that to which everything appears—becomes a genuine epistemic possibility. Let me emphasize, though, that I am not assuming that appearances are themselves entities ("qualia" or "sensa"). Nor am I assuming, in this section, that we are in any way integrated selves. We might be nothing more than causally connected bundles of conscious events. I am pointing to one striking fact of which we are aware by introspection—the fact that things appear, or the fact of consciousness.

Even as regards this one striking fact I ask for charity from readers. The words used, such as "appearance" and "conscious," are no doubt capable of interpretation by physicalists so that they can understand the world of "appearances" or that suitably complex systems are "conscious." My aim is to point to a striking, but hard to articulate, fact that physicalism does not enable us to understand, not to engage in disputes about the possible interpretations of the words used. Nonetheless some further clarification is in order. There is a (not necessarily precise) distinction between phenomenal *appearings*, on the one hand, and doxastic *seemings*, on the other. Consider a detailed visual scene, say ridge after ridge of tree-covered hills with a plume of smoke rising up on the right. I have a tendency to form verbal beliefs about what is in front of me. Yet I cannot put into words all that I see, so there is a nonverbal awareness of how things appear. The tendency-to-form-verbal-beliefs sense of the word "seem" I call the doxastic sense. But when I say there is a nonverbal awareness of how things appear, I am using the word "appear" in its phenomenal sense. I stipulate that I use the word "appear" only for the phenomenal and restrict the word "seem" to the doxastic. The striking fact, then, is that things *appear* in this stipulated sense. There are, no doubt, inter-mediate cases. Thus I might form the partially verbal belief that the plume of smoke is *that* shape, where I cannot describe but can imagine the shape. Nonetheless I think the distinction is clear enough.

It should not be necessary to draw this striking fact to our attention, but we can do so by considering patients whose brain damage results in blind sight, namely the formation of beliefs as a result of information conveyed by the optic nerves to the brain but without introspectible visual appearances. These patients lack the visual appearances of things.

When I deny there is a physicalist understanding of appearances, I am not, however, denying that physicalists could explain the functional role of ap-pearances. For example, some more sophisticated version of the following account would be plausible for visual appearances:

> The visual processing of information proceeds in stages leading even-tually to tendencies to believe and, in normal circumstances, to beliefs. If visual information affected other brain functions only after it had been fully processed into beliefs, then there would be neither appearances nor doxastic seemings. If it had effects on other brain functions only after it was processed as far as the tendency-to-believe stage, then there would be doxastic seemings but no visual appearances. In that case it would be like blind sight, which, I assume, occurs because there is a secondary route for processing visual information which operates even after the primary route is destroyed and which indeed has no effects prior to the tendency-to-believe stage. There are visual appearances precisely because an earlier, preverbal, stage of the processing of visual information, has effects on various other brain functions in addition to the route via beliefs. In particular, visual memories are laid down which

are not themselves remembered as beliefs but which can lead to beliefs on later occasions.

I do not dispute, therefore, that we can offer a functional characterization of the states in which there are appearances. What I claim, though, is that the functional characterization of those states does not enable us to *understand* the quality of those appearances, unless we supplement functionalism with some further metaphysical speculation.

I support this claim by means of a version of Jackson's argument that knowing everything there is to know about the physical description of things would not enable us to know what it is like to be in various states (Jackson 1982). Unlike Jackson, though, I aim neither to establish the existence of qualia (reified appearances) nor to refute physicalism as such. Instead I am arguing that reductive physicalism is incorrect and that no knowledge of the physical, whether in functional or neurophysiological terms, can without further speculation enable us to understand appearances. I therefore develop my argument in a rather different way from Jackson, by making an appeal to an *informed ignorance*.

Consider, then, a reply to the argument from evil based on the claim that the creator of this universe—God or a lesser god, it does not here matter which—does not feel any pain and so cannot know what it is like to be in pain, which is why the creator tolerates pain in creatures. Now I reject that reply chiefly on the grounds that all pain is divine pain in addition to being the pain of individual creatures. Let us ignore my objection, however, and suppose that indeed the creator could not feel pain. And further suppose that the creator knows the functional role of pain in perfect detail and every detail of human physiology. Finally suppose, although this is something else I do not accept, that this creator does not merely know these things but thinks about them, much as we do, but without any human limitations. If reductive physicalism were correct, or if physicalism provided us with a way of understanding appearances, then the creator would know what pain is like and so have just the sort of motive we have for not creating a universe with pain in it. I now ask, *Would* such a creator know what pain was like, and so be moved to prevent it, merely by knowing the functional roles of pain and the accompanying neurophysiology? I claim that we do not know the answer; we can only speculate.

This ignorance provides a case against the completeness of physicalist understanding. For if it were complete, then we should know the answer; we should not have to speculate. In response, reductive physicalists must say that if we only knew more details about the brain, we would be able to answer the question. That amounts to saying that physicalist understanding will be complete one day. The weakness of that response may be illustrated by making the counterclaim that, if we only knew, we could see that it is true by definition that there is a God (as in some versions of the ontological argument). Here and now, however, we do not know.

There is a temptation to say that for good theoretical reasons we should accept reductive physicalism and hence cease to proclaim the ignorance I have been commending. We should especially resist that temptation in the present context because we are deciding, among other things, between two rival scientifically oriented world views, antisupernaturalist theism and naturalism. I have already presented reasons why if God is a genuine epistemic possibility (and if the argument from evil can be answered), we should prefer theism to naturalism. So it is premature for naturalists to say that for "good theoretical reasons" we should embrace reductive physicalism.

Another reason for resisting the temptation is that, if it is not resisted, we would be saying there are good theoretical reasons for supposing that our theory enables us to understand the phenomena to be explained. We should not, I say, use a theory to theorize about what that theory could explain. Instead we should go ahead and explain it.

6. Consciousness

I claim, then, that there is a striking fact, the fact that things appear, which we cannot now understand in purely physical terms and have no good reason to believe we ever shall. As far as I can see, this is the same fact as the fact of consciousness. And it might be worth drawing attention to it in this way also. Let us consider, then, a robot with inner states causally connected in ways similar to, but not exactly the same as, that of a human being. This robot would exhibit similar behavior to a human being. I ask, Would it be a real or just an imitation person? By that I mean, Is the robot consciously aware of anything? My point is not that the answer is negative. Even if it is negative, it is not obviously so. Rather my point is that the answer is not obviously affirmative either—it is a matter of speculation. We do not *know* whether the robot would be conscious or not. I grant that maybe it is necessarily the case that such a robot is conscious. But if so, the necessity is neither analytic nor of similar ease of understanding. For if it were we should know.

Against this it could be urged that there are adequate functionalist accounts of consciousness. One attempt is to think of the conscious self as a monitor. In that case being conscious would amount to having suitable monitoring devices integrated into the system of brain processes that is the mind. I have no difficulty with that as an account of self-consciousness, given that we take consciousness and appearances for granted. But what I am seeking to understand is not the wonderful reflexivity by which the self is said to know itself. Rather I am concerned with something that strikes me as far less controversial than self-consciousness, namely the fact of conscious awareness itself—that there is something it is like to be aware of things. And, as I have already said, I do not take this to be anything more than the striking fact that things appear. But perhaps physicalists are claiming that conscious awareness of something is an awareness of being aware of that something, and that such a reflexive awareness is indeed just a matter of a physical self-monitoring device.

I am prepared to concede that the *appropriate* sort of self-monitoring might be sufficient for conscious awareness, although I am not convinced. But if it is sufficient, then we cannot understand why it should be sufficient. Consider an automated factory with a television camera that scans everything in the factory including itself, which it sees in a mirror. A computer then checks the match between the picture on the screen and images of how the factory should look. If there is a mismatch, then a human being is summoned to find out what has gone wrong. Such a factory contains a self-monitoring system. But it is not, presumably, conscious. Hence a self-monitoring device, though enough to turn consciousness to self-consciousness, cannot explain consciousness. Even if the self-monitoring device was increased in sophistication, it is by no means obvious that the system would be conscious. If, for whatever reason, we came to believe it was conscious, then, I submit, we would not understand why it was. For, as I have already urged, the mere fact of self-monitoring, as in the simpler device, does not result in consciousness.

This may be reinforced by a consideration of the peculiar but possible case in which human introspection is itself unconscious. An example is someone subject to heart attacks who has been told to take aspirin whenever even a slight pain is felt in the chest. This could become so habitual that the aspirin is taken without thinking about the pain. Indeed such a person could reason thus: "I have just taken an aspirin. Therefore I must have had a slight pain." The only plausible explanation of this is that the self-monitoring device responsible for introspection of pain is functioning without the person being conscious of the pain.

What I have been doing is drawing attention in various ways to the fact that things appear, which is, I submit, the same fact as that there is consciousness. This fact cannot, I say, now be understood in physical terms, and we have no good reason to believe it ever could be. Physicalists can grant all I have said by insisting that if the functional role of an inner state is as it is, then it necessarily appears as it does, where the necessity is metaphysical rather than analytic. Let me remind readers, therefore, that my aim is not to refute physicalism but to exhibit a gap in the physicalist understanding of human beings. And I claim that this gap in understanding is not diminished by saying that the connection between the way mental states appear and their functional roles is a necessary one. Its modal status might determine whether or not the resulting theory is to be called a physicalist one, but labeling it *necessary* does not enable us to understand it. (See my discussion of necessitarianism in Chapter 3.)

All the above, including our judgment of hypothetical examples, is based on a reliance on introspection, not, to be sure, as regards details but as regards such striking facts as that there are appearances. But does that not show I still have Cartesian hangups, ignoring the "Death of Self"? To take a well-articulated and fairly moderate expression of current anti-Cartesianism, consider Daniel Dennett's method of heterophenomenology (1991, chap. 4). Dennett tells us that in philosophical discussion it is not the appearances that should be taken as data but verbal reports, and that there is in principle no difference between my own verbal reports of how things appear and anyone else's. So we might as well take as our data the fact that other people sincerely report various states, and seek the theory that best explains those reports while cohering with everything we know about the brain. If we can explain why the reports are mistaken, then that is as satisfactory as accepting them as correct.

Heterophenomenology seems to be an excellent way of investigating the functional roles of mental states, and an effective antidote to the excesses of folk psychology. But if taken as a serious attempt at complete understanding, it would require the denial that we have any capacity to introspect the way things appear, and require the insistence that all so-called introspection is just a matter of having various tendencies to believe and hence that all appearings are really just doxastic seemings. I reject that position and invite readers to reject it, even though I myself have doubts as to the *precision* of the distinction between appearings and doxastic seemings. Perhaps, as Dennett urges, there are no "raw feels," that is, pure phenomenal appearings. (See 1991, pp. 331–33.) Perhaps there is merely a continuum from the medium rare to the overcooked. But we can live with vagueness, so doubts about precision do not make a distinction worthless. And even if there are no appearances free from some preconscious inference, physicalists can no more understand medium rare feels than they could understand raw ones.

A further criticism of Dennett's method of heterophenomenology is that it reflects the verbal chauvinism so characteristic of "Western" thought. Insistence on filtering *everything* through the medium of words can be guaranteed to distort our perspective on things.

7. The Unity of the Mental

Because introspection is fallible when it comes to details, I have been emphasizing only the most striking features of the mental. And the fact of appearances (or of consciousness) is one of these striking features. Another striking feature of the mental is its (admittedly fragile and imperfect) *unity*. By this I mean whatever mental states require in order to be states of the one mind at a given time. (Personal identity over time is a similar feature of the mental.)

The physicalist account of the unity of various mental states is, presumably, in terms of the degree of integration of the total system to which these mental states belong. (See Shoemaker and Swinburne 1984.) Provided there are enough causal connections and they are of the right kind, the system will constitute a single mind, rather than several minds or a collection of mental states not even forming minds. Call this the Integrated System Thesis. In accordance with my overall purpose, I am not rejecting the Integrated System Thesis. That thesis may well be a necessary, but nonanalytic, truth. My aim is to show that it fails as a way of understanding mental unity. One way of showing this is to consider the question of group minds and to rely once again on an informed ignorance.[4] Suppose the World Association of Telepathists achieves a highly integrated system made up of the mental states of all its members. Or suppose we link the brains of thousands of people using millions of artificial nerves. We could reasonably ask the question, Would there be a group mind? My point is not that the answer is obviously negative. My point is that the affirmative answer is not something we could know but rather a piece of speculation.

I conclude that if physicalism is correct, then the necessity whereby a highly integrated system of brain processes comes to have the unity of a single mind lacks the comprehensibility of an analytic truth. If we can understand it, that will be only by considering some further metaphysical speculation.

8. The Argument from Introspective Understanding

I now provide an indirect argument for the incompleteness of physicalist understanding. Knowing the way things appear enables us to understand our own behavior in a different fashion from knowing functional roles. Consider, for example, children who pinch, tickle, and tease their friends, who resist pinching, tickling, and teasing. In all three cases we could explain the resulting

---

[4] This argument is based on the sort of puzzle cases considered by John Searle (1980; 1984, chap. 2) and Ned Block (1978).

behavior, namely resistance, causally. But there is a difference between the extent to which behavior can be understood simply by knowing what it is like to be pinched or tickled or teased. To know the (mild) pain of being pinched enables us to understand pinch-avoidance. To understand the reaction to teasing, however, requires some thought, and the explanation is more complicated. Tickling is puzzling not because something subtle is going on but because knowing what it is like fails to enable us to understand why children avoid being tickled. The contrast among pinching, teasing, and tickling is intended to illustrate how the way things appear can, in some cases at least, enable us to understand behavior. There is an obviousness to pinch-avoidance that tickling-avoidance lacks.

To be sure, we are told how people who are given morphine after the onset of pain report that the pain is still there, although they do not care. Initially this is puzzling, but it is no counterexample to the thesis that knowing how pain appears enables us to understand pain behavior. For I favor the interpretation according to which we can, and in unusual circumstances will, distinguish between the pain itself and how the pain appears (Nelkin 1986). Pain under the influence of morphine is then rather like blind sight—you know the "object," in this case the pain, is there, without it appearing as it usually does. And it is not the having of the pain but how the pain appears that explains the pain behavior.

A rival explanation, due to Armstrong (1962, pp. 106-8), is that normal pain sensations "involve *both* the having of a certain sort of bodily sense-impression, *and* the taking up of a certain attitude to the impression." In that case pain under the influence of morphine consists only of the first component. Although this is entirely satisfactory as a way of handling the problem of pain under morphine, it does not offer us an understanding of the obviousness of our dislike of the bodily "sense-impression." For on Armstrong's account it just happens that the "sense-impressions" of pain cause us to have a marked antipathy toward them. The point of my contrasting pinches with tickles is that only in the case of tickles is Armstrong's account adequate— the "sense-impression" causes the antipathy without its being obvious that it should.

I claim that knowing how pain appears provides a way of understanding the pain-avoiding tendency not provided by knowing how the correlated brain processes tend to cause that behavior. If I am right, then physicalism omits an important way of understanding, namely the understanding of behavioral tendencies by knowing the way in which various mental states appear. But if the physicalist understanding of the way in which things appear was complete, then there could be no such omission. Therefore the physicalist understanding of the way in which things appear is incomplete.

It could be objected that the understanding of the pain-avoiding tendency which is provided by knowing how pain appears is not something in addition to the understanding a cognitive scientist would have who knew all about the functional roles of mental states. In both cases, the objection continues, we understand by discovering the functional role, although that role is known in different ways.[5] In the next chapter I myself speculate that a mental state just is how the functional role appears. (This is my version of the double aspect theory.) So I do not dispute the importance of functional roles. I grant that we might, perhaps, explain the tendency toward self-obsession that is one of the effects of pain, by noting that the functional role of pain is to remove its own cause, and it cannot perform that role effectively unless it dominates our consciousness. My objection is to the attempt at an understanding of pain-avoidance by appealing to the functional role of pain. For that is circular. The functional role of pain just is the removal of its own cause. And that is one reason why I chose the example of pain. It is the sheer simplicity of its functional that which prevents any illuminating functional explanation of it.

9. Unrestricted Consciousness

Things appear to us. Our minds have a certain unity. These facts about ourselves may well be compatible with physicalism, but, I have argued, they cannot be understood in physical terms. And if we cannot understand our own minds merely by describing the physical world, then, I say, we have no right to dismiss the speculation that there is a unified consciousness to which all things appear. Let us call this *unrestricted consciousness*. If we also grant, as I argued in Chapter 2, that our own freedom is to be understood as the special case of a general principle governing the power of any conscious being, then this unrestricted consciousness should have power only restricted by what is already the case.

I identify this unrestricted consciousness with God, who is the creator of physical structure. Now, in our cases, the details of our mental states depend on the functional roles played by various brain processes, which themselves depend on the brain's physical structure. We have, therefore, no reason for holding a thoroughly anthropomorphic account of the divine mind. What, then, would this unrestricted consciousness be like if, prior to creation, it lacks the features that, in our case, depend on the details of the brain? Some further

---

[5] Compare Lewis's (1990) reply to Jackson (1982). One response to that debate is to agree with Lewis that there is nothing that we know and Mary, the complete neurophysiologist, does not. However, the way we have of knowing, which Mary lacks, itself constitutes a gap in physicalist understanding.

account of this is required if I am to establish the genuine epistemic possibility of a personal deity, which, I have argued, explains more than an impersonal one. I begin, therefore, with an account that, if accepted, would undermine best-explanation apologetics, by identifying unrestricted consciousness with an impersonal deity. It is based on a reversal of the scholastic position that the soul stands to the body as form to "matter," or content. Scholasticism Reversed, as I call it, is the position that consciousness lacks intrinsic structure and that the structure of the human mind is due to the way consciousness is structured by the detailed workings of the brain. If we held that view, then an unrestricted consciousness would be an unstructured consciousness. The God of Scholasticism Reversed would have no knowledge of this rather than that and hence no reason to create this rather than that.[6] Such a God would have no providential concern for what has been created and hence would give no commands. In short such a God provides no explanation of the various things for which I have provided a theocentric understanding.

Scholasticism Reversed might indeed be a genuine epistemic possibility. To defend best-explanation apologetics I require an alternative speculation about human minds, one compatible with the personal character of a God who is consciousness unrestricted by any physical brain or brain analog. Perhaps we should consider the neo-Cartesian speculation. On it a something-or-other—the Self—is directly aware of the mental states. Or, as I would urge, it is directly aware of brain processes, and the ways these appear are the mental states. Descartes is no doubt "outmoded," but that does not keep us from recycling worn-out old Cartesian dogmas as neo-Cartesian speculations. Let us persevere for a while, then, with the neo-Cartesian response to the gaps in physicalist understanding. On it the physical structure of the brain provides a complex system of representations (of a body and of that body's environment). The Self is directly aware of these representations and hence indirectly aware of what they represent. A mechanism is, therefore, required for indirect awareness, which is one reason why we have such complicated brains. But no mechanism is required for direct awareness.

To forestall one objection let me note that indirect awareness does not mean coming to believe as a result of making an inference from what we are aware of. It means being aware of something by being aware of a representation of it.

On the neo-Cartesian speculation an imitation human being has a system of representations just like ours and behaves in ways based on connections

---

[6] The same problem arises in the context of divine simplicity. If readers think the problem can be solved in that context, and that the solution transfers to Scholasticism Reversed, then my further speculations about the divine nature are redundant.

between representations. There is, however, no awareness of the world around the imitation person or of the goals the behavior is directed toward. For such awareness, in the human case, requires a direct awareness of the system of representations.

Perhaps the neo-Cartesian speculation is a genuine epistemic possibility, but it has an obvious defect. For it postulates a nonphysical Self. And that in turn raises the question of why a given Self is, ignoring telepathy, directly aware of only one of the billions of collections of brain processes. In the absence of a satisfactory answer it is preferable to modify the neo-Cartesian speculation so as to remove the Self. What we took to be the relational fact that the Self is aware of X is now taken as a nonrelational fact that there is a way X appears. The astounding fact of consciousness is then interpreted as the fact not that each person has a conscious Self but that there are ways things appear. A mind is then interpreted as a *suitably unified* bundle of such ways things appear. I call this the neo-Humean speculation.

The neo-Humean speculation is no less plausible than Scholasticism Reversed. And on it there is a niche for unrestricted consciousness thought of as the sum or bundle of all the ways things appear. Let us identify unrestricted consciousness, interpreted in accordance with the neo-Humean speculation, with God. Provided we include among the things of which there is consciousness the *possibilities* for creation, and the value or disvalue of these possibilities, it then follows that, even prior to creation, God could indeed have knowledge of possibilities and so have a motive for creation. (For further speculations about both the neo-Humean God and the possibilities for creation, I refer readers to the next chapter.)

10. Physicalism—The Hard Case

I have argued in general terms that there is indeed a theoretical niche for unrestricted consciousness and that gaps in physicalist understanding can be used to support the neo-Humean speculation that unrestricted consciousness is an awareness of all things, not a totally unstructured consciousness. I now supplement this general argument by considering some more detailed responses to the gaps in the physicalist understanding of ourselves: nonreductive physicalism, substance dualism, and attribute dualism. I argue in all cases that there is a niche left for unrestricted consciousness as I have described. I begin with nonreductive physicalism, which can be expressed thus:

> Yes, we humans are indeed just "meat in motion," but it is incomprehensible how this meat in motion results in a unified, free, conscious mind.

I claim that such nonreductive physicalism leaves a niche for an unrestricted
consciousness interpreted as the awareness of all things and so having the
power to bring about whatever is still possible. In support of this claim I note
three considerations. The first is that if we do not understand the occurrence
of consciousness, then we are in a singularly weak position to deny with any
confidence that there is unrestricted consciousness. It would be as if opponents
of the theory of evolution granted that new varieties of a given species of
organism could evolve from old varieties, admitted that they did not understand how such new varieties could evolve, but were nonetheless quite confident that no new species or genus of organism could evolve.

The second consideration has to do with a remarkable convergence between nonreductive physicalism and a central tenet of classical theism, namely
the divine noncontingency. I have characterized nonreductive physicalism as
the thesis that all truths about human beings follow *of necessity* from a physical
description of human beings. I have rejected, however, the reductive thesis
that this necessity is analytic. Now classical theists say that necessarily there is
a God. But, unless they accept an ontological argument, they should likewise
insist that this necessity is not analytic. Both nonreductive physicalists and
classical theists, then, rely on a something holding of a necessity that is not
analytic. In both cases we could use the phrase "metaphysical necessity." Now
necessities should not be multiplied more than necessary. So why should we
not identify these two metaphysical necessities? In that case both theism and
a physicalist theory of human beings could well be special cases of a general
thesis that the only metaphysically contingent truths are those about the physical structure of the universe(s), including the truth that there are no other
universes.

In this way nonreductive physicalism, far from being incompatible with
theism, should reconcile us to the claim that God is a necessary being, which
so many philosophers have found baffling. (See Forrest 1996b.) In addition
there is a remarkable agreement between nonreductive physicalists and many
theists over what cannot be comprehended. Nonreductive physicalists should
concede that the dependence of the mental on the physical surpasses all understanding. "That is just what I think about God," the faithful are all too
ready to say. Physicalists and classical theists could even agree on a non-
Kantian mixture of Kantian themes: the things we humans cannot even in
principle understand are just those truths that hold of necessity without being
analytic.

My third consideration is that non-reductive physicalists are, just like dualists, realists about the fact of consciousness. They differ in denying the possibility of replicas of human beings who lack consciousness. Hence they can
accept the neo-Humean speculation, provided they insist that the ways things

appear supervene on the things that appear. Combined with the second consideration, this supports the speculation that in addition to all the minds composed of direct awareness of brain processes there is the direct awareness of all things, which I take to be God.

In sum, even physicalism provides a niche for unrestricted consciousness, because:

(i)   Physicalists should accept, without understanding, the fact that things appear some way or other, that the mental has unity, and that we are physically free. Given their lack of understanding of restricted consciousness, they are in a weak position to reject unrestricted consciousness.

(ii)   There is an interesting convergence between nonreductive physicalism and the classical theistic doctrine of divine noncontingency.

(iii)   The neo-Humean speculation can be interpreted by physicalists as the positing of ways things appear supervenient on the things that appear that way. This leaves a niche for the neo-Humean God.

11. Substance Dualism—The Easy Case

I have argued that even physicalism provides a niche for unrestricted consciousness and for the identification of unrestricted consciousness with God. That is the hardest case, but we must check the seemingly easier case of dualism. This is especially important for those who are not persuaded, as I am, that physicalism leaves a niche for theism. For the gaps in physicalist understanding should undermine confidence in physicalism to the extent of granting that it is at most an initially probable thesis. Provided dualism leaves a niche for theism, the non-negligible probability that dualism is correct would itself establish that theism is a genuine epistemic possibility.

The natural classification of dualist positions is into those according to which there is a nonphysical *substance* and those according to which there are merely nonphysical *attributes*. So I examine these two forms of dualism in turn, starting with substance dualism. Substance dualists believe that a human being is composed of two substances, one physical and one nonphysical. The former is the body, which might, I am prepared to grant, include rather subtle physical components as well as the organism known to current physiology.[7]

---

[7] Such phenomena as telepathy, clairvoyance, and memory of past lives, if they should turn out to be genuine, would, I think, best be explained as an extension of such phenomena as hyperacuity and sensitivity to minimal perceptual cues. Failing that, they could be explained by assuming there are structures which are physical but too subtle to have been discovered yet and which interact with the brain processes we do know. Thus I do not take the paranormal as evidence for anything nonphysical.

The latter substance is often called the *mind*, but I prefer to call it the *soul*, because the mind might well have to be identified, even by a substance dualist, with a combination of the brain and the soul. The term "substance" here is used in the technical sense, not as in, "What is this sticky green substance oozing out of my hot dog?" It means a thing capable of existing by itself, as opposed to such entities as properties and relations, which are widely taken to be capable of existing only as attributes of some substance or other. The substance dualist, then, takes it that some mental attributes could occur without any physical basis because they belong to a nonphysical substance, the soul.

Initially substance dualism makes the task of arguing for the genuine epistemic possibility of God seem an easy one. Surely, we think, if there are souls in the human case, then we can, without adding to the burden of mystery, posit God as a supersoul, a powerful entity belonging to the same kind as our souls. But things are not quite so easy, for, as I have said, the mind might not be the same as the soul. Substance dualists need not, and perhaps should not, treat all the attributes we commonly call mental as attributes of the soul. Indeed substance dualists might agree sufficiently with my speculations of the next chapter to claim that the only attribute of the soul is consciousness itself. The human soul would then be a pure, but restricted, consciousness. As a consequence, the mind would not be identified with the soul. In fact the mind would be, as both Kant and many Indian thinkers before Kant held, yet another collection of appearances. So even given substance dualism, the supersoul that could be reasonably identified with God might lack the full range of human mental states. In that case substance dualists should not in fact propose the neo-Cartesian speculation but, like physicalists, accept a neo-Humean God as a genuine epistemic possibility.

Might there be substance dualists who nonetheless eliminated consciousness from their description of things? If so, then they could object to my labeling substance dualism the "easy case." Such heterodox dualists might, for instance, reject physicalism because they are so impressed by artistic and intellectual creativity that they consider the imagination to be something nonphysical. My response to such heterodox dualists is not that their speculations are out of order. Rather it is that for a substance dualist to reject the genuine epistemic possibility of consciousness as nonphysical, while insisting there is a soul with some nonphysical attributes, would be a case of "Satan rebuking sin." I conclude, therefore, that substance dualism does indeed lead to the genuine epistemic possibility of an unrestricted consciousness, which would have all those attributes that in the human case lack a physicalist understanding, such as being aware, having sufficient unity to be described as a mind, and having the power to act.

12. Attribute Dualism

There is a further obstacle in the path from dualism to the genuine epistemic possibility of theism. For the dualism we start from might well be attribute
dualism, namely the thesis that a human being is a single psychophysical substance that must possess both physical and nonphysical attributes if it is to
exist. According to attribute dualism, there are no human souls and hence no
obvious precedent for the neo-Cartesian speculation. But neither is there a
precedent for the neo-Humean speculation, for there is a Self, according to
attribute dualists, namely the psychophysical substance that is a human being.
The problem, then, is that attribute dualism seems to provide neither the neo-
Cartesian nor the neo-Humean precedent for theism.

Before I propose a solution to this problem, I briefly consider two points
that might seem relevant but only serve to distract us from the main issue.
The first is that we might well insist that the disembodied soul of a human
being is no longer a human being. But that is not the issue. For what attribute
dualists deny is that there could be a disembodied, once human, soul.

The second issue is whether there is any empirical evidence for survival
after death. I think that whatever evidence there is for such survival could
quite reasonably be interpreted as showing that there is something physical
that survives, although it is something that cannot easily be detected by the
obvious physical means. Hence our survival of death does not imply substance
dualism. Since my aim is to argue for the genuine epistemic possibility of an
unrestricted consciousness and since attribute dualism threatens this possibility,
that interpretation is a concession on my part, so I need not undertake the
difficult task of providing a careful argument for it.

There are two ways of replying to the threat of attribute dualism. One is
to argue that, contrary to what has been suggested, attribute dualism provides
a precedent for God as a supersoul. The other is to argue against the supposed
advantages of attribute over substance dualism and hence argue that the assumption that some form of dualism is correct must leave substance dualism
about as probable as attribute dualism.

First, then, suppose attribute dualism is correct and there are various nonphysical attributes. In the human case they cannot have instances without
various physical attributes such as the patterns of neural activity. Why not?
One answer is that we should, if we can, explain how human beings are
individuated as distinct persons. Although we might follow Scotus and insist
that the distinctness comes from a special *thisness*, it is surely more economical
to follow Aquinas and hypothesize that persons are individuated by their bodies. So, attribute dualists may maintain, the reason our mental attributes must
belong to bodies is not that the mental attributes could not occur without

physical attributes but that the resulting entities would have nothing to make them distinct persons. If this is the reason for attribute dualism, then it leaves a niche for just one exception. For it is enough that all other minds be distinct from unrestricted consciousness. There is no need for something additional to distinguish unrestricted consciousness from other minds. Hence all the minds except unrestricted consciousness might have to be embodied, to prevent them being swallowed up by it. In this way attribute dualism in the human case leaves a niche for God.

Against this it could be objected that it would be excessively complicated to have a theory in which some entities, namely we embodied persons, have both physical and mental attributes, but another, God, had mental attributes only. But that is not a complaint attribute dualists should make. For they already grant that some entities have only physical attributes whereas we embodied persons have both physical and mental attributes. It would be as if physicists granted that there were particles with spin but no charge, and granted that there were particles with both spin and charge, but rejected, as excessively complicated, the supposition that there were particles with charge but no spin. Here, once again, a careful consideration of theoretical niches is less drastic than Ockham's razor.

I submit, therefore, that attribute dualism is not as serious a difficulty for theism as it might seem. In any case, as I now argue, the advantages of attribute over substance dualism have been exaggerated. As a preliminary, I would like to point out that metaphysical theses such as substance dualism should not be judged by what they suggest or by the metaphors they generate. I say this because substance dualism suggests a certain sort of attitude toward ourselves, one of nonidentification with our bodies and one of identification of ourselves with the intellectual. However, such "physical" items as our bodily feelings and our body image may be treated by dualists as the mental accompaniment of brain processes. The mental is not restricted to the intellect.

It could be said that attribute dualism has the advantage of simplicity, because it posits no soul. In reply I point out that the one psychophysical substance posited by attribute dualists is just as novel as the spiritual substance of the substance dualists. Both, by having special nonphysical properties, differ from any substances required in our account of the physical world.

Attribute dualism does not, therefore, have much of an advantage as regards simplicity. There is, however, a rather different line of argument for preferring it to substance dualism.[8] Do we not, it might be said, experience ourselves as a single thing with mental and physical attributes? I suspect that the widespread rejection of substance dualism as incorrect, or even unhealthy, derives from

[8] Derived from Armstrong 1968, p. 25. Armstrong, though, is a physicalist.

the thought that if there are two substances, then the *real me* is nonphysical and my body is mere clothing. But there is nothing of weight in that line of argument. Substance dualists can identify themselves with the unions of something physical with something nonphysical, and they can interpret their experience of unity as an experience of the intimate causal connections between the two. Alternatively, substance dualists could claim that the experienced unity of body and mind is a unity of the intellect with body image—a unity mediated perhaps by the emotions. And the body image would itself be something nonphysical, an attribute of the soul. There is, then, little reason to prefer attribute to substance dualism. So there can be no threat to theism from the supposed superiority of attribute dualism.

13. The No Planning Thesis

There is a problem with the identification of God with unrestricted consciousness, which I now discuss. It is that we tend to imagine God as a designer or architect planning a universe. Or we imagine God as thinking through the mathematical details of various possible physical theories deciding which should turn out to be true. Such activities require a complex structured mind, leaving theists open to the retort, "Who designed the designer, then?" More pertinent, designs and plans are mental representations of what is to be brought about, and it is implausible that unrestricted consciousness has such representations. I am committed therefore to the No Planning Thesis for creation, which I now expound.

Something of the immediacy of the act of creation is conveyed by the words of Genesis: God said, "Let there be light. And there was light." But it is even more direct than that. There need be no distinction between the awareness of a possible universe as of great value and the act by which it comes to be, past, present, and future. We humans need to design and plan precisely because we are not able directly and effortlessly to achieve what seems good to us. And that is one reason why we need immensely complex brains. God, as unrestricted consciousness, does not have to plan. Therefore God needs no representations. Therefore God needs no brain.

God creates, I am submitting, out of a nonverbal awareness of what various universes would be like if they existed and out of a nonverbal awareness of the goodness of various possible universes. There is no need for design, no need for planning, no need for theoretical physics, no need even for the *thought* that what is being created is a good universe. Indeed there is no need for any means to the chosen end. God is aware of what would be good, and that awareness, without more ado, causes it to be. Now I grant that if there is no conceptualized thought, then it might be somewhat inappropriate to speak of God's *reasons*. Creation would be, then, like the spontaneous altruism of the Good Samaritan, who in the parable did not reason anything out but simply had compassion. Or it would be like the spontaneous desire of the happy that others be happy too. This direct awareness of the situation and of its excellence provides quite as good an explanation of creation as positing a God who relies on a mathematical grasp of the possible laws of nature, or a God who has mental representations of the ways universes might be.

Perhaps there is a residual opposition to the No Planning Thesis based on the idea that it is better to achieve things with effort than effortlessly. That may be so in our case, but it would be anthropomorphism to assume to that God is like us in needing to "mix our labor" with things in order to appreciate them, use them wisely, and so on.

Any remaining objections to the No Planning Thesis would be based on its philosophical commitments, which I now investigate. The creator would have to be aware of all the universes there might be and would have to be aware of the goodness of those that were good.[9] And, of course, the creator must have the power to create. (I am not, however, supposing some distinction among the mental states of knowing, judging good, and deciding to create.) What I have posited is sufficient for the theocentric understanding even of such things as moral supremacy. For part of what God sees to be good is that when morally responsible animals such as ourselves evolve, we do so with moral convictions.

The power of unrestricted consciousness to bring universes into being follows from the account of physically free action I gave in Chapter 2, to which I refer readers. That power greatly exceeds ours for two reasons. The first is that with our more limited direct awareness of things, there are fewer things we can act upon. The second is that no one can bring about what is no longer possible, so we cannot act in ways that are contrary to the laws already brought into actuality by unrestricted consciousness.

The remaining philosophical commitments of the No Planning Thesis are (i) that unrestricted consciousness knows all there is, where that includes possibilities as well as what is actual; and (ii) that some of these possibilities are known to be good. For without the knowledge of possibilities and the knowledge of some of them as good, unrestricted consciousness would have no motive, in even the broadest sense, for creating some rather than other universes. It would be nothing more than a blind creative force, reminiscent of the Will in Schopenhauer's speculations. But such a blind creative force could

---

[9] I am not necessarily attributing to God *middle knowledge*, that is, knowledge of what would happen as a result of free decisions if a given universe were to be created. The knowledge of the possible universes does not have to be knowledge of them as determinate.

not enable us to understand the things for which I have provided a theocentric understanding.

There are, then, two significant philosophical commitments of the No Planning Thesis. One, which I call the Knowledge of Possibilities, is that unrestricted consciousness is aware of the possible physical universes in a way that does not depend on the actual existence of any of them. The other, which I call Evaluative Awareness, is that unrestricted consciousness is also aware of the value of these possible universes. In the next section I defend the first of these theses, leaving the defense of the other until the next chapter. My only reason for postponing that discussion is that I prefer not to assume, but rather to argue for, the objectivity of values. The objectivity of values is, however, something we might instead take as a basic belief that requires no argument. If so, then in some sense the possibilities of which God is aware are already good or bad prior to any creative act by God. In that case it is a genuine epistemic possibility that God, in knowing the possibilities, also knows their goodness and creates accordingly. Hence, if the speculations of the next chapter are rejected, all I forfeit is the ability to provide a theocentric understanding of things without assuming the objectivity of values. This weakens the case for theism, but only slightly.

14. Knowledge of the Possible

The remaining task for this chapter, then, is to defend the thesis that God knows the possibilities prior to any act of creation. Now the Theoretical Niche Argument leaves it quite open whether unrestricted consciousness should be interpreted narrowly as the conscious awareness of all that is actual or, more broadly, as the conscious awareness of everything without qualification. Granted that the physical possibilities would somehow be *there* to be known even if no actual physical universe had come into existence, there is no reason for denying that unrestricted consciousness would know the physical possibilities even had there been no actual physical universes. Hence the Knowledge of Possibilities is itself a genuine epistemic possibility. Putting the point in temporal terms, we can say that even before the (perhaps infinitely old) physical universes came into existence, unrestricted consciousness was aware of the ways they might be.

It remains, then, to defend the Priority Thesis for possibilities, namely that even without there being any actual physical universes, there would still have been possibilities.[10] In Chapter 2, I characterized the powers of any conscious

---

[10] Unlike Lewis, though, I am not suggesting that possibilities are *things*. For one alternative account, see Forrest 1986 and Bigelow 1988.

being in terms of what was still possible, where after an act less is possible than before. It follows that prior to any creative act the range of what is still possible coincides with the range of ways universes might be. Hence there does not have to be any actual physical universe for there to be the possibility of one or more physical universes. And that is all the Priority Thesis amounts to.

The chief rival to the Priority Thesis would seem to be actualism, the position that without an actual physical universe, there would be no ways such a universe might be.[11] One argument for actualism is based on the observation that we decide what is possible largely by combining elements of what is actual. This could be used to support the combinatorial theory, according to which the possible is determined by the ways the constituents of what is actual could be recombined (Armstrong 1989). For example, because the actual world contains blue parrots and brown bears, then, according to the combinatorial theory, there is the possibility of brown parrots and blue bears. This is an appealing account of possibility, but it is a version of actualism and so threatens the Priority Thesis. The threat is that if there is nothing that is yet actual, there cannot be the recombinations of the actual that constitute the possible. So it would not be the case that various universes would be possible independently of the existence of an actual one.

Let me grant, then, that, in one version or another, actualism has considerable intuitive appeal. In order to defend the Priority Thesis and hence the No Planning Thesis, I now argue that actualism can be modified so as remove all threat to the Priority Thesis, without losing its intuitive appeal. This modification is based on the traditional idea that although God creates only what is contingent, necessities depend in some other way on, and "reflect," the divine nature. Thus God does not choose which possibilities there are to be, but rather the range of possibilities is as it is because of what God is. That position is compatible with the Priority Thesis, but it retains the underlying intuition of actualists that all possibilities depend on something actual, in this case the divine nature. It is also the position I assumed when giving an account of the serendipity of mathematics in Chapter 4.

An alternative defense of the Priority Thesis is to exhibit its compatibility with actualism, by invoking the maximal indeterminacy speculation of Chap-

---

[11] Moderate actualists believe there are many possible ways a universe might be but only because there is at least one actual universe. Extreme actualists treat the merely possible as fictitious. The difference is not here important, although a highly heterodox theist who was a moderate actualist might say that God starts creating at random, having no knowledge of ways universes might be, but that any actual universe then generates all sorts of ways other universes might be, giving God the opportunity for a motivated creation.

ter 2. If prior to creation there was something physical, namely something indeterminate between all possible determinate universes, then the nature of the actual universe prior to creation would already, in a fashion, contain all possibilities. (We could, but do not have to, combine this defense with the previous one by thinking of the initial maximally indeterminate state of the physical universe as the divine body prior to creation, and think of creation as the self-determination of God in a manner reminiscent of process theology.)

Thus far in the discussion I have been assuming that actualism is being proposed on intuitive grounds, and I have, in various ways, defended the Priority Thesis from the threat of actualism. But perhaps actualism is being argued for rather than merely proposed as intuitively plausible. Now the only argument for actualism I know of is based on the Causal Razor. By that I mean the principle that there is a strong presumption against positing entities that do not affect either ourselves or that which we observe. The Causal Razor might well permit belief in electrons, because they affect us when we get electric shocks, but it would not permit belief in numbers, because they do not affect us. It could be deployed by actualists to argue against possibilities that exist independently of what is actual. I myself reject the Causal Razor on the grounds that all understanding, not just causal explanation, is the guide to truth, and that knowing what is possible helps us understand the actual (Forrest 1993a).

But I do not rely on anything as controversial as that. Instead I show that the Causal Razor does not threaten theocentric understanding. In passing, it is worth noting that the Causal Razor is a greater threat to evaluative understanding, for it is more plausible that God is literally a cause than that goodness is.

The Causal Razor is open to two interpretations. On the first it warrants belief only in the entities that affect us, and treats as mere speculation the theory of how those beliefs affect us. On the second it warrants the belief in the whole theory as to how we are affected causally. On the former interpretation it is indeed a threat to the Priority Thesis, if that is treated as anything more than mere speculation, but it does not threaten theism itself. For God would be in much the same position as the electrons. And all my speculations about how God creates would then be treated like the theory of how electrons affect us. But I never claimed to be doing anything more than speculating when discussing how it is that unrestricted consciousness has power to create. On the other interpretation of the Causal Razor the Priority Thesis would be warranted as part of the causal explanatory account, just as a theory of how electrons behave would be warranted. In neither case is there a genuine threat to theocentric understanding. I conclude that the threat of actualism is not a serious one and that we are entitled to rely on the Priority Thesis and hence on the No Planning Thesis as part of a speculation establishing the genuine epistemic possibility of God.

I have argued against reductive physicalism. And I have argued that not merely substance dualism but also attribute dualism and even nonreductive physicalism leave a theoretical niche for unrestricted consciousness, which I identify with God. I have also argued that, although God has no mental representations, God is aware of the ways universes might be even prior to creation. So God has the capacity to create out of an awareness of the goodness of what will be created. This establishes the genuine epistemic possibility of theism, provided we assume the objectivity of values, perhaps relying on the argument of the next chapter.

[7]
Speculating about Consciousness

In the previous chapter I presented the Theoretical Niche Argument for the genuine epistemic possibility of an unrestricted consciousness. That argument, based on the rejection of reductive physicalism, may be strengthened by means of a more detailed speculation about what we human beings are and hence about the divine nature.

1. A Double Aspect Theory

Double aspect theories tell us that the one item can have two "aspects"— the physical and the mental. The item in question could be the whole human being or, if we are concerned with details, some state or process of the mind/brain. If the "aspects" are considered distinct properties, this amounts to a version of attribute dualism, which I have already discussed. My version of the double aspect theory is, however, compatible with physicalism.[1] It differs, though, from the position of reductive physicalists in its emphasis on the way things in general, and brain processes in particular, *appear*.

I am proposing a functionalist double aspect theory. The brain processes appear as they do, not because of their intrinsic nature as patterns of spiking frequencies but because of the functional roles they perform. As I understand it, the functional role performed by a mental state is the tendency that state has to result in behavior or to affect other mental states (conscious or unconscious). It is widely assumed, although not essential to functionalism, that the

---

[1] Thus I have shifted from my position in 1993b.

mental states are the states of subsystems (the *homunculi* of homuncular functionalism) and the functional roles are the ways these subsystems tend to behave, affecting each other and the environment.

The functional role of a mental state is, therefore, an extrinsic or relational property of that state, to be contrasted with the intrinsic nature it has as a pattern of spiking frequencies. And, I submit, the way a mental state (identified with a brain process) appears is largely independent of its intrinsic nature and depends instead on the extrinsic property of performing a certain functional role. The introspectible character of a mental state is thus constrained by the way it forms part of a larger system, namely the total mental state in its context. (The context is a human being in a society, not an isolated individual, let alone an isolated brain.)

Later I generalize this double aspect theory and say that *everything* appears and that the way things appear is always constrained by the way they belong to larger systems. But for the moment I am concentrating on human mental states. And I ask, Is there more than one way in which a state playing a given functional role could appear? If so, I would have a further argument against the completeness of physicalist understanding, provided physicalists are committed to functionalism. My double aspect theory would not, however, be undermined—I am quite neutral on whether functional roles determine appearances or merely constrain them. For example, consider one of the more puzzling cases for functionalists. It could be said that the functional role of our awareness of colors is concerned only with our ability to discriminate between them. If that was so, then there could be someone with brain processes playing the same functional roles as mine but to whom red objects, such as ripe tomatoes, appear the way green objects, such as unripe tomatoes, appear to me. The functional roles of the states involved in color perception require that visual appearances differ in some way or other, without, it might be said, requiring that they have the character they do have. (See Bradley 1963.)

As I have said, that is a conclusion that need not bother me, for perhaps the functional roles do not fully constrain the way brain processes appear. Nonetheless I submit that discrimination is not all there is to color perception. The full functional role of color vision must include the connections of color with mood and with certain rather primitive aesthetic responses, such as a preference for green with splashes of red over red with splashes of green. Perhaps those differences between colors amount merely to what was common when a child. But that too can be incorporated into a functional characterization of colors. We may speculate, therefore, that a full functional characterization of the states involved in color vision will specify which state is seeing red and which is seeing green. Because that is just speculation, I am, however, quite neutral about which conclusion we should draw. Functional roles might or might not fully specify the way brain processes appear on introspection, but at least they constrain them.

2. A Solution to the Correlation Problem

How is it possible for the mental to interact with the physical? If that question is a rhetorical one intended to embarrass dualists, then we might well respond in a similarly rhetorical fashion: "But how is it possible for the physical to interact with the physical? Things just do affect each other." There is, however, the less "deep" but more serious *correlation* problem, noted by Smart (1963, p. 90): the interaction of the brain processes with mental states is too complicated to be treated as a fundamental psychophysical law of nature. Thus even an apparently simple mental state such as savoring the taste of a piece of fruit is correlated with highly complex patterns of spiking frequencies in the brain.

We have the problem, then, of finding some suitably simple principle governing the correlation of brain processes with the ways they appear. The first step toward a solution is to insist it is their functional roles that are directly correlated with the ways they appear. The brain processes that perform those roles are then indirectly correlated with the ways they appear on introspection, precisely by performing those roles. I describe this as a step toward a solution because I am convinced that the principles governing the correlation of introspectible appearances with functional roles are far less complicated than any that would directly correlate them with patterns of spiking frequencies. My conviction is due to the comparative ease of giving functional characterizations of the states we know by introspection. To be sure, I have rejected the claim that such functional characterizations by themselves enable us fully to understand that which we introspect. There remains something both wonderful and mysterious in the way things appear which cannot be understood just by understanding the functional roles. But partial understanding can be provided by finding a simple constraint on the correlation.

My proposed constraint is the Principle of Harmony, inspired by the Davidsonian Principle of Charity. I generalize it in Section 6, but in its ungeneralized form it says that the way a brain process appears on introspection must be *appropriate* to its functional role. The reason I call this the Principle of Harmony, not the Principle of Charity, is that I am not proposing it as a principle for interpreting the behavior of oneself and others. I am proposing it as a constraint on how things appear.

In order to illustrate the Principle of Harmony I begin by relying on the oversimplified characterization of the functional role of a mental state as its aptness to cause behavior of a certain kind. Consider, then, the contrast between an enthusiastic and a world-weary person. If we sought some direct correlation between the intrinsic character of the brain processes as patterns of spiking frequencies and the associated ways they appear, we would indeed have a difficult task. For the patterns of spiking frequencies are of immense complexity. However, the correlation between being in a state apt to cause enthusiastic behavior and what it is like to feel enthusiastic is remarkable only for its obviousness. "Of course," we think, "if you feel that way you will behave enthusiastically." More cautiously, I say enthusiastic behavior is inappropriate to feeling world-weary. The Principle of Harmony is, then, the modest claim that brain processes appear in ways appropriate to the functional roles they play.

Again, consider the hypothetical case in which something appears to you as severe pain but you are not in a state apt to cause screaming and so on. This is not the case in which, because you are paralyzed, you feel the tendency to scream out but nothing happens. I am considering the case in which there is not even a tendency. Nor is it the case of those given morphine for whom it (doxastically) seems they are in pain but there is none of the characteristically horrible way that severe pain appears. In the hypothetical case under consideration the way the pain appears would be inappropriate to its functional role. The Principle of Harmony tells us that this hypothetical case cannot occur.

The Principle of Harmony provides at least a partial understanding of the correlation between brain processes considered as patterns of spiking frequencies and the ways those processes appear. If there could be more than one appropriate way some process playing a given functional role could appear on introspection, then the constraint is incomplete and the understanding is indeed partial. In that case, as I have said, I have even more reason to reject reductive physicalism, but I would still claim that the Principle of Harmony constituted progress toward a solution to the correlation problem.

There are further principles that could be proposed to supplement the Principle of Harmony. One would be that if a given functional role is performed on two occasions by sufficiently similar underlying processes, then they should appear similar on introspection, even if the way they appear is not fully constrained by the Principle of Harmony. So even if the requirement of appropriateness to functional roles fails to determine the way colors appear, then we should expect colors to appear much the same to us and to monkeys, because we have similar brain processes.

It could be objected that familiarity results in an illusion of understanding and so the Principle of Harmony is worthless. On this view, a feeling of warmth would have been judged quite as appropriate to pain behavior as does the way pain appears, if a feeling of warmth had been regularly correlated with it instead. My reply to this objection is that there are many familiar phenomena that, instead of being judged appropriate just because they are familiar, cry out for explanation. For example, when students relax for the first time in weeks after working hard for their examinations, they often experience depression. This is surprising, because they so looked forward to the relaxation. It can, however, be understood in terms of a sudden drop in various hormones, but it is not understood just by being familiar.

A more serious objection is that there are prima facie exceptions to the Principle of Harmony, namely cases in which the ways brain processes appear to us are not appropriate to the behavior. In such cases we are often the embarrassed spectators of what we do. For example, an adolescent might tell a risqué story to a prudish relative without any conscious intention to offend. Such instances become more effective as prima facie counterexamples to the Principle of Harmony if we are prepared to grant that in some cases there are subconscious desires that really do explain the behavior. In such cases what would be appropriate to the behavior would be the way the subconscious states would appear. But, being subconscious, they do not appear any way at all.

These prima facie exceptions to the Principle of Harmony can be handled by abandoning the approximation in which the functional roles of mental states are characterized only in terms of the behavior they are apt to cause. Consider again the adolescent telling a risqué story to a prudish relative. The desire not to offend does not cause the behavior, but it does cause another mental state, namely embarrassment at what is being said. In a case such as this there is a lack of integration of the various mental states. For the desire not to offend has made no impact on the verbal behavior, perhaps because it is overruled by a subconscious desire. This can be understood in homuncular fashion, by saying that whenever the normal causal pathway from the mental state being considered to behavior is blocked, then the "behavior" the mental state is appropriate to is merely the behavior of some subsystem. And the tendency of a subsystem to behave in a certain way is the functional role of some mental state. Thus consideration of the functional roles rather than mere behavioral tendencies serves to defend the Principle of Harmony against the prima facie exceptions.

Even though the prima facie exceptions can be handled, there is one further objection to the Principle of Harmony which should be discussed. I am committed to the thesis that we are aware of the functional roles. Now the analysis of functional roles is a large part of cognitive science. Does not the absurdity follow that anyone can be an instant cognitive scientist? My reply is to rely on the (no doubt imprecise) distinction between appearances and seemings. Just as when we look at the scene around us there is a gap between what we see and what we can describe, so there is a gap between the introspective

awareness of how functional roles appear and our ability to describe them—
how they seem, in my terminology. We have a sense of the appropriateness
or inappropriateness of various descriptions to the appearances. Provided we
have the relevant concepts, we can begin to describe what we are aware of,
but there is no infallible method for arriving at these descriptions. And that
explains why we are not instant cognitive scientists. I believe, then, that by
introspection we are indeed aware of functional roles, but we are aware of
them as appearing a certain way and hence in a largely preconceptual fashion.

The position I have been describing is distinct both from reductive physicalism and from dualism. For I neither contrast appearance with reality nor
embrace realism about appearances. Appearance is nine-tenths of Reality, but
there are no such *things* as appearances.

At this point those with stronger dualist instincts than my own will be
bemused. How could a brain process appear anything like a pain? Part of my
reaction to such dualists is to say that a brain process must appear some way
if it is to be present to consciousness. How do they expect it to appear? Like
a moving picture of neurons with varying electric potential indicated by different colors? But what I would like to emphasize most in reply to such
bemused dualists is that it is the functional roles of the brain processes that
appear as they do, rather than the patterns of spiking frequencies.

My first step toward a solution of the correlation problem was to note that
there is less of a problem if we correlate the appearances with functional roles
than if we directly correlate them with patterns of spiking frequencies. The
second step was to propose the Principle of Harmony, namely that the appearances must be appropriate to the functional roles.

3. The Unity of the Mental

In the previous chapter I argued that the physicalist understanding of the
unity of the mental is incomplete. My aim in this section is to give an account
of that unity. Before I do so, however, I distinguish the *positive unity* of a
mind, namely its being a single mind rather than a mere collection of mental
states, from its *negative unity*, namely its distinctness from other minds.

It is immensely plausible, and amply confirmed by neuroscience, that the
brain processes of a human being interact in complex ways. Physicalists might
claim there is nothing more to the positive unity of the mental than this
sort of causal integration, and nothing more to the negative unity than the
lack of causal integration with other mental states. And if our belief in the
unity of the mental was merely inferred from our own behavior and that of
others, then the physicalist understanding of the unity of the mental as just a
matter of causal integration would be complete. I submit, however, that I am

aware of the positive unity of my mental states in a more direct fashion than that provided by inference from behavior. And it is this awareness of positive unity that lacks a physicalist understanding. The awareness of brain processes playing a certain functional role is an awareness of them as having a certain phenomenal character—pain, for instance. Likewise, the awareness of the integrated system of brain processes is an awareness of it as having a certain character, namely the positive unity of the mental.

There are three points of further clarification required here. The first is that although I claim to be aware of the positive unity of my mind, I do not claim to be aware of the distinctness of my mind from others. Indeed I am thoroughly suspicious of such resorts to negative phenomenology. The second point is that I am not assuming a Self to be aware of the causally integrated system of brain processes. Rather what we call the self is the unified system of mental states where the characteristic mental unity just is the way the causally integrated system appears.

My third point is that although I am providing a neo-Humean No Self theory, I reject the thesis that what we call the self is entirely a social construct. For neither the integrated character of my brain processes nor the unity that derives from the way this integrated system appears depends on the details of my interactions with others. I grant, however, that there is more to talk of the self than merely asserting its unity. The topic of adolescent anxiety and of midlife crises is a "self" that is indeed plausibly thought of as a social construct—although the society in question includes God, I say.

My speculation concerning the positive unity of the mental, then, is that, in the human case, it is just the way a causally integrated system of brain processes *appears*. This speculation about the unity of the mental should be contrasted with the Cartesian account in which the unity is explained by the existence of a single mental substance. My speculation has the advantage that on it there is a messy sort of unity, admitting of degrees. Either because the brain processes themselves are connected to differing degrees or because there is awareness of a greater or a lesser proportion of these connections, it happens that there are degrees of integration, which accords with our experience of ourselves and others. The unity of the mental is not an all-or-nothing affair.

On the proposed account of the unity of the mental there could be overlapping minds, provided the same physical items (brain processes) can participate in more than one integrated system of which there is awareness. In particular, there is nothing to exclude conscious homunculi, that is, subminds consisting of some of the states I am aware of together with others I am not. And again there is nothing, in principle, to prevent group minds made up of different persons and the relations between them. Indeed, if there are conscious homunculi, then they do form group minds, namely us.

The speculation that the unity of the mental is precisely an appearance, but not thereby unreal, is open to the objection that the self or mind whose unity we are considering must also be the one to whom there appears the unity. And that seems circular. This objection depends on the assumption that *appearing* is a relation between the self and that which appears. I have already rejected that assumption in giving a neo-Humean account. Appearing may be thought of intransitively. (See the next section for further discussion of this point.) In that case there is no circularity in treating a mind as nothing more than the way a suitably integrated system appears. Strictly speaking it is not that something appears to me; rather the way something appears is part of me. I hasten to add that if my reply is unsuccessful, then we would have reason to adopt a neo-Cartesian position, believing there is indeed a Self to whom things appear. In that case most of the discussion of this chapter becomes irrelevant, and I refer readers back to the previous one.

4. To What Category Does Consciousness Belong?

On the speculation I have been developing, brain processes have as one aspect their intrinsic character as patterns of spiking frequencies and as the other aspect the way their functional properties appear. If we could ignore the need to give an account of the fact of consciousness or of the way things appear, this double aspect theory would clearly amount to a form of physicalism. But what of consciousness itself? What kind of entity is it?

Perhaps the most natural speculation concerning the kind to which consciousness belongs is to say that it is a relation between something that is conscious and the thing that appears a certain way. We might take the thing that is conscious to be the brain of the person concerned, or some brain process or some system of brain processes. In that case consciousness might turn out to be a nonphysical relation between physical things. Alternatively, consciousness could be thought of as a relation between a nonphysical Self and the ground of appearances.

In neither case, however, does the thing that is conscious play any role in the speculation I have presented. If Hume was looking for this Self, I concur with his inability to find it. What I can find is the small "s" self, which is just a suitably unified system of mental states. Perhaps I could also discover something like the Freudian *ego*, but I would say that this ego is itself a subsystem of the total system of brain activity and is thus an object of consciousness rather than something that is conscious. I find no need, then, to posit a nonphysical Self as that which is conscious. Nor do we have much reason to treat consciousness as a relation between the total brain process and that which appears.

I had found it tempting to treat consciousness as a relation between the thing that is conscious and the object of consciousness. But the thing that is conscious (the Self) is redundant. Therefore it is a genuine epistemic possibility that the thing of which there is consciousness has a nonrelational property, which we could describe as the property of *there being consciousness of it*, or, less awkwardly, the property of *appearing*. Those descriptions of the property make it sound as if the property is in fact a relational one. Here we should, however, learn from Locke and distinguish the real essence (true nature) of something from its nominal essence (how we define it). For example, following Saul Kripke (1980), I take the nominal essence of gold to be that stuff which is of the same kind as the examples used to introduce the word "gold." Its real essence has been discovered by scientists to be that stuff consisting of atoms whose nuclei have seventy-nine protons. It is the rule rather than the exception for things initially to be characterized in a relational way and for their real essences to be discovered only later. And to reject the speculation that *appearing* is a nonrelational property just because we initially describe it in a relational way would be like thinking that the planet Venus can exist only if there are mornings or evenings on Earth because it was initially described as the Morning Star or the Evening Star.

It is a genuine epistemic possibility, then, that *there being consciousness of it* or, more briefly, *appearing* is a nonrelational property of the thing that appears, and in particular a property of the integrated system of brain processes, the awareness of which is the unity of the mental. In that way my double aspect theory would become a version of attribute dualism when we come to consider consciousness itself. There would be no such things as appearances, just the one nonphysical attribute of *appearing*.

What alternatives are there to positing a property of *appearing*? I have Ockhamist objections to treating consciousness as a fundamentally new category. And I would be prepared to do so only if that would help us understand consciousness, which it does not. Could we treat consciousness, then, as a property of a complex physical system comprising both the thing that is conscious and the thing that appears? That speculation is open to exactly the same charge of redundancy I raised against the relational account. There just is no need to put the Self in the picture at all.

Is there no alternative, then, to the position that *appearing* is a property of the thing that appears? A position worth considering is that we have no need to find a category for consciousness, because it is not an entity at all. Let us reflect on the project of ontology. An ontology consists of a list of the basic kinds of entity, such as substances, properties, and relations. We have to supplement it, though, with a discussion of the way the entities are, as it were, tied together. For instance, if we have an ontology of substances and properties, then it is a matter of some importance that properties *belong* to sub-stances but not vice versa. Thus the "tie" or "nexus" by which properties belong to substances can be used to characterize the substances as precisely the entities not capable of belonging to other entities in the way properties can belong to other entities. But what are these "ties"? To reify them as further entities belonging to some category, say that of relation, would require the "tie" to be itself tied to what it was intended to tie together, as in F. H. Bradley's regress (Bradley 1908, chap. 2). And the least of criticisms is that this is an extravagant speculation.

Are the ties, then, merely what we *say* of the entities in the categories? Surely not. The fact that a property belongs to a substance is as objective as the fact that the substance in question belongs to a certain kind. (Please do not read more into this claim of objectivity than I intend. The conceptual scheme whereby we think in terms of properties and substances need not itself correspond to some feature of a mind-independent reality. But if we take that scheme for granted, the fact that some property is "tied" to this rather than that substance is quite objective.)

When it comes to the "ties" that join properties to substances, even realists about properties should accept the position that there are some predicates that do not correspond to entities but whose application is nonetheless objective. We could call this a *moderate nominalist* attitude toward these predicates. Com-pare W. V. O. Quine, who adopts a moderate nominalist attitude toward enough predicates to avoid positing any properties or relations as basic enti-ties—basic as opposed, in his case, to set-theoretic constructs (1953a, 1953c, 1987). If we adopt such a moderate nominalist attitude toward the ties, we might extend it to other rather special predicates, including "appearing." So it would seem quite appropriate to refuse to treat consciousness as an entity but nonetheless insist that there are objective truths about what appears. In this way the superficially atheistic assertion that there is no such entity as God would be considered true, although misleading, by those theists who identified God with the consciousness of all things. Such nonobjectual but objective theism would be compatible not merely with physicalism as I have charac-terized it but with the stronger physicalist thesis that every fundamental cat-egory of entity is a physical category.

To sum up my speculations concerning the category to which consciousness belongs: on Ockhamist grounds I am reluctant to treat consciousness as a totally novel kind of entity; we could, instead, posit the property of (intran-sitive) *appearing*; or, impressed by the special character of consciousness, we could adopt the moderate nominalist strategy of saying there is no property of *appearing* even though there are objective truths about what appears.

5. Of What Is There Consciousness?

I now ask, Of what is there consciousness? Or, equivalently, What appears?
Thus far I have assumed only that there is consciousness of some brain processes, which appear in ways appropriate to their functional roles. So one answer to my question might be that there is consciousness of anything that
plays a functional role in a brain or something like a brain. But that answer
exhibits an arbitrary and anthropocentric limitation. How "queer" it would
be if consciousness was restricted to brains. It would be like insisting that only
the observable part of the universe is made of familiar matter but that the
parts too far away to be observed have a quite different constitution. We
might perhaps be driven to such hypotheses, but there is surely a presumption
in favor of uniformity. Likewise, there is a presumption in favor of the thesis
that all things without exception appear.

A certain sort of empiricist—Mackie perhaps—would have said that because the familiar examples of conscious beings have brains, we have no right
to believe in consciousness that is not dependent on brains or brain analogs.
This objection would be appropriate if our discussion of consciousness was
more like geology or botany than physics. If we discover that many oceanic
islands are of volcanic origin, we might extrapolate and hypothesize that most
of them are, but it would be rash indeed to suggest that islands on the con-
tinental shelf are of volcanic origin. Moreover, geologists would be unim-
pressed by the claim that it was ad hoc not to generalize in this way. By
contrast, extrapolation is second nature to physicists. The difference is that
geology and botany are concerned with local details of great interest, but not
the nature of things, which is the topic of physics—and metaphysics. When
I am speculating about consciousness I am not concerned with the details of
the brains of certain mammals on planet Earth; I am concerned with a fundamental fact about the universe, that there is consciousness. For that reason
it is eminently appropriate to speculate that all things without exception appear.

My double aspect theory leads, then, to the position that, although there
are several things that cannot be *understood* in physicalist terms, the only omission from the physical *description* of reality is the fact of consciousness. In this
way it raises the question, Of what is there consciousness? I appeal to readers
to grant that the most satisfactory answer is to allow that there are no limits
to that of which there is consciousness.

It should now be fairly clear how I intend to complete the Theoretical
Niche Argument. Human beings are living organisms that generate complex
brain processes of which there is consciousness—it is that which gives us

minds distinct from one another and with the positive unity we experience. But there is consciousness of all things, and as I argued in the previous chapter this unrestricted consciousness can perform the role of God in theocentric understanding. So my double aspect theory, though strictly compatible with physicalism, establishes a theoretical niche for a God who is identified with unrestricted consciousness.

I am proposing, then, that there is consciousness of all things. If we think of *appearing* as a property, then it would be a property all things have. Provided we distinguish properties from concepts, so that the one property can correspond to two concepts, we could then identify this property with *being*. To those to whom the idea of *being* as a property is repugnant precisely because it would belong to everything, I would suggest that *appearing* is problematic as a property in exactly the same way. That would be a further reason for denying that consciousness is an entity while granting the fact that there is consciousness of all things.

If I had posited a Self as that to which things appear, then there could be many different Selves to which things appear differently. But I saw no need to posit any such Selves. It follows that different minds must be distinguished in some way other than by their identification with different Selves. That might seem perplexing, but I have already given an account of the unity of the mental which requires no Self. The differentiation of one mind from another is a corollary of this account. Because a mind is the conscious awareness of a whole formed out of a suitably integrated system, there is a different mind for every integrated system. In particular, our minds are distinct from the divine mind just because our minds are integrated subsystems of the totality of things. But this distinction is the difference of the part from the whole, not the difference between two nonoverlapping things. That is because our minds are parts of the content of the divine mind. The divine awareness of the things you and I are aware of is numerically, not just qualitatively, identical to your or my awareness. So I arrive at a version of panentheism in which God literally shares our joys and sorrows. The divine mind, which is the conscious awareness of all there is, thus includes our minds, which are the conscious awareness of certain causally integrated subsystems of all there is, namely the systems of interconnected functional roles that depend on incredibly complicated patterns of brain activity.

One obvious objection to my proposal is that there will be minds all over the place. For there is consciousness of all things, and so whenever there is a suitably integrated system, there will be consciousness of that system as a unity, and such a consciousness is just what I have been saying a mind is. In reply to this objection I note that if this is a difficulty with my double aspect theory, it is just as much a difficulty with physicalism. For all I am doing is saying there is a unified mind whenever there is consciousness of the sort of system physicalists claim is already a unified mind. If there is a genuine difficulty here, that is a reason for preferring a more overtly dualist account, in which case I refer readers back to the previous chapter. Even though I do not know what sort of integration is required for there to be a unified mind, I do not, however, think there is a difficulty here. A certain degree of complexity in the subsystem would seem to be required for there to be a mind distinct from other minds. For that reason individual minds are a rare phenomenon, requiring that the universe be suited to life.

I have provided two distinct speculations about consciousness. One is that it is not an entity and so belongs to no category. The other is that it is a property of whatever there is consciousness of. On the latter speculation we have a position that could be mistaken for panpsychism. The difference is that I am suggesting not that all things have the property of being conscious but rather that all things have the property of there being consciousness of them.

6. Generalizing the Principle of Harmony

My refusal to limit consciousness arbitrarily to brains or similar complex systems requires me to generalize the Principle of Harmony so that it is not restricted to functional roles. I first note that the functional role of a state is merely the way it is incorporated into a larger system. Thus the functional roles performed by our brain processes are just the ways these processes form part of a larger system, which is, roughly speaking, an individual human being. (I say "roughly speaking" because I am, for simplicity, ignoring the social dimension.) I suggest that the Principle of Harmony should be interpreted as the principle that the way a state of a system appears must be appropriate to the way the whole system appears. For example, the way pain appears is appropriate to the way I *appear* (to myself and others) as a pain-avoiding organism. This is a minor modification of the earlier account I gave, according to which the way pain appears is appropriate to my *being* a pain-avoiding organism. I make the modification in order to arrive at the Generalized Principle of Harmony:

> All things appear and the way the parts appear must be appropriate to the way the whole appears.

But what is this appropriateness? Never loath to speculate, I propose that we extend the logical vocabulary of consistency and entailment so as to cover the

way things appear. It is not just that being a square is logically inconsistent
with being a circle.[2] There is something about the way a circle appears and
the way a square appears which provides the (perhaps fallible) basis for the
judgment that there cannot be a square circle. Let us say, then, that the way
a square appears is *phenomenally inconsistent* with the way a circle appears.

Now consider a simplified version of the functional role of hunger, namely
that being hungry is the relational property H of tending to cause eating. So
H has the form, standing in relation C to an E. There are, of course, far more
complicated examples we could discuss, but this serves as an illustration. And
let us suppose I am consciously aware of a brain process as having the relational
property H as well as being aware of something standing in the relation C
and being aware of something as having the property E. Then there are three
items I am consciously aware of, but they are not three independent items.
For the occurrence of the relational property H requires for consistency the
occurrence of the relation C and the property E. It would be surprising if, in
spite of this dependence, the way these three items appear were independent.
Instead, I suggest, the ways the components C and E appear put constraints
on the way H, namely standing in relation C to E, has to appear. Violating
these constraints would be a matter of phenomenal inconsistency.

I speculate, therefore, that if complex structures appear a certain way along
with their components, then the way the complex structure appears is constrained by the requirement of phenomenal consistency. For the structure to
appear other than it does while its components appear as they do is as absurd
as for something to appear as both a square and a circle. This is the required
generalization of the Principle of Harmony. It applies to functional roles because the functional role performed by a state is precisely the way the state is
incorporated into a larger system. The principle is not, however, restricted to
mental states. Everything appears, so the principle applies to everything.

7. Theistic Eudemonism

I have yet to provide a theocentric understanding of the good, namely what
is valuable not just as a means but as an end in itself. This is of independent
interest but is also required to complete the discussion of the previous chapter.

To understand the objectivity of the good I begin by expounding a version
of eudemonism. There is a state of well-being that we might call happiness
but that I prefer to call joy. The best example is not perhaps anything ecstatic
but the state of joie de vivre when we think to ourselves, "How good it is

---

[2] More accurately, the following form an inconsistent triad: (i) region V is either exactly or
approximately Euclidean; (ii) B is a square in region V; and (iii) B is a circle in region V.

to be alive!" My initial suggestion is that the end that is objectively worth-while is something like joy. I say "something like joy" because this state could well be rather richer than the word "joy" and the example of joie de vivre suggest. It includes the state in which you know, understand, and love, and in which you enjoy knowing, understanding, and loving. Our normal ways of conceptualizing our own mental states result in a division between the intellectual states of knowing and understanding on the one hand and the affective state of loving on the other. The sort of joy I have in mind is not, however, divided in this way. Fortunately my suggestions as to quite what this state of joy amounts to are not crucial to my discussion of the objectivity of values. My initial eudemonist proposal, then, is that the good can be iden-tified with joy. Similarly evil can be identified with suffering.

Like any eudemonistic theory, this has the advantage of making it rather obvious that what I have identified with the good is to be pursued and what I have identified with evil is to be avoided. But philosophers being what they are, there may be some who will say it is still quite subjective to prefer joy to suffering. To say it is subjective would, in this case, amount to saying that different people judge differently on the matter. Masochism might here be produced as an example of such a preference. I have three things to say about this. The first is that masochists in the strict sense derive sexual pleasure from pain, so they get joy out of it which balances the suffering. Second, there may well be those (masochists in a less strict sense) who inflict pain on them-selves without any apparent compensation and not even as a means to some, perhaps illusory, end. Such "masochists," unlike the genuine ones, need not be interpreted as desiring pain but merely as being caused by irrational forces to do what they would prefer not to do. I fail to see how they threaten the objectivity of the goodness of joy. Finally, I grant that there is no self-contradiction in supposing there might be a person who preferred suffering to joy and whose preference was not the result of causal processes interfering with freedom. But the mere lack of self-contradiction in a contrary judgment to mine does not show that different people judge differently.

Eudemonists have, then, a position that is objectivist in the sense that there is no subjectivity in pursuing joy and avoiding suffering. But typically eude-monism is threatened with a different sort of subjectivity, namely the apparent variations in what results in joy. Here theism can supply an objectivist account by saying that the things which are good as ends are those which are good as judged by God, that is, which give God joy.

Why, then, did I not provide this theocentric understanding of objective values in Chapter 4? My reason was that there is a residual problem with theistic eudemonism. It is plausible as an account of what is good only if we assume that our natures are such that we shall in fact find joy in only the things that give God joy. (So our varying preferences are often based on ignorance: we do not know what will give us joy.) Otherwise awareness of the same thing might give me sorrow and you joy, without either of us being in error, in which case it could be objectively good only in the sense that God happens to share your taste. I believe, indeed, that there is value in diversity, so we might have expected God to create different kinds of person who enjoy different things, thus undermining the objectivity of values. I am now in a position to solve this residual problem and so provide a theistic account of the objectivity of values.

I ask, then, What sort of thing is joy? On the account I have given it should be considered not a thing at all but a way things appear, although none the less real for being a way things appear. More significant, the joy you feel is not something that only you feel. The numerically identical joy is also part of the divine mind, here identified with unrestricted consciousness. I propose therefore that what is good is just anything the consciousness of which is joyful. Because there is no multiplicity of consciousnesses (but only a multiplicity of minds), there is no difficulty in accounting for the agreement between what gives us joy and what gives God joy.[3]

Here it might be objected that different things can give different people joy. And so they can. But *that* is no threat to the objectivity of values, provided what they are directly aware of differs. And because, I am claiming, there is no multiplicity of consciousnesses, it follows that this proviso is satisfied.

Obviously we could be mistaken about the effective means of achieving a good end. Perhaps it is not so obvious that, on the account being proposed, we could be mistaken even about the value of the ends we seek. Such mistakes can arise in one of two ways. The first is that in which we misarticulate our experience. I might think my consciousness is joyful when it is sorrowful or vice versa. This is, no doubt, uncommon when it comes to intense joy and sorrow. But it is easy enough for people to enjoy a gentle melancholy, the enjoyment of which would be spoilt by recognition. The second way of being mistaken about what is good is that in which the thing whose value I am judging is not something I am myself conscious of. That is, the consciousness of it is not part of my mind. So it could be good in that there is joyful consciousness of it even though I judge it not to be good, because I mistakenly infer that there is no joyful consciousness of it, from the true premiss that there is no joyful consciousness of it that is part of my mind. In spite of the possibility of these mistakes, it is not surprising that we are able to judge goodness. We do not need a special faculty to intuit transcendent values, but merely a fairly reliable capacity to introspect joy.

---

[3] I am indebted to R. J. Kearney for the suggestion that the objectivity of values ultimately rests on some sort of monistic identification of all of us.

It could be objected that joy can arise in ways that are manifestly not such as would be shared by a good God. There can be genuine joy, for instance, in murder. Yet how could God do other than sorrow at such evil? I say that which is in itself evil about the situation, the pain and death of the victim and the malice of the murderer, is indeed sorrowful to any who are consciously aware of it, but that the exhilaration, if that is what the murderer feels, is good and hence on my account a joy for God. The balance, presumably, is sorrow for God. Moreover, when I say evil is sorrowful for any who are aware of it, I do not mean that it causes sorrow in any who happen to know of it. I am here concerned with direct conscious awareness, not an indirect or discursive knowledge.

In Chapter 2 I discussed God's power to create, using a general account of action that applied to both the human and the divine case. I am now able to comment further on this. There were two requirements on actions. The first was that the state of affairs brought about must be still possible. The second was that the agent must be directly aware of something as satisfying, or tending to satisfy, the motive for acting. God's motive for acting is presumably the recognition of the value of the state that is to be brought about. For the sake of definiteness let us concentrate on what I take to be the chief purpose of creation, namely God's wanting to share the divine joy with others. God's consciousness of the joy to be had by others is itself potential grounds of joyful consciousness and as such is good. God's recognition of this goodness is the motive for creating, and this motive is satisfied if the sharing of divine joy comes about. What this amounts to is that the consciousness of the possibility of sharing joy results in the creation of a situation in which that joy is shared. In this way the account of creation in terms of a motive for creating converges with the other account I gave, according to which the divine joy overflows without any need for explicit motives. For in the case of God the motive amounts only to the recognition of what is good in itself, and that recognition just is joyful consciousness of the possibility of the spread of joyful consciousness.

But whence comes the joy God shares? My answer here is not based on some further speculation about appearances. I offer no way of understanding the divine joy. Rather I submit that our own experience of ourselves shows that, in the absence of pain and sorrow, consciousness is joyful—it is good to be alive. And the joyful character of consciousness is corroborated by a certain kind of mystical experience, from which is derived, I take it, the characterization of Brahman as *ananda* (bliss) as well as *sat* (being) and *cit* (consciousness).[4]

---

[4] Brahman thus characterized should be distinguished from Nirguna Brahman, by which is meant ultimate reality devoid of all attributes.

8. But Is Unrestricted Consciousness the Same as God?

I have argued that unrestricted consciousness can play the role of God in theocentric understanding. That is because at a stage at which every kind of universe is still possible we can understand the coming into existence of some but not others as the result of the awareness of some but not others as good. Now I have argued for the superiority of a personal over an impersonal deity as a way of understanding. I need, therefore, to return to the question of whether unrestricted consciousness is a personal deity—whether Brahman characterized as *sat-cit-ananda* is the same as the God of theism.

There are, in fact, two questions here, one to do with understanding, the other to do with emotional attitudes. Concerning our understanding of things, it suffices to say that every recourse I made to a personal God requires nothing more than unrestricted consciousness, provided that, even prior to creation, there is awareness of possible universes and of their value. In addition I have assumed that the value of the whole depends on that of the parts in such a way that the recognition of value will result in not a utilitarian creation but one that exhibits concern for the well-being of individuals. As regards the understanding of things provided by anthropic theism, it is of no further consequence whether we take unrestricted consciousness to be a personal God. In particular, it is of no further consequence whether God has anything like the human emotions involved in care and concern. Nonetheless *our* emotional attitudes of awe, gratitude, and devotion, and in some circumstances, fear, would seem essential for most theistic religions. It is important, then, to decide whether unrestricted consciousness is the proper object of such attitudes. And even if I were to restrict myself to purely intellectual aims, the question of the proper attitude toward unrestricted consciousness is relevant to the defense of theism against the threat of agnosticism. For I do not think the case I have presented for theism is strong enough to defend theism against that threat in an emotionally neutral context. (See the Concluding Remarks.)

I ask, then, whether a God who is identified with unrestricted consciousness is the proper object of such religious attitudes as awe, gratitude, and devotion. And I begin by granting that, quite obviously, there are ways in which unrestricted consciousness is unlike you and me. First, God, as unrestricted consciousness, is aware of all things and has power over all things. Those are traditional divine attributes and add to a sense of awe without lessening the personal character of the deity. Next, prior to creation, the divine mind, unlike our minds, lacks the sort of structure that derives from our brains. As a result, we may speculate that God neither has nor needs thoughts and memories. God is just aware of all. That should prevent too anthropomorphic a conception of God.

Another respect in which unrestricted consciousness is unlike us is the lack of the precise sort of unity our minds have. Our mental unity is a matter of causal integration of states together with a separation from other minds. And that depends very much on there being highly complex systems of brain processes. The divine awareness of all things might have a unity of its own, especially if unrestricted consciousness is considered one of the "things" of which it is itself aware. But it lacks our sort of unity.[5]

Without further discussion the considerations above might seem to undermine devotion. I have, however, two reasons in favor of the propriety of devotion to this God who is unrestricted consciousness. The first is that God quite literally shares our joys and our sorrows, rather than merely knowing of them. For all our mental states are parts of the divine consciousness. This provides ample motivation for religious emotions and the consequent devotion, even without belief in divine incarnation. The second is that, however much I have avoided anthropomorphism, I have insisted that God is like the ways in which we humans are not purely physical. This results in a more personal conception of God than, for instance, the neo-Pythagorean deity of Leslie's extreme axiarchism. The contrast is that, on my speculation, God creates out of awareness of what is good, whereas on Leslie's account goodness itself brings about the existence of what is good without any awareness.

In conclusion, then, I submit that, even without reliance on revealed religion, God is worthy of both awe and loving devotion. Nonetheless—excepting divine incarnation—it is as anthropomorphic to think of God as having something like a human mind, with its capacity to represent the world, as to think of God as having something like a human body.

A rather different problem with the identification of unrestricted consciousness with God is that, following the speculations of this chapter, consciousness either is not an entity at all or, it might seem, is a property. So, if God is unrestricted consciousness, then God is not an entity, which is peculiar enough, or, it seems, God is a property, which is absurd. The solution to this problem is to exercise some care. Strict theists (as opposed to verisimilitudinarians) are committed to the objective fact that there is a God. And this, it is being speculated, is the fact that there is consciousness of everything. If consciousness were an entity, then we could identify God with unrestricted consciousness, and, for ease of exposition, I have tended to talk that way. But I am not treating consciousness as an entity even if I am supposing there is a property things have when there is consciousness of them. Hence on either of my speculations about consciousness we have an objective but nonobjectual

[5] If God did have a human-type mental unity, I suspect there could not be a Trinity of divine persons.

theism. A corollary is that the fact of there being a God does not have the structure or "logical form" that it might seem to have, namely the instantiation of the property of divinity.

To what, then, are we devoted if there is no entity that is God? The answer is that devotion to God, like the fact that there is a God, need not have the "logical form" it seems to. Being devoted to God is not standing in a *relation* with God in the strict sense. That does not keep it from being a *relationship* with God in something like the popular sense. And the reason this can be so is that, I would suggest, the content of an emotion is often a proposition, not an object. For instance, the fear of death is the fear containing the thought expressed by saying, "I may shortly be dead." It is not the standing in some direct relation with a thing called "death."

9. The Point-of-View Problem

I now consider one last objection to my identification of God with unrestricted consciousness, namely the point-of-view problem. If God is unrestricted consciousness, things appear to God. From what point of view, place of touch, and so on do things appear to God? It is surely naive to think of God as seeing, feeling and hearing everything from up above, but what is the alternative?

My answer to this question is based on the assumption that the point of view, place of touch, and so on is part of the appearance, not a location from which the appearance is somehow perceived. For example, in out-of-body experiences it seems to people that they see things from above. We might be tempted to interpret the experience by saying that the Self to whom things appear is now located outside the body. Clearly that is contrary to the speculations of this chapter. I therefore assume an alternative interpretation, which in any case I find more plausible. Out-of-body experiences involve a systematic illusion in which the appearances are distorted in that things are as if seen from above. Thus the point of view, place of touch, and so on is part of the appearance, not a location from which appearances are viewed.

Containing a point of view is characteristic of visual appearances, at least in the human case. It could, however, appear (auditorily) to someone that space is full of music without any spatial variation. I conclude, therefore, that some appearances contain a point of perception but others do not. Because everything appears to God, we may say that things appear to God from all points of view, insofar as the point of view is part of the appearance. But we may also say that much of what appears to God has no point of view at all.

No doubt it is puzzling how God could have visual appearances from all points of view. I submit, however, that the fact that a human being has a single point of view is an evolutionary accident, related to having only two eyes and using these for binocular vision. The aliens who inhabit other planets—or just B-grade movies—can have six eyes at the ends of ten foot stalks and so have multiple points of view just as easily as we have multiple places of touch.

That God sees from all points of view, feels from all places of touch, and so on might seem to threaten the unity of the divine mind. According to pantheism, God is all over the place and so the various parts of God cannot communicate if they are moving apart faster than the speed of light. My panentheistic speculation seems to be threatened with a similar problem in that the divine mind, by incorporating all points of view, is, in a different way, all over the place. How can such a mind be unified and so truly a mind? The answer lies in those appearances that do not contain a point of view. God does have a nonspatial atemporal "view," but in addition to, not instead of, the multiplicity of spatio-temporal points of view. Because God has more than a multiplicity of points of view, the unity of the divine mind is not threatened.

Thus God transcends space and time in that things appear to God in ways that require no point of view, but God is also immanent in space and time in that the divine mind contains all points of view. This parallels the way God transcends individual minds in that much of the divine consciousness is not part of any other mind, although God is immanent in individual minds because all our mental states are parts of the divine mind.

I am now in a position to offer a summary of the speculations of this and the previous chapter. I began by pointing out various gaps in the physicalist understanding of human beings, gaps that could be filled by acknowledging the mysterious fact that there is consciousness. I insisted, however, that consciousness need be neither reified as a thing among other things nor treated as a contingent fact. So my emphasis on consciousness is quite compatible with nonreductive physicalism.

Initially it might seem fairly obvious that consciousness must be associated with a brain or similarly complex structure, but I pointed out how arbitrary it would be to insist that the fundamental description of the way things are should make a distinction between different types of material object. I speculated, therefore, that there is consciousness of all things and that part of the importance of having brains is that the consciousness of a suitably integrated system provides the sort of unity we know ourselves to have. Consciousness is thus individuated by its objects, which in our cases are physical systems centered on our brains.

The thesis that consciousness is not arbitrarily restricted to an awareness of just some physical systems leaves a theoretical niche for God as unrestricted consciousness—the consciousness of all things. Although I use the phrase "unrestricted consciousness" to refer to consciousness itself, I hope it is clear that we humans do not have any separate, restricted consciousnesses; our consciousness is just the consciousness of various physical systems. So unrestricted consciousness just is consciousness, and our minds are parts of God.

In this way we have a further argument for the conclusion that there is a God, namely that the attempt to understand our own natures suggests that there should be an unrestricted consciousness, which may be identified with God. That is, of course, a rather weak argument, because of the speculative character of that attempt at understanding. But my chief purpose in this chapter has been to supplement the argument of the previous one, the conclusion of which was that God is a genuine epistemic possibility. And for that purpose even a rather speculative argument suffices.

The speculations of this chapter are also relevant to our understanding of the divine motive for creating a physical universe. I assume that God creates primarily to share the divine joy and that this goal is achieved by creating minds that are not God. On my speculation every mind is part of God. Something is required, therefore, to separate the mind thus created from God. One, though perhaps not the only, way to achieve this goal is to ensure that there are suitably complex physical systems, the consciousness of which results in minds that are not God, even though they depend on God and are indeed parts of God.

A Speculative
Understanding of Evil

Belief in God enables us to understand much, and it is a genuine epistemic possibility even before we take note of all it enables us to understand. My case against atheism follows provided there is no unanswered objection to theism. But, of course, there is a serious and well-known objection, the argument from evil. It is to this I now turn.

The argument from evil is based on the puzzlement—to put it with offensive mildness—that a God who creates for the sake of the well-being of creatures permits or even causes various evils, notably suffering and malice. Even if we are convinced that some such evils are necessary for a greater good, there remains the puzzlement as to why God creates a universe containing our own planet, which has *so much* evil. Swinburne, for instance, argues persuasively that there is need of "a substantial amount of various kinds of evil in order to provide the opportunity for greater goods, and in particular a choice of destiny" (1979, pp. 218–19), but he goes on to confess "considerable initial sympathy" for the claim that there is just too much evil.

I am not going to attempt an actual understanding of all the appalling evil around us in just one chapter. Rather my aim is to provide a speculative understanding of evil. That is, I answer the question, How *could* a good God allow suffering and moral evil? not the question, Why in fact *does* God allow suffering and moral evil? The force of the word "could" in the question, How could a good God allow evil? is not merely a matter of establishing the logical consistency of various evils with the existence of a good God. Such consistency has, I take it, been established by Nelson Pike (1963) and Plantinga (e.g., 1974, chap. 9). Rather what I need for my apologetic purpose is something stronger, namely a way of establishing the genuine epistemic possibility that a good God would allow the evils that disfigure this otherwise surpassingly beautiful world of ours.

1. Should We Seek to Understand Evil?

Should we seek to understand evil? Would it not be less arrogant to say we should not expect to understand God's purpose in creating and hence should not expect to understand evil? Indeed there is a cautionary tale on the topic of theodicy. When discussing evil I have heard quoted the anecdote about Alfonso X of Castile, who said he could have given God some good advice about creation. The intended point of the quotation was that even a mere human being could have done better than produce this universe with its evils. But, according to the anecdote, Alfonso X made that remark not about any of the evils that puzzle us but about the epicycles used by the astronomers of those days: why did God not decree that the planets move in perfect circles? We can now laugh at this, and no one these days would raise the aesthetic defects of the universe as an argument against theism, because such "defects" as the noncircular motion of the planets are now seen to be superficial and derived from underlying principles of great elegance. The moral for the project of theodicy is that our current understanding of evil could be as primitive as our understanding of astronomy was in the thirteenth century.

I accept that moral: considerations of our own ignorance might absolve us from any requirement to provide the true explanation of suffering and moral evil. It does not, however, absolve us from the requirement to provide a speculative understanding of evil. Why not? Consider the recent debate between William Rowe and Stephen Wykstra. Rowe has argued on several occasions that probably there exist evils that God could have prevented and had they been prevented the world as a whole would have been better. And, he goes on to say, God would prevent such evils. So probably there is no God (Rowe 1986). Several philosophers, including Wykstra,[1] have suggested that Rowe's first premiss amounts to an appeal to ignorance: we just do not know of any good for the sake of which God would permit the suffering of animals or other apparently pointless evils. Wykstra makes the further comment that we would expect God to be able to grasp goods "beyond our ken" and hence expect that many of the evils permitted by God for the sake of a greater good would seem pointless.

[1] In an unpublished paper cited by Rowe (1986, p. 236n), "Difficulties for Rowe's Case for Atheism." See also Wykstra 1984.

If I totally agreed with Wykstra, then I would grant that even a speculative understanding of evil was unnecessary. But that would be to ignore Rowe's dilemma, as I call his response to Wykstra and others. The dilemma is that theism should be interpreted as either *restricted* theism (i.e., theism without any other religious claims) or *expanded* theism (i.e., theism supplemented by other religious claims). Rowe is prepared to grant that expanded theism might indeed imply Wykstra's claim that God can grasp goods beyond our ken. But he notes that there is a cost to expanding theism, namely that the more detailed a hypothesis, the less probable it is.[2]

Now I grant that according to the calculus of probabilities, adjoining any hypotheses to theism will indeed reduce its probability. But calculations with probabilities are based on the idealization that we can survey all hypotheses. And I interpret Wykstra's response as based on our inability to survey the hypotheses about the possible goods for the sake of which God creates, rather than itself being the hypothesis that God knows of goods "beyond our ken." Rather than try to settle the issue by appealing to the calculus of probabilities, we require some guidance as to how we should reason in situations of radical ignorance, where we cannot even begin to survey the hypotheses. My story about Alfonso X was intended to persuade that we might indeed be in such a situation of radical ignorance.

How, then, are we to reason in a situation of radical ignorance where the calculus of probabilities fails us? I have already discussed this in Chapter 1, where I made a case for the use of speculation to reply to objections. The speculation acts as a representative of many replies we do not know of. Without even such a speculation we would lack grounds for believing there are any replies to be had, were we able to survey the hypotheses.

I provide two speculations, both of which cohere with the scientific theism developed in this work. One is a somewhat Leibnizian plenitude theodicy; the other is a panentheistic variant on John Hick's Eirenean, or "soul-making," theodicy. That is not to say that I reject other theodicies. The more speculations the better. I should also add that, like faith itself, our response to evil has a strong emotional component. My discussion is of the intellectual component by itself and is in that way unsatisfactory. Let me emphasize, therefore, that my purpose is a limited one, namely to provide a speculative understanding that removes an intellectual obstacle to theism. The emotional component is best handled, I believe, in the context of the Christian doctrine of Redemption.

[2] Swinburne shares Rowe's sensitivity to the calculus of probabilities and is reluctant to appeal to an afterlife in order to explain why God permits so much evil, because this is to add to the theistic hypothesis. See Swinburne 1979, pp. 221–22.

2. Plenitude Theodicy

My first speculation, then, is a version of plenitude theodicy, which I now introduce. This is based on the speculation that God can create, and probably has created, universes of many different types. Initially this speculation might be rejected using the principle that we should seek elegant or simple hypotheses in science. Now that principle might in turn seem to be refuted by the sheer complexity of the mathematics used by physicists and by the astounding amount of detail to be found in chemistry and biology. But what is being enjoined is simplicity of the hypotheses used to explain this mass of detail, not some simplification of the description of these details. Likewise, reliance on best-explanation apologetics requires that God be thought of as lacking the sort of complex structure our brain-based minds have. Such fundamental simplicity is quite compatible, though, with the speculation that God creates universes of many types, rather than creating only the best.

The Neoplatonist version of plenitude, which influenced both Augustine and Aquinas, seems to imply that every possible type of situation would be created, which would no doubt explain why there is suffering and wrong-doing, since these are possibilities.[3] But that is inconsistent with the belief that God creates out of an awareness of the goodness of various possibilities, rather than out of self-love. Moreover, it is open to the same objections as I raised to metaphysical plenitude in its unrestricted form. Instead, then, of claiming that every possible type of situation is created, I rely on a much weaker and quite negative assumption of plenitude, namely that God is not restricted to creating just one type of universe. God could create, and for all I know has created, universes of many types. (See McHarry 1978; Forrest 1981.)

This provides a reply to those who object that God would surely have created a universe of a better type instead of this one, even if this one would be worth creating were it the only type of universe there could be. I later discuss a refined version of that objection as the *minor adjustment argument*, but here I consider the unrefined version. The failure is important because the complaint that God should have created a better universe is likely to occur in any discussion of the argument from evil.

Here is an analogy. Suppose I was puzzled at the fact that wealthy friends who enjoyed surfing had a holiday home in the mountains. Why not have one by the sea? My puzzlement would disappear if I was told they had holiday homes in both locations. Likewise, it is as easy for God to make any number of universes as to make just one. Apart, then, from the minor adjustment

[3] See Hick 1968, chap. 4, for a critical discussion of Neoplatonist plenitude.

argument, comparisons are irrelevant. We should concentrate on *this* type of universe. Was it genuinely worthy of creation?

We may use plenitude theodicy as part of a reply to Rowe's empirical argument from evil. Until Section 5 I suppose, contrary to my belief, that God creates in a utilitarian fashion. This simplifies the discussion. As an initial further simplification let us suppose God has, for all we know, created universes of all the on-balance-good types, no matter how trivial the difference between the types of universe. Then I could reply to Rowe as follows:

> God could indeed have prevented the seemingly pointless evils around us but only by not creating a universe of our type. For our precise type of universe is one with a planet like ours in which all the various evils we know of occur.[4] But if God did prevent these evils by not creating a universe of our precise type, then the world as a whole would not be better because by the world as a whole either: (i) we mean this universe, which, being on balance good, would not be better for not existing, or (ii) we mean the sum of all things, in which case the world as a whole would not be better, because it would have one on-balance-good part the less.

This reply invites the rejoinder that the world, meaning the sum of all things, would be better if a better type of universe were created *instead* of this one. It is here that plenitude theodicy is relevant. God has, for all we know, created that type of universe *as well* as this one.

The above is probably oversimplified, for it is counterintuitive to suggest that God creates universes that are too similar to each other. This Not Too Similar constraint on creation forms the basis for the minor adjustment argument of the next section. It also requires me to restate my reply to Rowe:

> There are indeed many types of universe so like ours that God would not create them as well as ours and which have none of the seemingly pointless evils we know of. They are universes very like this one except either they have no counterpart of Earth or no sentient life develops on that counterpart. But these universes are, on balance, less good than

---

[4] Unless, that is, the precise type of universe created by God leaves some things up to either chance or the decisions of nondivine agents. In that case the evils, insofar as they are not part of what God has created, are due to either chance or freedom, which *are* part of what God has created. The only difference this makes is that it raises the question why God did not subsequently intervene to prevent evils. I discuss this in Section 4. Here I am considering the act of creation itself.

ours, because our planet even with its many evils is on balance good. So God has good utilitarian reasons for creating this type of universe rather than ones without sentient life on Earth. If it is now asked why God did not create a different type of universe in which there is a counterpart of Earth with all the good things on our planet but none of the seemingly pointless evils, then I reply that this could occur only in a significantly different universe. And God has, for all I know, created that universe as well as ours. Indeed one of my speculations about an afterlife requires there to be just such a paradise counterpart of Earth in another universe.

Notice that this reply combines plenitude theodicy with the claim that preventing seemingly pointless evils on a planet like Earth would require a significant difference to the type of universe. It is here that scientific progress has helped solve the problem of evil. We now understand why, on a planet like this in a universe like ours, evolution results in beings who feel pain when burned and why, on a planet like this in a universe like ours, climatic and meteorological conditions result in forest fires.

My talk of other universes might alarm some readers, even though these universes would be related to one another indirectly as all being created by the one God. Part of this worry might be semantic. Should not the word "universe" be reserved for the sum total of the physical? That is not how I use the word, but there is no need to quibble. What most people take to be the whole universe might merely be one subuniverse, unrelated spatially or temporally to other subuniverses. But there is a more serious worry. For many have found the idea of anything not directly related to us in a spatio-temporal fashion incoherent. Quite why they find this incoherent is something I have never grasped. But rather than argue the point, I could grant that there is just one universe and consider regions of this universe. Instead of saying that, for all we know, God has created other and better universes as well as ours, I could say that, for all we know, God has created this universe with other and better regions as well as ours. Indeed perhaps the least controversial form of plenitude theodicy concerns planets. Perhaps there could be a planet inhabited by beings rather like us, who suffered no evils and yet enjoyed everything good that we can enjoy. If someone suggests that God should have created that planet instead of this one, I can quite reasonably reply that, for all we know, God has created it in addition to ours, either in some distant galaxy or in a different subuniverse connected to this one by a sort of umbilical cord of spacetime.

Perhaps the most basic laws of nature have to be the same throughout a spatio-temporally connected region. If so, then the supposed incoherence of multiple universes, not connected to one another, would force God to choose one rather than another set of the most basic laws from all that are possible. But how could anyone presume to say that some other set of basic laws would have been a better choice? Some might suggest that, for some reason, a deterministic universe would be preferable to the one we have, governed as it is by quantum mechanics. I disagree, but, in any case, the manifestation of quantum mechanics at the macroscopic level is so subtle that underlying quantum mechanical laws admit both situations where the macroscopic indeterminism is significant and situations where it is negligible. So God does not have to choose between deterministic and nondeterministic subuniverses. By instituting quantum mechanics, God can create both kinds of subuniverse.

In the above I have assumed the Not Too Similar constraint on the creation of universes. Some might deny this and suggest therefore that God would create many instances of just one type of universe instead of different types. And in that case the question would again arise as to why God did not create a better type of universe. To this I reply that creating many different instances of a single type might well have less aesthetic value than creating different types of universe, but there is no need for this appeal to aesthetic considerations. Even if God decided to create infinitely many instances of a universe of a certain type, God can still create many different types of universe and so has a reason to create at least one instance of any creation-worthy universe. The number of instances of other types of universe is irrelevant.

3. The Minor Adjustment Argument

I have conceded the Not Too Similar constraint on creation. This suggests another version of the argument from evil, which concerns not the prevention of all seemingly pointless evils but merely the creation of a universe with fewer or less serious evils. This minor adjustment argument, as I call it, asserts that, because God will not create universes of all possible creation-worthy types, God should create a somewhat better universe that is very like this one. For instance, even if God could not eliminate dysfunctional pain on a planet like this in a universe of our type, God could lessen the amount of dysfunctional pain by means of frequent violations of the laws of nature. Such a universe might be very like ours in all other respects, and so, the argument goes, God would have to choose between it and ours. That God chose ours would then appear to be a callous preference for the aesthetic value of exceptionless and simple laws.

My reply to the minor adjustment argument is that things are not so simple. Suppose we live in universe U and there is another universe V that is rather like U but just different enough for God to create it as well as ours. Then the minor adjustment that would result in the better universe U* instead of U might prevent God creating V, because U* and V would then be too similar for both to be created. So God might have to create V* instead of V. But that might, in turn, prevent the creation of a third universe, W, because now W and V* are too similar. Therefore it is not just this universe that is adjusted. There might well have to be adjustments to many other universes as well. And though it might be obvious that there is a universe U* that is better than ours but very like it, we are in a situation of total ignorance when it comes to adjustments to a whole range of universes.

A geometric analogy might be useful. Suppose we represent possible universes by points on the surface of a globe, and suppose we represent their overall value by the height above sea level. Then universes that are not creation-worthy are represented by points below sea level. God does not create these. But God does create many universes represented by points above sea level. Now the closeness of two points represents how similar the universes are, so God will select a set of points above sea level that are no closer than, say, one hundred yards apart. (For definiteness, assume the distance apart is measured at sea level.) We could therefore work out the optimal choice of universes, by maximizing the sum of the altitudes above sea level of a set of points no closer than one hundred yards apart. (In the actual case of creation there may well be no optimal choice, because God creates infinitely many universes. That does not affect my reply to the minor adjustment argument, merely the accuracy of the illustration.) If you like, we could think of these points as sites for houses, where the aim is to live at the highest possible altitude subject to the constraint that we cannot live nearer our neighbors than one hundred yards. Now consider a very simple case. An island is in the shape of a cone, of height sixty yards and radius one hundred and twenty yards. We could arrange house sites so that there is one at the top and six at an altitude of ten yards. Any owner of one of the six sites at an altitude of ten yards could protest that it would be easy enough for that home site to be a few yards higher up. But in that case the total altitude would be less. If, for instance, one site was one yard higher, both the topmost site and the one diametrically opposite would have to be one yard lower, with the remaining four sites each just a fraction of a yard lower.

As this simple example illustrates, to decide whether some other choice of universes would be better overall, we have to know about the other universes. There is one respect, however, in which this example is misleading. For it might seem unfair that there is one site right at the top. A variant of the example without that feature might be helpful. With mountains of a certain shape it could easily happen that the optimum arrangement of house sites had five about halfway up but with a sixth much lower down. Thus the mountain might rise steeply and then suddenly even out to a gently rising plateau. Five points might then fit quite comfortably on the plateau, leaving room for a sixth point far below. Yet the attempt to arrange six points at equal altitude might force them all to be near sea level. Our universe could be like the sixth house site. In that case it would be easy for God to create a better universe instead of ours, but only by creating worse universes instead of many others.

We have, then, a speculative understanding of the evils around us. It is a genuine epistemic possibility that the minor adjustments required to replace this universe by a slightly different one would require minor adjustments to other universes, making them less good.

4. On Divine Intervention

My discussion thus far has concerned the divine act whereby the universes were created. But why, you might ask, does God not intervene subsequent to creation in order to lessen suffering? Here I distinguish genuine from "as if" intervention. God could have so ordered the universe that without any exception to the laws of nature, or indeed any further divine action, it would be as if God intervenes in answer to prayer or to alleviate suffering. For example, God could have ensured in the one and only act by which this universe was created that if enough people prayed, then the nuclear war that would otherwise have occurred in this century never happened. That would be an "as if" intervention only, not an act subsequent to the creation of the universe. Quite clearly, to ask why there is not more "as if" intervention of this sort is to ask why God did not create a slightly different universe in the first place. That is the minor adjustment argument, which I have already discussed.

The scope for genuine divine intervention is restricted by God's capacity to know what will result from creation without having to observe what did happen. For suppose God had known of some suffering when creating the universe. Then what reason could God have for intervening in a subsequent act rather than creating the universe slightly differently? In the human case there can indeed be a reason for intervening in response to events that were anticipated and could have been prevented, namely that the compassion resulting from experience of the suffering of others could outweigh the predicted value of ignoring that suffering. Thus parents might predict that sending a child to a school notorious for its Spartan regime would result in considerable suffering but decide it was good for the child. Nonetheless on coming to be actually aware of the child's suffering, they might change their minds. It would be too anthropomorphic to think of God as somehow needing to "see" suffering before being moved by compassion to alter the divine plan.

If God does intervene, therefore, it must be for some other reason. The obvious suggestion here is that God cannot know what creatures will freely decide to do. Hence, it could be suggested, circumstances might arise in which God would subsequently intervene to correct the mistakes we have made. Even this suggestion is problematic. For the only freedom I have assumed is that of acting for reasons where the outcome is not *causally* determined. I have not rejected the position that our free acts are "determined" by the reasons we have for acting. If in fact our actions are thus "determined," then God could know what reasons we would have and so know how we would freely decide if a universe of this type was created, and God would use that knowledge to decide whether to create it or not. In that case God could not have any reason subsequently to intervene.

The suggestion, then, as to why God might intervene requires that the sort of freedom we have is such that not even God knows what we shall do. In that case God might intervene to prevent the suffering that our free acts would otherwise cause, or God could intervene by alleviating suffering when freely requested to do so in prayer. But there is a cost as well as a benefit in intervening to prevent us suffering the consequences of the acts, whether our own or others: it detracts from human responsibility. There is also a cost to intervention in response to prayer, chiefly that it discourages us from solving our own problems. Such familiar enough remarks might seem inadequate because it is hard to believe that the cost of intervention outweighs the benefits. We are, however, considering only those rather restricted cases in which divine providence has been frustrated by our freedom. So we are not concerned with such topics as the excessive character of pain or the fact that humans have the *opportunity* to inflict grievous harm on one another and on the rest of creation. For those evils are such as can be taken into consideration by God when creating and so are not the present topic.

My discussion of divine intervention was based on what I took to be a restriction due to God's capacity to know what would happen if a universe of a certain type was created. I took such intervention to be restricted to responses to free acts by creatures. There may be some who would deny this restriction. It is worth, therefore, providing an alternative discussion that allows that God might—why, I do not know—allow room for subsequent intervention in a universe, even though it was foreknown what would happen but for intervention. Such room for intervention must itself be considered a feature of the universe which is fixed by the act of creation. In that case God does not intervene more often, precisely because the amount of intervention is already fixed. And if the lack of other opportunities for intervention is itself proclaimed an evil, I reply that it would be an evil that could not itself be alleviated by divine intervention. So the resort to plenitude theodicy, and my reply to the minor adjustment argument, apply to it.

5. Plenitude, Care, and Respect

Assuming, then, that the unit of creation is a whole universe and that God acts in a utilitarian fashion, plenitude theodicy provides a way of understanding why God has created this universe with its many and grievous evils. It is on balance of positive value, and, for all we know, creating a similar universe instead would not improve the total situation made up of many universes. Of these two assumptions, that the unit of creation (what God creates in a single act) is a whole universe is harmless enough. But if it is insisted that God somehow creates the universe a planet at a time, then plenitude theodicy will still succeed, provided it is granted that, on balance, this planet is of positive total value. For we may replace the word "universe" by "planet" in the discussion.

The most persuasive objection to plenitude theodicy, however, is that God is not a utilitarian. There are two ways of making this objection, of which I endorse only the second. The first is to argue that God must act with moral righteousness and that, for familiar reasons, we should reject a utilitarian account of morally right action in favor of one with *side constraints*, such as never bringing about what would in itself be bad even if it leads to something of great goodness. That specimen of a side constraint would not in fact apply to God, provided the unit of creation is a whole universe or even a whole planet. For God would not be creating one thing in order to bring about another— God would be creating the whole situation with its good and bad components. There are, however, other widely accepted side constraints, and perhaps some of these would prevent the creation of this universe or of this planet. We might, for instance, insist it was wrong deliberately to put others in a situation in which they were tempted to do serious wrong even if we judged that their doing so was for the general good and even if we were prepared to do what we could to rectify the harm done.

The first reason for not appealing to just any side constraints we find convincing is that they may well be based on some of the contingent features of the human condition. For example, we have special obligations to our children. This obligation is, presumably, dependent on certain features of human nature. Hence we should not be scandalized to discover a race of extraterrestrials who were like us in most respects but who found our partiality to our offspring to be nothing but a dereliction of utilitarian duty. It is likely

224] God without the Supernatural

that many of the other side constraints we rely upon are similarly restricted to human beings and so not applicable to God.

My second, and more fundamental, reason for not appealing to just any intuitively plausible moral rules when considering creation is that theists are entitled to explain side constraints, although perhaps not the whole of morality, as due to the prohibitions of a God who is morally good in some way that is not defined in terms of keeping these rules. I have already discussed the divine command theory when explaining the resiliency of moral supremacy, and I shall not repeat myself. Here I merely point out that if God were a utilitarian, then God might, for excellent utilitarian reasons, impose on us humans all sorts of side constraints.

Theists do not even have to rely on the divine command theory to explain why a host of nonutilitarian side constraints are inapplicable to God. It suffices that God is taken to have revealed that certain kinds of behavior almost always have harmful consequences. Given our tendency to deceive ourselves about consequences when there is something we are inclined to do, it then follows that it is rash to back our own utilitarian judgments against revealed rules. For example, students are often tempted to cheat in examinations, but most are restrained by moral intuitions. A utilitarian student might be further tempted to reason that better consequences follow from success than failure, thinking, "I have to pass my medical examinations; otherwise I cannot help others by being a doctor." This reasoning may be countered by suggesting that moral intuitions, especially if derived from God, are a source of information about the likely consequences of various kinds of act which, given our capacity for self-deception, should override our own estimates of the consequences.

I am suspicious, therefore, of any reliance on our *moral* intuitions in order to reject the thesis that God is a utilitarian. Nonetheless I am committed to the claim that God cares not just for the overall goodness of what is created but for the individual creatures. For a start I have chosen to defend just such a version of theism. Moreover, as I explained in Chapter 2, the total value of creation might well be infinite with or without embodied persons. This threatens the coherence of the utilitarian motive for creating a universe suited to life. In addition the divine care for individuals was an important part of my explanation of moral supremacy.

I am committed, therefore, to the divine care for individual creatures. And that shows there is more work to be done. Plenitude theodicy has focused our attention on the individual, and on societies, precisely by dealing with issues to do with the universe as a whole, ignoring societies and the individuals who make them up. I do not foresee special problems to do with societies, so I consider two nonutilitarian constraints concerning individuals. These are not moral obligations so much as the consequences of the caring nature of God. They are to do with recompense and with consent.

The first constraint, then, is that we might well expect a caring God to ensure that every creature should receive ample recompense for the suffering undergone. To count as recompense a good state of affairs should be not just something that is in fact good but something that the creatures can recognize as good for them. We Christians believe that indeed there is a very great good in store for us, namely a sharing in the divine joy. Nonetheless we might recoil from the suggestion that God owes us this by way of recompense. Given my reluctance to apply nonutilitarian side constraints to God, I am not, however, arguing that God has a moral obligation to compensate those who suffer. Rather it is that, if God cares for us, then God will respect how we, the creatures, think of these matters. And, I suggest, it is in no way a defect or fault of those human beings who suffer much to demand recompense from God. The demanded recompense need not, however, be the fullness of joy to which Christians look forward. That is indeed more than we could reasonably have demanded.

Without subscribing to the doctrine of Hell as a place of unending suffering due to frustrated evil desires, I hold that we might have within us the terrible power to deprive ourselves of an infinitely great good. So there may be those whose lives have left them unwilling or unable to enjoy the company of God. How could they be recompensed for their suffering in this life? I do not in fact think there should be recompense for the suffering of those—if there are any—who have deprived themselves of the good that God intended for them. For I agree with Swinburne that they might justly suffer a finite amount more (Swinburne 1989, pp. 180–84). But if such recompense is required, then I suggest that Hell might be a place of intense physical pleasure unmixed with affection. The damned might be precisely those who find this preferable to a joy that requires total unselfishness. (See Walls 1992, chap. 5.)

Nonhuman animals who suffer would, I suggest, be recompensed in a sort of limbo. They would feel good without, we might suppose, enjoying the company of God. Alternatively, for a nonhuman animal the company of God might not be more than feeling good. Against this there is the argument from animal suffering, based on the claim that there are life forms which are capable of genuine suffering but for which the idea of an afterlife is rather implausible. A giant leech, for instance, with its neural network of only a few dozen neurons, shows aversive behavior and might well be in pain. But could such a lowly organism be compensated in an afterlife? And if not, is not there something unfair or even cruel about God's bringing these organisms into existence knowing that for many of them their lives will be painful ones?

In answer to these questions I first submit that the argument from animal suffering is based on some rather dubious premises. We do not know enough about what it is like to be a giant leech, or even a turtle, to answer either the question, Does it have a mental life sufficiently like ours for it to be capable of an afterlife? or the question, Does it have a mental life sufficiently like ours for it to be capable of genuine suffering and not mere pain? As I understand it, the distinction made here between pain and suffering is that pain is a characteristic sensation that normal human beings desire not to have and desire to be free from. Suffering is the accompaniment of any frustrated desire, and so, for those in pain, suffering accompanies the normal human desire not to be in pain. But for rather lowly animals the pain sensation might well be the accompaniment of behavior unaccompanied by desire. For desire typically requires a way of representing what is desired, so only rather sophisticated living organisms have desires and can therefore suffer. No doubt when it comes to our treatment of various animals we should behave as if we knew they could suffer, just to be on the safe side morally, but this need not reflect a belief that there are organisms too lowly to be recompensed in an afterlife but sophisticated enough to be capable of genuine suffering.

An appeal to ignorance, then, may be used, quite properly, to reply to the argument from animal suffering. I shall, however, speculate further about the topic. If an animal suffers, it should have sufficient unity for there to be a mind that suffers. Without that unity all we can say is that there is suffering, not that this animal suffers. Perhaps it is ownerless suffering. But in that case there is no problem based on the impossibility of recompensing individual animals for their suffering. If there can be ownerless suffering, then this might add to the overall evil in the universe. So it would need to be balanced by some good or other, notably human joy. The question of recompense can arise, then, only for animals whose neural networks are sufficiently developed to integrate their mental states into a single mind. But where there is sufficient unity at a given time for there to be a single mind, not a mere collection of mental states, an animal could come into existence again and be recompensed in a fashion appropriate to its status. Indeed it is in the spirit of antisupernaturalism to suppose that our human survival is based on laws of nature that would automatically tend to ensure the survival of other animals too.

The first constraint, then, on the actions of a caring God is that there should be recompense for all living organisms who have suffered in this life. The second constraint is that, out of respect for the persons who have been created, God should not inflict suffering without at least *virtual* consent. Here virtual consent is said to be given if would be irrational to withhold consent were it asked for and were all the relevant facts provided.[5] Because I am concerned, among other things, with our consent to be brought into existence, I stipulate that the consent may be retrospective. In that case consent amounts to subsequent agreement that the benefit is such that it has always been worth the suffering. So in the case of our being brought into existence, virtual consent is given if it would be irrational not to grant that the sufferings consequent upon existence have been worthwhile for the sake of the benefits. The background for this requirement of virtual consent is the discussion of the rights of children. In particular, because we cannot expect children to be rational, we do not in fact ask for their actual consent before we inflict upon them painful medical treatments. And of course we cannot ask children's actual consent before bringing them into existence.

The virtual consent requirement is a significant constraint, provided it is realized that in many situations it might be morally wrong to withhold consent without its being irrational. For example, if someone needs some of my bone marrow to live, I would consider it morally wrong but not irrational to withhold consent to its donation. That there is ample recompense is part of what is required to ensure virtual consent. For without ample recompense the refusal to suffer for the sake of others would not be irrational.

Another requirement for virtual consent, I suspect, is that every evil suffered is necessary in the circumstances for the good of someone or other, and not just for, say, aesthetic reasons. In any case a God who cares for individuals is unlikely to inflict suffering for aesthetic reasons and then compensate. So the evils should not just have a point but have as their point the welfare of either the one who suffers or others. Indeed, because virtual consent requires that it would be irrational, not merely selfish, not to consent, we should be careful about the case of suffering for the sake of the welfare of others. Consider, for example, the Permaculturalists. They live in "gardens" that look like patches of rain forest, provide them with food and other necessities, protect them against extremes of heat and cold, and require no work to maintain. Unfortunately these gardens do not last forever. So the Permaculturalists must, from time to time, set up new gardens. And new gardens take so long to come into production that they themselves will not benefit, only their descendants. Moreover, there is not merely hard work in establishing a new garden but considerable suffering. Although the Permaculturalists have nothing themselves to gain in setting up new gardens, I would judge them irrational not to do so for the sake of future generations. For they themselves have benefited

[5] Must animals be considered as giving virtual consent? Presumably any requirement that those who suffer give virtual consent would apply to animals only if it makes sense to think of an animal consenting. I see no problems that would arise if that is the case.

in just that way from the labor and suffering of past generations. Those who disagree with me about this should treat this as a stipulative extension of what is to be considered irrational for the purposes of characterizing virtual consent. I would invite them to grant that a God who cares for individuals might inflict suffering where there is virtual consent even given this stipulation.

We may contrast the above with the following example. Suppose some of the Permaculturalists propose an increase in the number of gardens so that, in some seventy years' time, there will be a surplus of produce that can be sold to buy marble for sculpture. It might be ignoble for a dissident faction of Permaculturalists to refuse to undergo the suffering involved in increasing the number of gardens, but even if compensated in some way they would not be irrational, even in the stipulated sense. We should not, therefore, say they have given virtual consent to the project.

I conclude that virtual consent is most easily established if what is consented to is for the benefit of the one "consenting." I extend this, however, to include the case where what is "consented" to benefits others in just the way the one "consenting" has been benefited.

We have, then, two conditions we might expect to be satisfied if this universe has been created by a God who exhibits care, respect, and even love for creatures. The first is that there be ample recompense for the suffering of this life. The second is that the one who suffers either benefits or has benefited in a similar way.

The first requirement is satisfied provided we accept the traditional idea of a heavenly afterlife in which, among other things, there is recompense for suffering. Against this there are two possible objections. The first is that, it might be claimed, we cannot take the idea of a heavenly afterlife seriously given what science has revealed of the universe. In reply to this I refer readers back to the antisupernaturalist speculations about an afterlife presented in Chapter 2. So I turn to the second objection, which is that no recompense would be adequate for the severe suffering some undergo. Virtual consent, I grant, requires ample recompense. Otherwise we may say only that someone might consent if they knew all the relevant facts, not that it would be irrational not to consent. Indeed I grant that no mere prolongation of earthly joys for an individual would ensure consent if those who suffer knew of it in advance.[6]

---

[6] Some readers might be curious as to how the damned (i.e., any who freely reject God) could be said to give virtual consent to suffering if the most they can receive by means of recompense are hedonistic pleasures. I would suggest that the coherence of the doctrine of damnation probably requires the possibility of freely choosing to be irrational, because it must always be irrational to reject the divine love. Such a free choice of what is irrational could occur as a result of self-deception. See Walls 1992, pp. 129–33. So even the damned give virtual consent to their sufferings of this life.

Here we may adopt a modification of Wykstra's point that God is able to grasp goods "beyond our ken." Using plenitude theodicy we can understand the point of evil, but even so we can only partially understand how a loving and caring God would allow evil, for we cannot fully comprehend the good of sharing in the divine joy, and so, faced with the undeniable horribleness of the suffering many undergo, we cannot comprehend a good that is so great as to provide abundant recompense.

My preferred position on the abundance of recompense, however, is that sharing in the divine joy is infinitely more than could be demanded, because there would be abundant recompense for suffering by participating in a human community that was not disfigured by selfishness, indifference, and malevolence. For the defect in earthly joys is that they cannot be shared widely. The difficulty in seeing how there could be sufficient recompense for suffering is, I think, based on too individualistic a conception of the good life.

Perhaps it is further objected that virtual consent requires the prospect of retributive justice. The Jews who were the victims of the Holocaust might not have given consent to their being allowed to suffer at the hands of the Nazis even if God had revealed to them abundant recompense. They might also have required that the Nazis be punished. I do not see that as a further problem, though. The traditional Catholic doctrine of suffering in Purgatory or a doctrine of finite suffering in Hell would handle this detail. For we can easily comprehend a suffering sufficiently great to be a fitting punishment for even the most vile wrongdoing, namely experiencing what those you wronged had to suffer.

The second condition required for our universe, with its manifold evils, to be the creation of a caring God was not merely that the evils have a point but that this point be the well-being of the one who suffers, or, with provisos, some other individual. This condition is satisfied provided, as Robert Adams (1979) has argued, the suffering is necessary for our existence. For given the relevant evidence, in this case knowledge of the joy of the life to come, our existence must surely be considered a benefit, so we would be irrational not to give retrospective consent to our being brought into existence.

It remains to show, though, that our suffering is necessary for our existence. There are two ways to argue for this. The first is to note that to come into existence in a universe like ours, each one of us requires just the parents we had and almost exactly the actual circumstances surrounding our conception. And the same, of course, applies to all our ancestors. The slightest change to history, for better or worse, would have resulted in a universe in which we, the actual human beings, had not existed. To be sure, the occasion of my suffering is not one of the events needed for my existence, but we have here a situation like that of the Permaculturalists, who suffer so others may benefit just as they have benefited. That is, I submit, sufficient for virtual consent. And if it be suggested that God should have ensured that we existed in a universe quite unlike ours where accidents did not have such consequences as to who should come into existence, I reply that I have already discussed the question why God did not create a universe of a better type instead of this one.

The other way of arguing that suffering is necessary for the benefit of existence is to consider again the minor adjustment argument. Perhaps all types of universe like ours but with less suffering are too like other universes that have been created. Hence, to prevent universes being too like one another, God may well have only one alternative to allowing suffering, namely not creating us at all. In that case the suffering each individual endures is necessary for the benefit of existence, and so we assume that virtual consent is given.

It might be objected that there is a minor adjustment God could have made to our universe to remove all suffering. Instead of creating this universe with its various evils, why not create one that is just like the afterlife we hope to achieve? In short, why not do without this life? I reply as follows. Unless some of the creatures living in the heavenly counterpart universe might turn out to be recognizable counterparts of some of us,[7] there is no reason God should not create the heavenly counterpart universe as well as this one, for they are dissimilar in many ways. For the proposed version of the minor adjustment argument to get going, we must suppose that the heavenly counterpart universe is such that counterparts of some of us might arise in it. So the argument amounts to considering some people who suffered greatly and asking why God did not instead create counterparts of them who did not in fact live an earthly life. Such counterparts would have had fake memories of an earthly life and would have characters and personalities that make sense only as having been formed by such a life.

What God is here being told to create reminds me very much of what Philip Gosse argued God actually did create, namely a planet that in fact had existed only some six thousand years but that had in it false traces of greater age, such as fossils. Gosse could have added that by creating in this way, God spared the suffering of countless generations of animals who lived before humanity arose. Our intuitive rejection of Gosse's ingenious hypothesis applies just as strongly to the suggestion that God should have faked earthly lives for the blessed in Heaven.

---

[7] I use the phrase "might turn out to be" because which human beings come to exist could be said to depend on free decisions God cannot control or random events God might choose not to control.

Another reason for rejecting the suggestion that God should have faked earthly lives for the blessed is that either they enjoy Heaven in ignorance of the deception, in which case there is something wrong with this situation of ignorance, or they know of it, which would, if they are like us, result in a diminution of their joy.[8] (And please do not say, "Well, then they should not be like us." I am considering counterparts of ourselves, so they have to be like us.)

My chief reason, however, for rejecting the suggestion is the following. If something is good, then it is better for us that we achieve it partly by our efforts than that it be given to us without effort. In addition, because of the characters we have come to have by the time of our deaths, we might only be able to appreciate a heavenly existence to different degrees. It is more just, and so preferable, that such differences arise from the ways we have lived our earthly lives than that they too be faked by God.

I have argued, then, that the two conditions are satisfied for us to say not merely that God creates so as to produce what is good but that God cares for, and hence respects, individuals. Is there more to the divine love than such care and respect? As a Christian I am inclined to say there is and to give as one reason for the Incarnation God's willingness to share our suffering more fully, both as an expression of divine love and as a revelation of what the fullness of love is like. But I am not here discussing specifically Christian doctrines, so it suffices to refer readers back to my reasons for rejecting the thesis that God is guided only by utilitarian considerations. I was committed to the thesis that God cares for and respects individuals. Such care and respect does not entail the depth of divine love ascribed to God by Christians.

6. Soul-Making Theodicy

Although the plenitude theodicy has been completed, it is worth showing how it can be used to fill in what I take to be a gap in Hick's Eirenean soul-making theodicy. As part of his theodicy Hick submits that evils occur because they are the inevitable result of various features of the world around us which are necessary for opportunities for individual and collective growth: "A world without pain . . . would lack the stimuli to hunting, agriculture, building and social organization, and to the development of the sciences and technologies,

---

[8] Perhaps something like this does happen to aborted fetuses or those who die as infants. Persons very like what those human beings could have become may, for all I know, enjoy the heavenly afterlife without the joys and sorrows of this life. They would perhaps have optimal physical and mental characteristics compatible with their short lives on Earth and thus be, in a sense, enviable. Nonetheless I do not envy them.

which have been essential 'foci of human civilisation and culture" (1968, pp. 323–24). In my opinion there are two difficulties with any Eirenean theodicy. The first is that the connection between experiencing evil and growth seems to be contingent upon our having the psychological constitution we humans have. Yes, we humans do need the stimuli provided by pain, but other and happier creatures might not. The second difficulty is that, like most other theodicies, it fails to come to grips with the sheer magnitude of evil. For although some suffering and some moral temptation seems required for individual and collective growth, the growth is not, it seems, proportional to the extent of the suffering. Hick recognizes this, granting that "excessive and undeserved suffering . . . remains unjust and inexplicable, haphazard and cruelly excessive" (1968, p. 335).

Plenitude theodicy is rejected by Hick, but largely because he is thinking of it in its Neoplatonic form in which all possibilities are said to occur, not in its more moderate form in which many but not all possible types of universe are created by God. I now apply plenitude to soul-making theodicy, in order to avoid the difficulties with Hick's version.

I begin with the example of identical twins, Susan and Barbara, who are separated at birth and adopted in different countries. By chance, successful Susan and battling Barbara meet many years later. They agree that it was worth having been born. That is not in question. But they had greatly differing fortunes in their adoption. Susan had everything a child should have, affection without being spoiled, the best possible education, and so on. She went on to be a successful lawyer and politician, noted for her honesty and zeal for justice. The other twin, Barbara, was far less fortunate. There was alcoholism at home, and she herself has had to struggle with a drinking problem. She has always been employed in dull jobs and has had a series of unsatisfactory relationships. None of this, we are to assume, is her fault. On the contrary she is a battler, doing her best in spite of everything.

Barbara could well be dearer to God than Susan, whom all look up to. For she might have more "soul." But I want to make a rather different point. What will Barbara think when she meets Susan? Initially she will be envious. "If I had only been adopted differently, I would be like Susan," she says to herself. She goes on, however, to think: "But then I would not have been the person I now am. There is no way in which I, the one I now am, could have enjoyed Susan's life." I say Barbara's thought is basically correct, in spite of the coherence of the supposition that she, not her twin—or as well as her twin—had been adopted so felicitously. For her thought is of something she values about herself, not a metaphysical thesis about individual essences. What Barbara properly values about herself is not something she has in virtue of having developed from these rather than those cells of the pre-embryo. The basis for a proper self-esteem is the thought that I am unique because of the history I have had.[9]

If we think of the "soul" as the conjunction of the features that make us individuals, then a case can be made for saying that our histories do not merely cause but constitute our souls. Hence the evils around us are soul-making in two ways. First, given the kind of creatures we are, then, as Hick has argued, some suffering and some moral temptation is required for maturity. But, second, the evils, even if very grievous, are like the good things of life in being part of the thoroughly contingent process by which we become true individuals each with a special history.

The obvious objection to this version of soul-making theodicy is that God created not for the sake of you and me but for the sake of whatever animals who are persons might come to exist. Had things been significantly different, *we* would not have existed, at least not as having the individualizing histories we have, but other and happier creatures might have existed instead. We are, as they say, part of the problem. It is here that plenitude comes to the rescue. This universe is not small, and there may well be many universes in addition to ours. There is indeed room for persons of all sorts, and so God's capacity to create other, happier, creatures is scarcely relevant unless there must be a choice. I do not see anything absurd about God creating a plenitude of lives, provided for each one there is the opportunity of ample recompense for suffering. In that context of superabundant creation we may rejoice that we, the people we are, exist in all our variety, even though the price for that is often grievous evil. And we may not only rejoice in this; we may understand the evils as making up the histories without which we would not be the individuals we are.

7. Panentheism and the Problem of Evil

Plenitude theodicy was based on the scientifically respectable hypothesis that the Universe as a whole is made up of many universes, or, at least, that the Universe is enormously large and varied. I would like, in addition, to develop a theodicy that relies on my panentheistic speculations. The divine mind, I speculated, was unrestricted consciousness, that is, consciousness of all things. Our minds are parts of the divine mind, namely consciousness of especially well unified subsystems of the "all things" of which God is conscious. This speculation provides one way in which God could be considered loving beyond having "mere" care and concern. For our suffering is our

[9] I am here indebted to A. B. Palma, who used to stress the value people have *as they are* with all their often comical but sometimes tragic faults and imperfections.

portion of the suffering awareness of things that, outweighed by the joyful awareness of things, makes up the divine consciousness. Hence God is not an aloof observer of our suffering. In addition my panentheism offers an alternative response to the problem of animal suffering. Previously I argued that animals could not suffer unless they had the mental unity required for recompense in an afterlife. Suppose, however, we thought there could be suffering without the requisite mental unity. Then, I submit, such suffering should be considered divine suffering, for without mental unity the animal concerned does not exist as a separate mind from God. So the suffering of the fawn burned in a forest fire is the suffering of God and has whatever point there is in God suffering for the sake of creating this universe, namely the point that in this universe there can arise minds that are truly separate from God.

The main effect of panentheism on the argument from evil is to offer us another variant on Hick's soul-making theodicy. Hick emphasizes the *distance* required for spiritual growth. God has reason to hide from us, so that the universe is "as if there were no God" (1968, p. 323). That is a valuable insight, which I would like to develop as follows. God wants to share something very good, namely the divine joy. To do this God requires there to be creatures who love God and one another and who are supremely happy in these loving relations. Now it is easy, we might think, for God to do this: just create some animals who are persons. On my panentheistic speculations, however, all minds are parts of the divine mind, so there are difficulties in creating other minds. Indeed there are not one but two kinds of imitation person. There is the kind that philosophers like to discuss, namely organisms that behave like persons but lack consciousness, but there is also the kind that are conscious but whose minds are insufficiently distinguished from the divine mind to count as separate persons. Such imitations would, I think, be considered incarnations in the Hindu but not the Christian sense. The problem for God is how there could be genuine nondivine persons, that is, ones that are imitations in neither sense. Only, I submit, by first being separated or split off from God in various ways can we be individuals with whom God shares the divine joy. Without the separation God would merely be creating more bits of God, as it were.

There are analogies with both parental and sexual relations. Parents are saddened if their children do not grow up to become their friends. Yet possessive parents who keep their children in some way from distancing themselves prevent the possibility of genuine friendship. Again, sexual relations at their best involve lovers acting as one. Yet if the lovers really did become a single person by some process of fusion, all we would have is a single individual enjoying itself, not the sexual expression of mutual love. In both cases, then, there is a dialectic to love in that the sought-after union has value only given an initial distancing or separation. It is, I submit, thus with God and us: nothing created could surpass in value the coming to be united with God of creatures who are distinct from God.

There may well be degrees of separation from God, so a rather lesser degree than that mature humans experience might be sufficient for eventual union with God. (That would seem to be the case with higher animals, small children, and the emotionally crippled.) But if the separation admits of degrees, then the value of a loving relation between individuals also admits of degrees. And it is not unreasonable to attach value to the degree of separation adult humans have, provided this is thought of not as an end in itself but as a temporary state of affairs that is a necessary condition for there being those who are not God but who love God and one another.

There are several factors making for the degree of separation we humans experience. One of these, which is a necessary condition for the others, is the possession of a distinct mind. That can be achieved without suffering. All that is required is a suitably integrated system of mental states. Another factor is, as Hick calls it, epistemic distance (1968, p. 323). Creatures who have always lived with the awareness of God would in some way be better and more beautiful than us because they would be more Godlike, but they would not be as separate from God.

There is more, however, than epistemic distance between us and God. There is *sin*, by which I mean the moral and spiritual distance from God due to the desire for that which is incompatible with what God desires, or, to avoid seeming to posit anthropomorphic feelings, what God judges good.[10] One of the ways in which we are truly separate from God is that initially our first-order desires are not God's desires.[11] This separation is increased by our sinning in the sense of giving in to sin. Because the purpose of sin is to provide a separate individual who eventually comes to love God, this increase of sin beyond our initial sinful state is not to be commended. Rather the best situation would seem to be that of someone whose first-order desires are temporarily other than God's but who always does what God desires.

Suffering may in turn be explained by sin. For suffering is an inseparable

[10] It is sin in this sense, not actually doing what is contrary to God's desires, which we can inherit by means of social forces. If in fact sin in this sense is the product of past sinning, then that sinning was indeed a "felix culpa." Likewise, Mother Julian was right to say, "Sin is behovely," if by sin she meant desiring to do what God does not desire and if by "behovely" she meant "for the ultimate good."

[11] First-order desires are desires the object of which is not itself a state of desiring or not desiring. For example, someone who desires to eat rich, fattening, unhealthful food, but who desires not to have that desire, has a potentially harmful or wrong first-order desire that might, however, be held in check by the second-order desire.

aspect of desiring to have what you do not have or to be free from what you desire not to have, especially pain sensations. Hence God could create a universe with sin in it but no suffering only if God provides us with all the things we desire even when that is contrary to what God judges good. In this way both our tendency towards wrong action and our suffering can be understood as the necessary means for the separateness from God that is not otherwise achievable. My point is not that in a paradise we would all be children but rather that in a paradise we would be prematurely divine.

There is, to be sure, a superficial air of paradox in my praise of sin. How could the divine consciousness be so lacking in unity that God judges good, and so allows to occur, that which is contrary to the divine desire? What is going on, I submit, is that we have a nested series of situations, some good and some bad. God has an overall joyful awareness of the exceeding good situation in which genuine individuals come to share in the divine joy. But part of that overall joyful awareness is the sorrow at our desires, which are desires for that which is not, all things considered, good. So though the desiring is, for a while at least, all things considered, good, what we desire is not. The situation is complicated further by the fact that what we desire is, I assume, good in itself and so something God judges good. It just happens to be incompatible with something God judges better.

In this chapter I have argued that suffering, wrongdoing, and other evils do not defy speculative understanding. They can be understood by means of a plenitude theodicy that directs our attention to whether or not the creatures we know of in our universe are worth creating. And, I say, these creatures are worth creating, not for this life, in which for many of them evil outweighs good, but for the sake of an afterlife. And if it is suggested that no one should inflict suffering on others without their consent, I submit that a virtual consent is all that is required and that we may all be deemed to have given virtual consent to the evils that befall us, even those of us—and pray God there are none—who freely reject God.

Alternatively, suffering and wrongdoing may be understood by a version of Hick's Eirenean, or soul-making, theodicy. If we incline toward panentheistic speculations about God, then God can bring about the immense good of love of others only by ensuring a distance or separation of the creature from God. This distance, I submit, is achieved by giving us longings or desires for things incompatible with what God desires. Both our suffering and our wrongdoing derive from the fact that we have these longings. Both these ways of understanding evil are speculative, to be sure, but, as I argued in Chapter 1, all we require is a speculative understanding in order to reply to objections.

Concluding Remarks

Other theists may well be able to articulate more of the theocentric understanding of things than I have. And other theists may be able to provide other and better speculations about such matters as the afterlife. Yet again there may be much theocentric understanding that resists articulation. In spite of this I claim to have shown that anthropic theism is somewhat superior to any rival view. Therefore the positive rejection of anthropic theism is unwarranted. Positive rejection is one thing, however; suspense of judgment, another. For various reasons, such as the threat of the unknown hypothesis, I have not been able to argue against suspense of judgment between anthropic theism and its rivals.

Although my primary apologetic purpose has indeed been to make out a case against atheism rather than against agnosticism, I think it is appropriate, in this concluding chapter, to discuss agnosticism. For simplicity I concentrate on suspense of judgment as a response to the dispute between theists and atheists. Everything I say may, however, be adapted to suspense of judgment as a response to the dispute between anthropic and ananthropic theists. I would like to remind readers, however, that in arguing against agnostics and atheists, I am not saying they are irrational or obstinate. Still less am I suggesting they have wickedly rejected a divine offer of faith. Rather I have put forward certain considerations that favor theism over atheism, and I now put forward some considerations which favor it over agnosticism. Concerning atheism, my position is that its defects should result in severe intellectual stress for atheists. The stress for agnostics is, I argue, an emotional, not an intellectual, one.

1. Compromise versus Commitment

Suppose, as I am granting, the other constraints on reason allow as warranted both theism and agnosticism, and suppose no appeal is made to further considerations, such as further arguments for theism, religious experience, or religious tradition.[1] Should we not then suspend judgment between belief and suspense of judgment, becoming a sort of second-order agnostic who is neither a straightforward agnostic nor a straightforward theist?

There are in fact two rather different interpretations of this suggestion. The cruder is to pretend, as Bayesians do, that we all have precise numerical degrees of belief in anything we have ever thought about. In that case to suspend judgment is to have a degree of belief of about 50 percent and to believe is to have a degree of belief near 100 percent. So first-order constraints, we are here supposing, constrain us only to the extent of forbidding the range of degrees significantly below 50 percent. Thus the range 90 percent to 40 percent might be permissible. Then one way of suspending judgment between suspense and judgment would be to recommend a degree of belief in the middle of the otherwise acceptable range, around 65 percent, say. That would be agnostic but inclined toward theism.

The less crude interpretation of the suggestion that we should adopt a second-order agnosticism would be to allow indefinite degrees of belief as well as definite ones, and to say that when other considerations suggest there could be a permissible range of definite degrees of belief from, say, 40 percent to 90 percent, then in fact we should have an indefinite degree of belief: 65 percent ± 25 percent. This would be not so much a Rule of Compromise as a Rule of Indefiniteness.

The appeal of both these further constraints is based on the intuition that in the absence of a reason to adopt one rather than another of the extremes, intellectual caution should make us reject both the extremes. So if either the Rule of Compromise or the Rule of Indefiniteness were the sole relevant consideration, then indeed the case for agnosticism would have considerable weight. These rules, however, although having much intuitive appeal, are not the only second-order constraints in circumstances in which all the ordinary constraints of reason leave the outcome undetermined. For there is a further consideration that tends to oppose both the Rule of Compromise and the Rule of Indefiniteness. It is the value of commitment and passion. There is value, although not a value subsumed under rationality, of being committed on matters of significance. It is not that there is anything irrational or unwarranted about the agnostic position; it is just that the agnostic lacks passion.

[1] This section overlaps part of Forrest 1994a.

Having said that, I would be among the first to note the vice of the many religious enthusiasts, patriots, and other zealots whose commitments are not within the bounds of reason. Nonetheless I would suggest that the Rules of Compromise and of Indefiniteness are balanced by the value of commitment and passion.

2. The Amphibious Character of Faith

Something like the Rule of Compromise has considerable intellectual appeal, and merely to note that we also value commitment and passion might seem a rather weak argument for preferring theism to the agnostic position. I should explain *why* I value commitment and passion when it comes to faith. And I begin by considering the emotions.[2] As so often in philosophy of mind, the undesirable states are easier to discuss than the desirable ones. So the typical emotions are often taken to be fear and hatred rather than love. It is widely noted that fear and hatred involve three components: beliefs about the object of fear or hatred, associated bodily feelings, and the tendency to behave in various characteristic ways (e.g., flight or fight). Presumably these components are not merely there at the same time. For example, it is not merely that (i) I believe the truck driving at eighty miles an hour on the wrong side of the road is a threat to the life of myself and my family; (ii) I have rather unpleasant bodily sensations; and (iii) I have a tendency to scream out to my wife, who is driving. Thus fear is a single mental state with three components, not just three different states that happen to coincide. This is brought out by contrasting this state of terror with a simultaneous noticing that the Sun has come out. That act of noticing would be something which just happened to coincide with the fear, without being integrated into the emotion.

Of the three components the bodily feelings seem to occur only in some, fairly strong, emotions. So perhaps we should distinguish the twofold combination of belief and behavioral tendencies from the full case, where there is also bodily feeling. A further complication in any attempt to analyze the emotions is that we would have to be more specific about the sort of behavioral tendency that is characteristic of an emotion. For even the highly unemotional belief that, say, Boston is farther south than Paris, is associated with various behavioral tendencies, such as those exhibited in a geography test. Finally, in some cases emotions seem to involve attitudes, which lead indirectly to behavior, rather than immediate behavioral tendencies.

---

[2] The sort of account of the emotions I am relying on has become something of an orthodoxy among English-speaking philosophers. For a recent account of the emotions, see Gordon 1987.

Fortunately I do not need to provide an analysis of the emotions. For I am not going to treat faith as an emotion but merely liken it to one. My purpose in talking of the emotions is to note that a single mental state can have several components, only some of which are beliefs. I call such a state *amphibious*. It should not be controversial that religious faith is also amphibious. I would suggest, though, that faith differs from emotions in several ways. First faith has a more detailed cognitive component. Again, some of the identifiable components in the state that is faith are indeed religious emotions and, as such, themselves amphibious. Among these we can list awe, gratitude, and love. And there are other mental states that can be incorporated, such as the "voice" of conscience. Finally, attitudes are far more central to faith than they are to "raw emotions." Yet faith is like an emotion in that it is not just a matter of having various beliefs, on the one hand, and having various other states, on the other. It is a single state with a substantial belief component and various other components.

My reason for noting that faith is amphibious is that this has implications for the topic of whether faith is warranted. Because of the belief component, it is constrained by the first-order constraints on belief. So no matter how desirable the other components, faith cannot be warranted unless its belief component is. But because an amphibious state is not just a belief, it is a mistake to assess its coming about, its maintenance, or its cessation as if it were nothing but a belief. So, provided we operate within the first-order constraints imposed by reason, the counsel of intellectual caution is no more appropriate to faith than to the emotions. That is, I submit, the context in which we should value commitment and passion—not as usurping the role of reason but because an amphibious mental state is not a mere belief.

I have yet to explain what I value in commitment and passion. I have merely stated the context for this evaluation. Now it would be silly to go out of our way to make a commitment and even sillier to cultivate passion. Rather the point of commitment and passion is that you let yourself be attracted to what is attractive. Respect for reason, morality, and any other constraints you recognize requires positive action, even courage. But, within these constraints, it is not a virtue but a subtle vice to hold back not "doing what comes naturally." When I say I value commitment and passion, what I value, then, is the ability to discern that the time has come to *let go*. Although religiosity is odious, the right sort of faith, with its tendency toward hope and love, is indeed attractive, and, as I have argued, it is within the constraints of reason. To remain agnostic is often to *hold back*.

I have defended theism against the charge that we should compromise between it and a clearly agnostic position. Such caution is admirable when, but only when, we are concerned with mere belief. Faith is not mere belief but an amphibious mental state. And it has paid its dues to reason, provided the first-order constraints have been satisfied. In particular, faith is warranted because it leads to understanding. If, as I urge, it is more attractive than the agnostic position, then its attractiveness should be allowed to have its natural effect untrammeled by further intellectual scruples.

Agnostics might respond to the above by adapting a moderate instrumentalism, which suspends judgment about the truth of a theory about unobservable entities while endorsing the implications of that theory for observables.[3] This could inspire a position I call attitudinal instrumentalism, namely suspension of judgment combined with the adoption of the attitudes and values appropriate for belief. Initially attitudinal instrumentalism might seem to combine the advantage of commitment with the intuitively appealing restraint of agnosticism and so threaten my case for the superiority of theism.

I have, however, two reasons for rejecting attitudinal instrumentalism. The first is that it is not just the religious practice and the attitudes associated with faith that are attractive. Faith itself is attractive. So the injunction to let go when all the first-order requirements of right reason have been met promotes theism over attitudinal instrumentalism.

The second reason for rejecting attitudinal instrumentalism is that the requirements of reason do not merely govern beliefs; they also put some constraints on the connection between beliefs and attitudes. For example, however attractive tree worship might be for someone, the worship of trees is hard to reconcile with our ordinary beliefs about them. Likewise, I submit, there is an intellectual strain in suspending judgment as to whether there is a God, at the same time as adopting the attitudes and values appropriate for theism. Perhaps some such strains are unavoidable in the intellectual life, but, given that theism satisfies all the first-order constraints of reason, it is surely preferable to embrace it rather than accept the strain of inappropriate attitudes.

3. My Project in Context

In order to defend theism against the agnostic position, I have put belief in God in the context of an amphibious mental state I call faith. I conclude this work by putting my project itself in a broader context. I suggest, although I have no way of persuading, that the articulate understanding offered in this work represents only part of the totality of theocentric understanding. Given that some of theocentric understanding has stood up to the test of articulation, we have reason to put our trust in the remainder. I am not, therefore, saying

---

[3] Such moderate instrumentalism, in the context of science, is one component of van Fraassen's constructive empiricism (1980).

the topics considered in this work exhaust the understanding that faith provides. Much of that understanding is a matter of faith making sense of our lives and of the world around us, in ways that are hard to express.

Another part of the broader context of best-explanation apologetics is the difficult topic of religious experience, which is beyond the scope of this book. It is worth mentioning, though, that it is peculiar to treat religious experience as merely something for which we seek understanding. It reminds me of a philosopher who argues that there is a cat sitting on the mat because that is the best explanation of why it looks as if there is a cat sitting on the mat. Instead we should think of religious experience either as confirming a faith in God that is already within the constraints set by reason or perhaps as converting someone from an agnostic position to that of a believer. Something analogous to scientific prediction is going on. Using what you already believe, you predict something experiential, and the confirmation of that prediction further supports the belief. Or, for the agnostic, the occurrence of a certain sort of religious experience previously considered a genuine epistemic possibility, although not actually predicted, turns suspense of judgment into belief.[4]

Finally, the power of theocentric understanding provides the background for any reasoned assessment of the claims of various religious traditions, including Christianity.

---

[4] As before, I refer readers to Alston 1991 for the case for the warrantedness of faith based on experience.

Works Cited

Adams, Robert (1979). "Existence, Self-Interest, and the Problem of Evil." *Noûs*, 13, 53–65.

à Kempis, Thomas (1952). *The Imitation of Christ.* Trans. Leo Sherley-Price. Harmondsworth: Penguin.

Almond, P. C. (1982). *Mystical Experience and Religious Doctrine.* Berlin: Mouton.

Alston, William P. (1985). "Functionalism and Theological Language." *American Philosophical Quarterly*, 22, 221–30.

——— (1991). *Perceiving God: The Epistemology of Religious Experience.* Ithaca: Cornell University Press.

Anscombe, G. E. M. (1971). *Causality and Determinism.* Cambridge: Cambridge University Press.

Armstrong, D. M. (1962). *Bodily Sensations.* London: Routledge and Kegan Paul.

——— (1968). *A Materialist Theory of Mind.* London: Routledge and Kegan Paul.

——— (1978). *Universals and Scientific Realism.* 2 vols. Cambridge: Cambridge University Press.

——— (1980a). "Acting and Trying." In *The Nature of Mind, And Other Essays.* St Lucia: University of Queensland Press, 68–88.

——— (1980b). "Naturalism, Materialism, and First Philosophy." In *The Nature of Mind, And Other Essays.* 149–65.

——— (1983). *What Is a Law of Nature?* Cambridge: Cambridge University Press.

——— (1989). *A Combinatorial Theory of Possibility.* Cambridge: Cambridge University Press.

Bigelow, John (1988). "Real Possibilities." *Philosophical Studies*, 53, 37–64.

——— (1990). "The World Essence." *Dialogue*, 29, 205–17.

Bigelow, John, Brian Ellis, and Caroline Lierse (1994). "The World as One of a Kind: Natural Necessities and Laws of Nature." *British Journal for the Philosophy of Science*, 45, 371–88.

Bishop, John (1990). *Natural Agency*. Cambridge: Cambridge University Press.

Block, Ned (1978). "Troubles with Functionalism." In *Perception and Cognition: Minnesota Studies in Philosophy of Science, Vol. 9*, ed. C. Wade Savage. Minneapolis: University of Minnesota Press.

Bradley, F. H. (1908). *Appearance and Reality*. 2d ed. London: George, Allen.

Bradley, M. C. (1963). "Sensations, Brain Processes, and Colours." *Australasian Journal of Philosophy*, 41, 385–93.

Calvin, Jean (1953). *Institutes of the Christian Religion*, trans. Henry Beveridge. London: James Clarke.

Campbell, C. A. (1957). *On Selfhood and Godhood*. London: George, Allen and Unwin.

Campbell, Keith (1970). *Body and Mind*. 2d ed. London: Macmillan.

Carter, Brandon (1990). "Large Number Coincidences and the Anthropic Principle in Cosmology" In *Physical Cosmology and Philosophy*, ed. John Leslie. New York: Macmillan, 125–33.

Cupitt, Don (1984). *The Sea of Faith*. Cambridge: Cambridge University Press.

Danto, Arthur (1973). *Analytical Philosophy of Action*. Cambridge: Cambridge University Press.

Dasgupta, Surendranath (1975). *A History of Indian Philosophy*, vol 1. Delhi: Barnarsidass.

Davidson, Donald (1967). "Causal Relations." *Journal of Philosophy*, 64, 691–703

—— (1980a). "Action, Reasons, and Causes." In *Essays on Actions and Events*. Oxford: Clarendon Press, 3–20.

—— (1980b). "Agency." In *Essays on Actions and Events*. Oxford: Clarendon Press, 43–62.

Davies, Paul (1981). *The Edge of Infinity*. London: J. M. Dent and Sons.

—— (1992). *The Mind of God: The Scientific Basis for a Rational World*. New York: Simon and Schuster.

Davis, Stephen T. (1986). "Is Personal Identity Retained in the Resurrection?" *Modern Theology*, 2, 328–40.

Davis, Wayne (1991). "The World-Shift Theory of Free Choice." *Australasian Journal of Philosophy*, 69, 206–11.

Dennett, Daniel C. (1991). *Consciousness Explained*. Harmondsworth: Allen Lane/Penguin Press.

Devine, Philip (1989). *Relativism, Nihilism, and God*. Notre Dame: University of Notre Dame Press.

Devitt, Michael, and Kim Sterelny (1987). *Language and Reality*. Oxford: Blackwell.

DeWitt, Bryce, and Neill Graham, eds. (1973). *The Many-Worlds Interpretation of Quantum Mechanics: A Fundamental Exposition by Hugh Everett III*. Princeton: Princeton University Press.

Dreyer, J. L. E. (1953). *A History of Astronomy from Thales to Kepler*. New York: Dover.

Ducasse, C. J. (1969). *Causation and the Types of Necessity*. New York: Dover.

Durkheim, Emile (1965). *The Elementary Forms of the Religious Life*. New York: Free Press.

Earman, John (1989). *World Enough and Space-Time: Absolute versus Relational Theories of Space and Time*. Cambridge, Mass.: Bradford/MIT.

—— (1992). *Bayes or Bust? A Critical Examination of Bayesian Confirmation Theory*. Cambridge, Mass.: Bradford/MIT.

Edwards, Paul, and Arthur Pap (1965). *A Modern Introduction to Philosophy*. 2d ed. New York: Free Press of Glencoe.

Ellis, Brian (1990). *Truth and Objectivity*. Oxford: Blackwell.

Ewing, A. C. (1973). *Value and Reality*. London: Allen and Unwin.

Foreman, Robert K. C., ed. (1990). *The Problem of Pure Consciousness*. New York: Oxford University Press.

Forrest, Peter (1981). "The Problem of Evil: Two Neglected Defences." *Sophia*, 20, 49–54.

—— (1982). "Occam's Razor and Possible Worlds." *The Monist*, 65, 456–64.

—— (1985a). "Backward Causation in Defence of Free Will." *Mind*, 94, 210–17.

—— (1985b). "What Reason Have We to Believe in Laws of Nature?" *Philosophical Inquiry*, 7, 1–12.

—— (1986). "Ways Worlds Could Be." *Australasian Journal of Philosophy*, 64, 15–24.

—— (1989a). *Quantum Metaphysics*. Oxford: Blackwell.

—— (1989b). "The Problem of Representing Incompletely Ordered Doxastic Systems." *Synthese*, 79, 279–303.

—— (1989c). "An Argument for the Divine Command Theory." *Sophia*, 28, 1–19.

—— (1991a). "How Can We Speak of God? How Can We Speak of Anything?" *International Journal for Philosophy of Religion*, 29, 33–52.

—— (1991b). "Aesthetic Understanding." *Philosophy and Phenomenological Research*, 51 (3), 525–40.

—— (1992). "Reference and the Refutation of Naturalism" In *Our Knowledge of God*, ed. K. J. Clark. Dordrecht: Kluwer, 65–85.

—— (1993a). "Just Like Quarks? The Status of Repeatables." In *Ontology, Causality, and Mind: Essays in Honour of D. M. Armstrong*, ed. John Bacon, Keith Campbell, and Lloyd Reinhardt. Cambridge: Cambridge University Press, 45–65.

—— (1993b). "From Difficulties for Physicalism to a Program for Dualists." In *Objections to Physicalism*, ed. Howard Robinson. Oxford: Clarendon Press, 251–69.

—— (1994a). "Why Most of Us Should Be Scientific Realists: A Reply to van Fraassen." *The Monist*, 77, 47–70.

—— (1994b). "The Mystery of Secular Ethics." *Australian Religious Studies Review*, 7, 1–8.

—— (1995). "Is Space Time Continuous or Discrete? An Empirical Question." *Synthese*, 85, 327–54.

—— (1996a). "Physical Necessity and the Passage of Time." In *Natural Kinds, Laws of Nature, and Scientific Methodology*, ed. P. J. Riggs. Australasian Studies in History and Philosophy of Science. Dordrecht: Kluwer.

—— (1996b). "Physicalism and Classical Theism." *Faith and Philosophy*, 13.

Gardner, Martin (1970). "Mathematical Games." *Scientific American*, 223 (4), 120–23.

Gordon, Robert M. (1987). *The Structure of the Emotions*. Investigations in Cognitive Philosophy. Cambridge: Cambridge University Press.

Gould, Stephen Jay (1980). *The Panda's Thumb: More Reflections on Natural History*. New York: Norton.

—— (1989). *Wonderful Life: The Burgess Shale and the Nature of History*. New York: Norton.

Grave, S. A. (1989). *Newman on Conscience*. Oxford: Clarendon Press.

Guth, Alan H. (1983). "Phase Transitions in the Very Early Universe." In *The Very Early Universe*, ed. G. W. Gibbons, S. W. Hawking, and S. T. C. Siklos. Cambridge: Cambridge University Press, 171–204.

Harré, Rom, and E. H. Madden (1975). *Causal Powers: A Theory of Natural Necessity*. Oxford: Blackwell.

Hart, Michael H. (1982). "Atmospheric Evolution, the Drake Equation, and DNA: Sparse Life in an Infinite Universe." In *Extraterrestrials: Where Are They?*, ed. Michael H. Hart and Ben Zuckerman. New York: Pergamon Press, chap. 17; reprinted in *Physical Cosmology and Philosophy*, ed. John Leslie. New York: Macmillan, 1990, pp. 256–66.

Hartshorne, Charles (1987). "Pantheism and Panentheism." In *The Encyclopedia of Religion*, ed. Mircea Eliade, vol. 11. New York: Macmillan, 165–71.

Hawking, Stephen (1988). *A Brief History of Time, from the Big Bang to Black Holes*. London: Bantam Press.

Heathcote, Adrian, and D. M. Armstrong (1991). "Causes and Laws." *Noûs*, 25, 46–53.

Hick, John (1968). *Evil and the God of Love*. London: Collins.

Hornsby, Jennifer (1980). *Actions*. London: Routledge and Kegan Paul.

Hughes, R. I. G. (1989). *The Structure and Interpretation of Quantum Mechanics*. Cambridge: Harvard University Press.

Hume, David (1962). *A Treatise of Human Nature, Book One*, ed. D. G. C. Macnabb. Glasgow: Fontana/Collins.

—— (1969). *Dialogues Concerning Natural Religion*, ed. Henry D. Aiken. New York: Hafner.

—— (1975). *Enquiries Concerning Human Understanding and Concerning the Principles of Morals*, ed. L. A. Selby-Bigge, rev. P. H. Nidditch. Oxford: Clarendon Press.

Jackson, Frank (1977). *Perception: A Representative Theory*. Cambridge: Cambridge University Press.

—— (1982). "Epiphenomenal Qualia." *Philosophical Quarterly*, 32, 127–36.

—— (1987). *Conditionals*. Oxford: Blackwell.

Jantzen, Grace M. (1984). *God's World, God's Body*. London: Darton, Longman and Todd.

Katz, Steven (1978). "Language, Epistemology, and Mysticism." In *Mysticism and Philosophical Analysis*, ed. Steven Katz. Oxford: Oxford University Press.

Kenny, Anthony (1989). *The Metaphysics of Mind*. Oxford: Clarendon Press.

Kripke, Saul A. (1980). *Naming and Necessity*. Cambridge: Harvard University Press.

Leslie, John (1979). *Value and Existence*. Oxford: Blackwell.

—— (1989). *Universes*. London: Routledge.

Levi, Isaac (1980). *The Enterprise of Knowledge*. Cambridge: MIT Press.

Levine, Michael P. (1994). *Pantheism: A Non-theistic Concept of Deity*. London: Routledge.

Lewis, David (1973). *Counterfactuals*. Oxford: Blackwell.

—— (1983). "New Work for a Theory of Universals." *Australasian Journal of Philosophy*, 61, 343–77.

—— (1986). *On the Plurality of Worlds*. Oxford: Blackwell.

—— (1990). "What Experience Teaches." In *Mind and Cognition: A Reader*, ed. William G. Lycan. Oxford: Blackwell, pp. 499–519.

Linde, Andre (1983). "The New Inflationary Universe Scenario." In *The Very Early Universe*, ed. G. W. Gibbons, S. W. Hawking, and S. T. C. Siklos. Cambridge: Cambridge University Press, 205–50.

Locke, John (1961). *An Essay Concerning Human Understanding*, ed. John Yolton. London: Dent.

Longair, M. S. (1993). "Modern Cosmology—A Critical Assessment." *The Quarterly Journal of the Royal Astronomical Society*, 34, 157–99.

Mackie, J. L. (1982). *The Miracle of Theism.* Oxford: Clarendon Press.

McCall, Storrs (1994). *A Model of the Universe.* Oxford: Oxford University Press.

McHarry, J. D. (1978). "A Theodicy." *Analysis,* 38, 132–34.

Menzel, Christopher (1987). "Theism, Platonism, and the Metaphysics of Mathematics." *Faith and Philosophy,* 4, 365–82.

Mitchell, Basil (1973). *The Justification of Religious Belief.* London: Macmillan.

Morris, Thomas V. (1986). *The Logic of God Incarnate.* Ithaca: Cornell University Press.

—— (1987). *Anselmian Explorations: Essays in Philosophical Theology Incarnate.* Notre Dame: University of Notre Dame Press.

Murti, T. R. V. (1980). *The Central Philosophy of Buddhism.* London: Unwin Paperbacks.

Nelkin, Norton (1986). "Pains and Pain Sensations." *Journal of Philosophy,* 83, 129–47.

Newman, John Henry (1970). *University Sermons.* London: SPCK.

Newton-Smith, W. H. (1981). *The Rationality of Science.* Boston: Routledge and Kegan Paul.

Nozick, Robert (1981). *Philosophical Explanation.* Cambridge: Harvard University Press.

Oddie, Graham, (1986). *Likeness to Truth* Dordrecht: Reidel.

Olding, Alan (1991). *Modern Biology and Natural Theology.* London: Routledge.

Parfit, Derek (1984). *Reasons and Persons.* Oxford: Clarendon Press.

Pike, Nelson (1963). "Hume on Evil." *Philosophical Review,* 72, 180–97.

Plantinga, Alvin (1974). *The Nature of Necessity.* Oxford: Oxford University Press.

—— (1980). *Does God Have a Nature?* Milwaukee: Marquette University Press.

—— (1979). "The Probabilistic Argument from Evil." *Philosophical Studies,* 35, 1–53.

—— (1983). "Reason and Belief in God" In *Faith and Rationality,* ed. Alvin Plantinga and Nicholas Wolterstorff. Notre Dame: University of Notre Dame Press, pp. 16–93.

—— (1986). "The Foundations of Theism: A Reply." *Faith and Philosophy,* 3, 298–313.

—— (1993a). *Warrant: The Current Debate.* Oxford: Oxford University Press.

—— (1993b). *Warrant and Proper Function.* Oxford: Oxford University Press.

Polkinghorne, John (1986). *One World.* London: SPCK.

—— (1988). *Science and Creation.* London: SPCK.

—— (1989). *Science and Providence.* London: SPCK.

Popper, Karl (1978). "On the Possibility of an Infinite Past: A Reply to Whitrow." *British Journal of the Philosophy of Science,* 19, 47–8.

Price, Huw (1994). "A Neglected Route to Realism about Quantum Mechanics." *Mind,* 103, 303–36

Putnam, Hilary (1978). *Meaning and the Moral Sciences.* London: Routledge and Kegan Paul.

Quine, W. V. O. (1953a). "On What There Is." In *From a Logical Point of View.* Cambridge: Harvard University Press, pp. 1–19.

—— (1953b). "Two Dogmas of Empiricism" In *From a Logical Point of View,* pp. 20–46.

—— (1953c). "Reification of Universals" in *From a Logical Point of View,* pp. 102–29.

—— (1987). "Universals." In *Quiddities: An Intermittently Philosophical Dictionary.* Cambridge: Harvard University Press, pp. 225–29.

Quinn, Philip P. (1985). "In Search of the Foundations of Theism." *Faith and Philosophy,* 2, 469–86.

—— (1993). "The Foundations of Theism Again: A Rejoinder to Plantinga." In *Rational Faith: Catholic Responses to Reformed Epistemology* ed. Linda Zagzebski. Notre Dame: University of Notre Dame Press, pp. 14–47.

Rowe, William L. (1986). "The Empirical Argument from Evil." In *Rationality, Religious Belief, and Moral Commitment.* ed. Robert Audi and William J. Wainwright. Ithaca: Cornell University Press, 227–47.

Schlesinger, George (1971). *Religion and Scientific Method.* Dordrecht: Reidel.

—— (1988). *New Perspectives on Old-Time Religion.* Oxford: Clarendon Press.

Searle, John (1980). "Minds, Brains, and Programs." *Behavioural and Brain Sciences,* 3, 417–24.

—— (1984). *Minds, Brains, and Science.* Harmondsworth: Penguin.

Sheldrake, Rupert (1985). *A New Science of Life: The Hypothesis of Formative Causation,* 2d ed. London: Anthony Blond.

Shoemaker, Sydney, and Richard Swinburne (1984). *Personal Identity.* Oxford: Blackwell.

Smart, J. J. C. (1963). *Philosophy and Scientific Realism.* London: Routledge and Kegan Paul.

Smith, Quentin (1993). "The Concept of the Cause of the Universe." *Canadian Journal of Philosophy,* 23, 1–24.

—— (1994). "Anthropic Explanations in Cosmology." *Australasian Journal of Philosophy,* 72, 371–82.

Steinhardt, Paul Joseph (1983). "Natural Inflation." In *The Very Early Universe,* ed. G. W. Gibbons, S. W. Hawking, and S. T. C. Siklos. Cambridge: Cambridge University Press, 251–66.

Swinburne, Richard (1979). *The Existence of God.* Oxford: Clarendon Press.

—— (1986). *The Evolution of the Soul.* Oxford: Clarendon Press.

—— (1989). *Responsibility and Atonement.* Oxford: Oxford University Press.

—— (1990). "Argument from the Fine-Tuning of the Universe." In *Physical Cosmology and Philosophy,* ed. John Leslie. New York: Macmillan, pp. 154–73.

Teilhard de Chardin, Pierre (1959). *The Phenomenon of Man,* trans. Bernard Wall. New York: Harper.

Tooley, Michael (1990). "The Nature of Causation: A Singularist Account." *Canadian Journal of Philosophy,* suppl. vol. 19, 271–322.

Tryon, Edward P. (1990). "Is the Universe a Vacuum Fluctuation?" *Nature,* 246 (5433), 396–97; reprinted in *Physical Cosmology and Philosophy,* ed. John Leslie. New York: Macmillan, pp. 216–19.

Underwood, Peter (1978). *The Dictionary of the Supernatural: An A to Z of Hauntings, Possession, Witchcraft, Demonology, and Other Occult Phenomena.* London: Harrap.

van Fraassen, Bas C. (1980). *The Scientific Image.* Oxford: Clarendon Press.

—— (1989). *Laws and Symmetry.* Oxford: Oxford University Press.

—— (1991). *Quantum Mechanics: An Empiricist View.* Oxford: Clarendon Press.

van Inwagen, Peter (1975). "The Incompatibility of Free Will and Determinism." *Philosophical Studies,* 27, 185–99.

—— (1988). "The Place of Chance in a World Sustained by God." In *Divine and Human Action,* ed. Thomas V. Morris. Ithaca: Cornell University Press, 211–34.

Wainwright, William J. (1986). "Monotheism." In *Rationality, Religious Belief, and Moral Commitment,* ed. Robert Audi and William J. Wainwright. Ithaca: Cornell University Press, 289–312.

Walls, Jerry L. (1992). *Hell: The Logic of Damnation.* Notre Dame: University of Notre Dame Press.

Watts, Fraser, and Mark Williams (1988). *The Psychology of Religious Knowing.* Cambridge: Cambridge University Press.

Weisheipl, James A. (1974). *Friar Thomas D'Aquino: His Life, Thought, and Work*. New York: Doubleday.

Wolterstorff, Nicholas (1976). *Reason within the Bounds of Religion*. Grand Rapids, Mich.: Eerdmans.

Wykstra, Stephen (1984). "The Humean Obstacle to Evidential Arguments from Suffering: On Avoiding the Evils of 'Appearance.'" *International Journal for Philosophy of Religion*, 16, 73–94.

Index

Cornell Studies in the Philosophy of Religion

EDITED BY WILLIAM P. ALSTON

God without the Supernatural: A Defense of Scientific Theism
by Peter Forrest

God, Time, and Knowledge
by William Hasker

On a Complex Theory of a Simple God: An Investigation in Aquinas' Philosophical Theology
by Christopher Hughes

Time and Eternity
by Brian Leftow

Rationality and Theistic Belief: An Essay on Reformed Epistemology
by Mark S. McLeod

Theology in the Age of Scientic Reasoning
by Nancey Murphy

Mystic Union: An Essay in the Phenomenology of Mysticism
by Nelson Pike

Divine Hiddenness and Human Reason
by J. L. Schellenberg

The Concept of Faith: A Philosophical Investigation
by William Lad Sessions

Reason and the Heart: A Prolegomenon to a Critique of Passional Reason
by William J. Wainwright

The Nature of God: An Inquiry into Divine Attributes
by Edward R. Wierenga